Catawba County North Carolina Marriages 1842[50]–1880

Volume 1

Elizabeth Bray Sherrill, RG

HERITAGE BOOKS
2012

HERITAGE BOOKS
AN IMPRINT OF HERITAGE BOOKS, INC.

Books, CDs, and more—Worldwide

For our listing of thousands of titles see our website
at
www.HeritageBooks.com

Published 2012 by
HERITAGE BOOKS, INC.
Publishing Division
100 Railroad Ave. #104
Westminster, Maryland 21157

Copyright © 1993 Elizabeth Bray Sherrill, RG

Other Heritage Books by the author:
Catawba County, North Carolina Marriages, 1842[50]–1880
Catawba County, North Carolina, Will Book 1

All rights reserved. No part of this book may be reproduced or
transmitted in any form or by any means, electronic or mechanical,
including photocopying, recording or by any information storage
and retrieval system without written permission from the author,
except for the inclusion of brief quotations in a review.

International Standard Book Numbers
Paperbound: 978-1-55613-897-3
Clothbound: 978-0-7884-9197-9

IN HONOR OF MY PARENTS

EDNA & HARRY BRAY
MARRIED 11 MAY 1940

MY PARENTS-IN-LAW

HAZEL & CLIFFORD SHERRILL
MARRIED 22 JULY 1950

AND MY BELOVED HUSBAND, SAMUEL F. SHERRILL
MARRIED 15 JUNE 1973

CONTENTS

Dedication iii

Introducton vii

Abstracts 1

Bride's Cross-Index 107

INTRODUCTION

Catawba County was established in 1842 from Lincoln County, NC; and, since its formation, the county has generated many marriage records. These documents are housed in the Catawba County Register of Deeds' Office in Newton, NC.

Over the years, the Register of Deeds' Office has seen many changes in procedures, recording, techniques, etc., and one such "improvement" was the undertaking of the tremendous job of indexing, alphabetizing, and placing in chronological order, the marriages of the county.

In June, 1976, **Rita Smith Beaver** began her career with the Register of Deeds. Rita is formerly from Little Mountain, Catawba County, NC, but now resides in Valdese, Burke County, NC. Although Rita had quite a bit of help with the marriage project, Ruth Mackie, Register of Deeds', informed that Rita was a most dedicated worker and still is. She is in the process of computerizing the marriage information, and Mary Rudisill and Irene Stephens of the office are taking upon the important task of proof-reading the data input. The computer project is said to be about a year or so away from completion, and it will cover the years 1842[50] through 1967 for bride entries. A bride index now exists for the year beginning 1968.

When asked how the early marriage information was stored and organized, Rita explained that a lot of the marriage papers were not indexed, they were handwritten; not in chronological order, nor even in order by year; and, they were not alphabetized. The licenses and paper work were folded up and stored. Each license was opened up and entered into a book, but the arrangement had no rhyme nor reason. From the book entries, 3 x 5 index cards were made up and arranged by alphabetized groom's surname.

Because of her relentless efforts, determination, dedication and concern, I dedicate any effort I have made with regard to recording this marriage information in a condensed form to Rita Smith Beaver.

The 1500 bride/groom marriage entries contained in this book are arranged in alphabetical order by GROOM'S name, with a separate BRIDE'S CROSS-INDEX located directly following the GROOM'S INDEX. Both the groom's and bride's names are listed surname first, Christian name, and middle name or initial. All other names are arranged in their natural order.

Entries can include the following information: name of the groom, name of the bride, groom's age, bride's age, race, date of marriage or bond issuance date, name of clergy or Justice of the Peace, place of marriage, witnesses names, names of the groom's parents, names of the bride's parents, location of the legal document of marriage or mention of non-extant documentation, and the book and page number where the original document can be located in the Register's Office.

The usual format of the abstracts, according to actual information recorded, is as follows:

Groom's name, age, parents' names, residence; bride's name, age, parents' names, residence; race; date the marriage took place; officiator's name; witnesses names; book and page number [e.g. 1-642 = Book 1, Page 642] of the original document.

All information herein contained was extracted from the MALE INDEX TO MARRIAGES volumes located at the Register of Deeds' Office in Newton, NC.

This researcher apologizes for any errors in the abstracted marriage records, and asks the readers to understand the nature of human error. Please note that any errors were unintentional.

The following is a list of abbreviations used within the entries:

Number within parenthesis	=	indicates age
M	=	marriage date/date of bond
JP	=	Justice of the Peace
Bapt. Min.	=	Baptist Minister
Luth. Min.	=	Lutheran Minister
Meth. Min.	=	Methodist Minister
Hky Twsp	=	Hickory Township
Cald. Twsp	=	Caldwell Township
Cat. Twsp	=	Catawba Township
Mt. Crk Twsp	=	Mountain Creek Township
JF Twsp	=	Jacob's Fork Township
n/k or n/g	=	Not known or not given
Names within []	=	Parents' names
NL	=	No License Issued

ABSTRACTS

ABEE, Ephraim (19); HAWN, Flora (17); M=15 Sept. 1878; Abel Whitener, JP, at Margaret Hawn's; JL Sigmon, CM Abee, MG Flanagar. NL.

  Jefferson (21) of Burke Co., NC; BRITTON, Annie E.; white; M=30 Apr. 1874; JW Bandy in Bandys Twsp; WS Burns, ZB Martin, WP Johnson. NL.

ABERNATHY, Adam A. (18) [n/g & Nancy]; CLINE, Rhoda E. (21) [Pink & Mary C.]; white; M=2 Oct. 1879; WC Caldwell, JP in Cald. Twsp; Matt A. Hewitt, WA Hewitt, JY Hewitt. 1-321.

  Adolphus S. [Alburt & Sophia]; SHUFORD, Alace [George P. & Eliza]; M=28 Feb. 1872; Robert Helton; no witnesses. 1-136.

  Cain [Frank Holdsclaw & Polly Abernathy]; SHIPP, Margaret [Jim Connor & n/k]; M=15 Mar. 1868; JW Gabriel, Esq.; no witnesses.

  Calvin L. (23); BAKER, Sarah (25); M=15 Sept. 1878; JC Clapp, Ref. Min. at Anna Baker's; Lee Lowe, Alfred Baker, William Killian; white.

  David A. (22) [John & Caroline]; WHITENER, Maggie E. (24) [Moses & Mary]; white; M=13 Aug. 1874; AG Corpening, JF Twsp; HG Seitz, DH Ramsour, S. Hawn. 1-260.

  David G. (23) [FM & Eliza]; FRY, Laura J. (21) [Monroe & Emeline]; white; M=10 Oct. 1880; Abel Whitener, JP in Hky Twsp; ML Fry, JP Whitener, John Whitener. 2-1.

  Ephraim (44); HINKLE, Eliza (25); black; M=4 Jan. 1877; William Brooks, Min. at Sid Reinhardt's; Sidney Reinhardt, McLain Abernathy, James Abernathy.

  F. M.; HUIT, Eliza; M=4 Aug. 1853; Thomas Ward, JP.

  Henry (29); SCHOFIELD, Alice (19); black; M=27 Apr. 1876; JB Turner, Min. in Hky, NC; JG Hall, JN Bohamen, F. Alexander. NL.

  Jacob [Nathan & Emeline]; GOODSON, Malinda [Mills & Violet]; M=5 Nov. 1868; DC Caldwell, JP.

  James (24); WITHERSPOON, Mary J. (22); white; M=17 Aug. 1875; JK Howell, Bapt. Min. at E. Witherspoon's; AH Houston, WL Moore, John Abernathy. NL.

  James H. (22); CHAMBERS, Elizabeth (21); black; M=20 Oct. 1878; Walace Shuford, Bapt. Min.; JA Cowan, A. Sherrill, Ed Thomas.

  James M. (51) of Gaston Co., NC; BRIDGES, Elizabeth (25); white; M=27 Feb. 1877; John B. Marsh, Bapt. Min. at A. Bridges'; James S. Bridges, JA Moore, AT Bridges.

  James W. (22) [William & Novella]; LAIL, Susan (18) [George & Melissa]; white; M=10 Aug. 1879; JM Smith, Luth. Min. in Cline's Twsp; LA Deal, I. Deal, Tolivas Moser. 1-323.

  Jerry J. (24) [Smith & Nancy] of Burke Co., NC; LINK, Emma (16) [Jacob & Ann]; white; M=13 Nov. 1879; William Abernathy, Bapt. Min. in Icard Twsp; DA Cook, CC Cook, Sidney Cline. 1-322.

  John P.; ABERNATHY, Nancy E.; M=19 Mar. 1862; JD Caldwell, JP.

  John Eli (24) [John & Stacy] of Gaston Co., NC; WILKIE, Mattie (20) [George G. & Ann] of Hamilton Twsp; white; M=5 Mar. 1873; JK Howell, Min. in Hamilton Twsp; IM Hildebrand, JM Miller, HA Danner. 1-224.

ABERNATHY, John P. [Miles C. & Nancy]; HARRIS, Yarmetty [Robert Bagle & Elizabeth Harris]; M=14 Apr. 1869; James A. Garvan, JP.

  L.; BUMGARNER, Nancy; M=17 Jan. 1861; JD Caldwell, JP.

  M. A. [Wilford & Polly]; MILLIGAN, Martha R. [GA & Cornelia]; M=23 Apr. 1868; BG Jones, Min.

  McClain (30) [Ephraim & Harriett]; LOWRANCE, Fannie (20) [Peter & Susan]; yellow; M=28 Nov. 1872; William Brooks, Min. in Hamilton Twsp; Peter Lowrance, Alfred Smith, James Smith. 1-137.

  Michael (22) of Cald. Twsp; TOLBERT, June (24) of Cald. Twsp; white; M=1 June 1873; JL Hunt, Luth. Min. in Cald. Twsp; Pat Clark, Robert E. Cobb, Jacob Abernathy. NL.

  Miles; BUMGARNER, Dovy; M=11 Mar. 1866; JD Caldwell, JP.

  Miles C. (68) [Seth & Polly]; CORRELL, Margaret M. [Joseph Williams & Polly]; white; M=23 Dec. 1875; HA Forney, JP in Newt. Twsp; WA Hewitt, Mary F. Forney, Daniel Barringer. 1-267.

  Milton A.; BRADY, MA; M=19 Jan. 1860; JHA Yount, JP.

  Mitten; BEATTY, M. J.; M=20 Dec. 1860; JA Sherrill, JP.

  Osburn F. (29); ABERNATHY, Sarah A. (33); white; M=21 Aug. 1875; GW Cansler, JP in Hamilton Twsp; Jacob Wycoff, John Lowrance, Charles Lowrance. NL.

  Pinkney (21) of Cald. Twsp; BUMGARNER, Camila M. (22) of Cald. Twsp; white; M=28 Sept. 1873; JE Greenhill, Min. in Hky Tavern Twsp; FM Hester, J. Oliver, Jacob Abernathy. NL.

  R. D. (22); ABERNATHY, Jenna (19); white; M=20 Mar. 1879; JC Clapp, Min. in Newton; AE Summerow, ES Abernathy, AP Rowe.

  Robert (30) [Tilmon Perkins & Violet Abernathy] of Newton, NC; ROBINSON, Catharine (21) [Ephraim & Fanny]; black; M=20 Jan. 1876; E. Harris, Min. at Snow Hill; Albert Abernathy, Catharine Wood, ML Wilson. 1-309.

  S. O.; ROCKET, Jane M.; M=17 June 1859; Rev. Joseph Parker, Min.

  Samuel; WHITENER, Jane; M=13 April 1864; PS Rowe, JP.

  Theodore R. (24); CAMPBELL, Janie (19); white; M=11 Dec. 1873; JC Clapp, Ref. Min. at AC Campbell's; DB Gaither, MO Sherrill, William Abernathy. NL.

  William; CLINE, Polly; M=5 June 1860; Daniel May, Min.

  William Albert (21) black; REINHARDT, Eliza (22) yellow; M=20 Apr. 1873; Edward Harris, Min. in Hamilton Twsp; Albert Shell, Ephraim Abernathy, George Hood. NL.

  William H.; LIMENTON, Jane [Robert & Susan]; M=24 Dec. 1868; Elijah Allison, Min.

  William L. (26); SEITZ, Pheribee C. (19); white; M=20 Feb. 1878; JB Marsh, Bapt. Min. in Cat.; John C. Moore, JQ Deal, JS Trollinger.

ABERNETHY, Mack R. (20) [Albert & Sarah]; KALE, Julia (23); black; M=13 Jan. 1876; William Brooks, Min. in Hamilton Twsp; Ephraim Abernathy, Pinkney Smyer, G. James. 1-310.

ALEXANDER, Daniel A. (22) [Rufus & Lettie Bandy]; BEAL, Mary (20) [Marcus & Elizabeth]; M=1 Apr. 1875; JL Hewit, JP in Cald. Twsp; David Caldwell, Marcus Beal, Adolphus Bandy. 1-269.

  F. B. (27) [TM & Nancy]; SUDDERTH, Minnie M. (20) [Stanhope & Martha]; white; M=11 Aug. 1880; FB Alexander, Min. in Hky Twsp; WH Ellis, William W. Wilson, JS Tomlinson. 2-2.

ALEXANDER, Henry (25) [n/k & Jimmina Alexander]; HARMON, Lina (25)
    [David & Mary Smith]; black; M=14 June 1879; JH Bruns, JP in
    Hky Twsp; CS Dwight. 1-324.
   J. Q. [Leander & Jane]; SIGMON, Lovina B. [? & Bettie Ann]; M=
    15 May 1868; PC Henkel, Min. NL.
   Julius (26); COLLETT, Harriett (22); black; M=1 Aug. 1876; AH
    Shuford, JP in Hky; AH Crowell, A. Hockins, Deby Shuford. NL.
   Yount [Miles & Emeline Wilson]; BOST, Ider S. [George & Sarah
    Ann Kinkade]; M=10 Oct. 1868; JH Bruns, JP. NL.
ALLEN, B. C.; FRY, Joanna; M=23 Jan. 1862; PJ Pitts, Esq.
   Bartlet [John & Nancy]; RUDISILL, ?; M=1871; record missing.
   J. A. [Jehu & Caroline]; WHITENER, Mary J. [David R. & Elizabeth]; M=17 Sept. 1871; JA Sherrill, Min. 1-48.
   John [John & Christina]; SIGMON, Mary Ann [William & Catharine];
    M=26 Aug. 1868; JA Sherrill, Magistrate.
   William E. (27); CRANFORD, Mary M. (19); white; M=27 Dec. 1876;
    JA Sherrill, Min. at JA Sherrill's; William Howard, SJ Whitener; EA Sherrill.
ALISON, Thomas A. (21); BOST, Ella Gertrude (23); white; M=13 Mar.
    1879; CM Anderson, Min. in Newton; MG Sherrill, George A.
    Warlick, George Setzer. NL.
ALLISON, B. L. [John & Elizabeth]; LITTEN, Sarah; M=1871; record
    missing. NL.
ANGEL, George [Abel & Sarah]; WILSON, Margaret [Davie & Polly]; M=
    20 Feb. 1871; EP Coulter, JP. 1-49.
   Henry M. (22); WILLS, Margaret (16); white; M=27 Jan. 1878; AC
    Corpening, JP in JF Twsp; James Love, Eddy Blackburn, Willie
    Shuford. NL.
   Lawrance W.; HOOVER, Anna C.; M-24 Sept. 1851; Rev. Adam Miller,
    Min. NL.
   Robert (21) [James & Eva]; ROBINSON, Fannie (22) [Thomas &
    Eliza]; black; M=17 Oct. 1880; AG Corpening, JP in JF Twsp;
    Max Shuford, Eliza Sigmon. 2-3.
ANTHONY, Churchill (21); ANGEL, Bena (17); black; M-3 Dec. 1877;
    Robert Helton, Min. at Robert Helton's; Rhoda Helton, Harriet
    Helton, Ima Helton. NL.
   R. L.; ABERNATHY, N. T.; M=27 June 1858; JD Caldwell, JP. NL.
ARMSTRONG, Daniel M. [Thad & Martha]; CARTER, Martha E. [CP &
    Lily]; M=5 Jan. 1868; H. Cline, Esq. NL.
   Joseph; PAINTER, Perlina; M=24 July 1856; JD Caldwell, JP. NL.
   W. B.; WILKINSON, Dancey; M=24 Feb. 1856; JD Caldwell, JP. NL.
ARNDT, George (21); SIGMON, Catharine (30); white; M=23 Nov. 1876;
    JL Huit, JP in Cald. Twsp; JT Hewitt, Perry Cloninger, Samuel
    Parker. NL.
   John Henry (51); ARWOOD, Anna (30); white; M=4 July 1875; NE
    Sigmon, JP in Cline's Twsp; Julius Sigmon, Mark Sigmon, Anna
    Deal. NL.
   John M. [Daniel & Margaret]; Smyer, Mary M. [Moses M. & Rhoda
    Huit]; M=22 April 1869; PC Henkle, Min. NL.
ARNEY, J. C. [RH & Elizabeth]; CHUMN, M. E. [Robert & Mariah]; M=
    11 Feb. 1869; Daniel May, Min. NL.
   John; PITTS, Sarah; M=5 Dec. 1865; E. Yount, JP. 1-5.
   Phillip; TINCK, Susan L.; M=26 Oct. 1865; Alfred N. Robinson. NL
   Pinkney M. (21) [Henry & Elizabeth] of Cald. Twsp; PROPST, Adoline (21) [Wallace & Abigale]; white; M=12 Dec. 1872; JL
    Hewitt, JP in Cald. Twsp; John Bumgarner, Jacob Bolch,
    Eleanor Propst. 1-138.

ARNT, Henry; MACE, Seana E.; M=8 Aug. 1852; Joshua Wilson, JP. NL.

AUSTIN, Larkbury; KAYLOR, Harriet; M=28 Oct. 1855; John Lantz, Min. NL.

BAILEY, John (55); CRUTCHFIELD, Elizabeth E. (22) of Iredell Co., NC; white; M=22 Feb. 1875; Daniel May, Min. at OG Ford's; OG Ford, Lucy L. Foard, LH Moose. NL.

    John (45); RECTOR, Camila (28); white; M=7 Dec. 1877; QM Smith, JP in Cline's Twsp; PK Little, SAE Smith, William McGee. NL.

    John (21); SETZER, Fannie (16); black; M=18 Dec. 1878; "Returned by mail and not signed by officiator," but married at John Bailey's; Alfred Sherrill, Abraham Turner, Andrew Setzer. NL.

    John; MATHEWS, Rhoda M.; M=4 Feb. 1864; JB Little, JP. NL.

    William (21) [Pinkney & Katy]; FRY, Laura (18) [Samuel & n/g]; black; M=25 July 1880; EJ Harris, Min. in Newton; Peter McCreey, Young Wilson, Lee Wilson. 2-4.

BAKER, Barney (29); KELLER, Emma L. (23); white; M=23 Aug. 1875; JK Howell, Bapt. Min. at MJ Livingston's; Alace Powell, Mrs. AH Houston, J. Livingston. NL.

    Barton (27); RAMSOUR, Jane J. (20); white; M=15 Feb. 1874; Robert Helton, Min. at JA Ramsour's; AG Corpening, JM Finger, DW Ramsour. NL.

    Barton (37); HUFFMAN, Amanda L. (21); white; M=4 Aug. 1878; GJ Wilkie, Bapt. Min. at Milas Huffman's; WP Sterling, J. Say, A. Baker. NL.

    Calvin (21); GOODMAN, Victoria (16); white; M=21 Jan. 1875; NE Sigmon, JP in Cline's Twsp; JB Ervin, Martha Ervin, F. Jones. NL.

    Calvin (24); SEITZ, Rosea (16); white; M=7 Nov. 1877; Robert Helton, Min. at Robert Helton's; DE Warlick, MM Warlick, Etta Gantt. NL.

    David J. [David & Sarah]; Whitener, Eliza Jane [George & Margaret]; M=6 Oct. 1870; JC Clapp, Min. 1-7.

    Fielden N. (22) of Lincoln Co., NC; SMITH, Laura A. (19); white; M=7 Feb. 1878; HA Forney, JP in Newton; EM Bollinger, Robert Baker, Mary Forney. NL.

    Franklin (54); HERMAN, Gracie (19); black; M=1 Oct. 1874; NE Sigmon, JP in Cline's Twsp; Cain Hunsucker, Peter Loretz, Cal Reinhardt. NL.

    Henry; JENKINS, Mary E.; M=5 Apr. 1855; John Lantz, Min. NL.

    John P.; HOKE, Emoline; M=20 May 1860; JB Little, JP. NL.

    Martin L. (22); DEAL, Laura A. (19); white; M=24 Dec. 1874; JM Smith, Luth. Min. at Sylvanus Deal's; CS Hefner, SD Little, AE Sipe. NL.

    Milas (22); BOST, Allace (19); black; M=4 July 1875; NE Sigmon, JP in Cline's Twsp; James Abernathy, John Herman, William Baker. NL.

    William [Clabern Patterson & Cela Thompson]; MARSHALL, Nelly; M=10 Dec. 1869; Elijah Allison, Min. NL.

    William (21) [Frank & Viola]; HUNSUCKER, Mary (18) [Elkana & Caroline]; black; M=21 Nov. 1879; CW Herman, JP in Newton; Pierce Herman, Miles Baker, Elcanah Hunsucker. 1-326.

BALLARD, F. A.; WEAVER, Jane; M=20 Mar. 1868; AJ Whitener, Esq. NL

BANDY, Daniel A. (22) [Rufus Alexander & Lettie Bandy]; BEAL, Mary (20) [Marcus & Elizabeth]; white; M=1 April 1875; JL Hewit, JP, Cald. Twsp; David Caldwell, Marcus Beal, Adolphus Bandy. 1-269.

BANDY, J. W. (50); WEAVER, Mary (20); white; M=21 July 1874; Jacob Mosteller, JP, Bandys Twsp; HM Johnson, Jacob Smith, J. Richey. NL.

Robert H. (22); BEAL, Anna E. (21); white; M=30 Apr. 1878; WC Caldwell, JP, Cald. Twsp; LW Bandy, Benjamin Beal, LS Caldwell. NL.

Theodore L. (20) of Cald. Twsp; DRUM, Mulvina (18) of Mt. Crk Twsp; white; M=8 June 1873; JL Huit, JP at JL Huit's; John Gant, George Arndt, Miles Huit. NL.

William; Huit, Emoline; M=30 Dec. 1851; Philip Burns, JP. NL.

BARGER, Abel; SEAPOTH, HE; M=21 Sept. 1854; E. Yount, JP. NL.

Allin; MILLER, Catharine; M=2 Jan. 1857; E. Yount, JP. NL.

Babel; JUSTICE, Mary Ann; M=18 Oct. 1855; E. Yount, JP. NL.

David; TURNER, B. C.; M=20 Dec. 1866; DA Little, JP. 1-2.

Hosea (35); KILLIAN, Rebecca (33); white; M=20 Aug. 1877; CW Herman, JP, Newton; JT Sullivan, GOW Lail, Rebecca M. Barger. NL.

John M. (21); NANGLE, Frances C. (18); white; M=4 Apr. 1878; JC Hartsell, Min. at Nancy Holder's; SE Killian, LL Deitz, SF Nangle. NL.

M. W.; SETZER, Catharine; M=15 Jan. 1860; PJ Pitts, JP. NL.

Marcus [David & C]; Hawn, Martha Ann E. [John & Elizabeth]; M=26 Nov. 1868; AJ Whitener, JP. NL.

Noah; POOVEY, A. M. C.; M=2 Sept. 1860; E. Yount, JP. NL.

BARKLEY, Henry C. (24); MUNDAY, Mary J. (26); white; M=25 Oct. 1876; JA Sherrill, JP at JA Sherrill's; GA Barkley, CL McCaul, JF Dellinger. NL.

John A.; BEATY, Elizabeth; M=6 Dec. 1855; H. Asbury, Min. NL.

John M. (19) of Lincoln Co., NC; GABRIEL, Laura M. (19); white; M=29 July 1875; JA Sherrill, JP at JW Gabriel's; Clay Barkley, John Gabriel, Edman Howard. NL.

BARRINGER, Noah; HUIT, Mahala L.; M=11 Dec. 1856; PC Henkle, Min. NL.

Noah (43) [David & Catherine] of Cald. Twsp; CLINE, Eliza (28) [Aaron & Melinda]; white; M=29 Dec. 1872; PF Smith, JP in Cald. Twsp; AM Huit, Hosea Deal. 1-139.

BASS, S. H. (22) [IF & Rachel] of Lincoln Co., NC; RHONEY, Sarah Susan (21) [IJ & MS] of Watauga Co., NC; white; M=9 Oct. 1873; JW Bandy, JP in Bandys Twsp; John Stamey, WW Barnes, JH Payne. 1-225.

BEAL, Aaron (21); Fry, Catherine (20); white; M=5 July 1874; JL Hewit, JP in Newton; Marcus Beal, John Cook, CA Gantt. NL.

Andrew (19) [Joseph & Mary]; TROLLINGER, M. Elizabeth (20) [James & Lodiaskie]; white; M=18 Sept. 1880; PFW Stamey, Min. in JF Twsp; Rev. JS Nelson, Rev. CA Gantt, James Keever. 2-5.

Daniel (21); SHUFORD, Laura (18); white; M=17 Dec. 1874; John A. Foil, Ref. Min. at Noah Shuford's; JP Keever, CA Gantt, WS Jarrett. NL.

Ephraim (23) of Cald. Twsp; ABERNATHY, Rhoda (21) of Cald. Twsp; white; M=15 May 1873; JL Hewit, JP at Miles C. Abernathy's; Adolphus Hewitt, John Caldwell, Marcus Hewitt. NL.

Marcus (25); TAYLOR, Sarah C. (21); white; M=5 Oct. 1876; JL Huitt, JP in Cald. Twsp; George Beal, Nancy Finger, PA Abernathy. NL.

William P. (28) [Joseph & Mary]; HUITT, Delphia (26) [John & Harriett]; white; M=13 Oct. 1879; WM Bagby, Min. in Cat. Twsp; PH Huit, JA Beal, JHC Huit. 1-327.

BEARD, Asbury (20); PITTS, Hattie (16); M=23 Aug. 1875; JH
    Bruns, JP in Hky; HE Sigmon, ML Fry, RW Wilson. NL.
  Asbury B. (22) [William & Sallie]; BEARD, Eva (26) [n/k &
    Eliza]; white; M=10 Feb. 1880; HA Forney, JP in Newton; AJ
    Helton, RF Campbell, JW Pope. 2-6.
  Blume (21); THRONEBURG, Mary (19); white; M=22 Aug. 1878; HA
    Forney, JP in Newton; George Throneburg, Adoline Throneburg,
    Fanny Throneburg. NL.
  Henry C. (21); Morrow, Emma (18); white; M=14 Nov. 1878; J.
    Ingold, Min. at Levi Yount's; Levi M. Yount, William Beard,
    Abel Helton. NL.
  J. F. (22); TRAVIS, Callie (18); white; M=1 Jan. 1879; PK
    Little, JP in Cline's Twsp; JB Barringer, PE Travis, HE
    Travis. NL.
  Jacob Waitsel (42); THRONEBURG, Margaret (23); white; M=8 Mar.
    1877; GL Hunt, Luth. Min. at GL Hunt's; Sidney Settlemyre,
    Frank R. Boyd, John Throneburg. NL.
  Julius (24) [William & Sarah]; PITTS, Malinda C. (24) [Conrad &
    Lydia]; white; M=13 Dec. 1875; Abel Whitener, JP in Hky Twsp;
    WM Turner, Pink ?; MC Turner. 1-271.
  Watsel; HICKS, Nancy; M=13 Apr. 1858; PJ Pitts, JP. NL.
BEATTY, Calvin; ABERNATHY, M. A.; M=12 Nov. 1857; H. Asbury, Min.
  NL.
BENFIELD, Noah (24); DRUM, Mary (18); white; M=16 Feb. 1879; PK
    Little, JP at PK Little's; EP Bolch, WP Smith, ML Benfield.
    NL.
  Perry (18); HUFFMAN, Francis (18); white; M=10 Sept. 1874; PK
    Little, JP in Cline's Twsp; CS Little, David Ingold, Silvanus
    ?. NL.
  Secrtus (Socrates) (19) [Riley & Susan]; of Cline's Twsp; FOX,
    Sarah (18) [Hugh & Sarah]; of Cline's Twsp; white; M=12 Dec.
    1872; PF Smith, JP in Newt. Twsp; Jacob Lee Hefner, David
    Shook. 1-140.
  Silvanus (22) [Jacob & Ruah]; POPE, Ruah (50) [Paul Shook &
    n/g]; white; M=21 Nov. 1872; PF Smith, JP in Newt. Twsp; JE
    Epps, AH Sherrill. 1-141.
  Silvanus (25); HEFNER, Linnie (22); white; M=17 Dec. 1874; PK
    Little, JP in Cline's Twsp; Daniel Roseman, DF Roseman, TS
    Little. NL.
BERRY, J. M. [Enoch & Amanda]; COULTER, Mary Ann [Eli S. &
    Harriett]; M=13 Oct. 1867; J. Loutz, Min. NL.
  Osburn [Ezekiel & Polly]; AKINS, Anna C. [Aaron & Eliza]; M=
    4 July 1872; JW Bandy, JP. NL.
  Pinckney; WARD, Catharine R.; M=25 Nov. 1862; PL Rowe, JP. NL.
BLACK, Samuel H. (26) [James & Harriet] of Gaston Co., NC; HOLLER,
    Belle (18) [Alfred & Ruana]; white; M=5 Dec. 1880; CW Herman,
    JP in Newt. Twsp; Robert Holler, Sidney Black, Martha Holler.
    2-8.
BLALOCK, Andrew A. (55); FISH, Eliza (45); white; M=30 Feb.?
    1878; W. Cranford, Min. at Susan Fish's; SA McGee, FW Drum,
    SE Drum. NL.
BLAYLOCK, Joseph H. (21); SIGMON, Catharine (21); white; M=10 Feb.
    1879; GW Ivey, Min. at Caroline Sigmon's; Robert Haynes,
    Caroline Sigmon, JMD Williams. NL.
BLANKENSHIP, Elisha; DETTER, Carolina; M=21 May 1851; Nathaniel
    Wilson, JP. NL.

BLANKENSHIP, George (21); SIGMON, Texas (22); white; M=4 June 1874; JL Hewitt, JP, Cald. Twsp; WA Hewit, Davy Sigmon, Mary Sigmon. NL.

BOLCH, A. J. [Andrew & Rosanna]; SIMMONS, Fanny [Daniel & Liney]; M=26 June 1870; JA Smith, Min. NL.

Abel [Elias & Catharine]; SIGMON, Catharine [Israel Deitz & Anna]; M=21 May 1868; William L. Mehaffey, Esq. NL.

Benjamin [David & Elizabeth]; DELLINGER, Catherine E. [David & Martha]; M=13 Feb. 1868; LN Wilson, Esq. NL.

Caleb M. (21) of Hky Tavern Twsp; LAIL, Catherine E. (22) of Cline's Twsp; white; M=16 Oct. 1873; NE Sigmon, JP in Cline's Twsp; Daniel Deal, JC Herman, George S. Herman. NL.

Cany; DELLINGER, Barbara C.; M=25 Jan. 1855; PC Henkle, Min. NL.

Christian F. (21) of Hky Tavern Twsp; SETTLEMYER, Alace (21) of Newt. Twsp; white; M=10 Aug. 1873; JH Bruns, JP in Hky Tavern Twsp; HC Bolch, A. Sigmon, Mat Deitz. NL.

Elcanah (19) of Cald. Twsp; KANUP, Malinda (19) of Hamilton Twsp; white; M=10 July 1873. NL.

Elcahan (20); HEDRICK, Lucinda (19); white; M=18 May 1875; JM Smith,, Luth. Min. at JM Smith's; JS Simmons, MM Smith, HS Smith. NL.

Elias P. (24); SIGMON, Sarah P. (20); white; M=20 May 1877; PK Little, JP in Cline's Twsp; DW Cline, LH Deal, David Hewitt. NL.

Ephraim (42); PROPST, Caroline R. (42); white; M=23 Feb. 1879; GL Hunt, Min. in Newt. Twsp; WF Hallman, GE Bollinger, LM Hunt.

Gerard (22); MILLER, Genela (21); white; M=4 Apr. 1875; PF Smith, JP in Newt. Twsp; Pink Miller, J. Bolch, A. Bolch. NL.

H. J. [Elias & Katy]; BOWMAN, Rhoda E. [Bostan & Molly]; M=22 Jan. 1868; EA Warlick, Esq. NL.

Henry C. [Phillip & Anna B.]; SIGMON, Margaret M. [Jesse & Adline M.]; M=21 Dec. 1871; JH Bruns, JP. NL.

Henry P. (47) of Hky Tavern Twsp; HERMAN, Louisa (19) of Hky Tavern Twsp; white; M=24 Sept. 1874; ML Bean, JP in Hky Tavern Twsp; John A. Dickson, ND Davis, DJ Bolch. NL.

Isaac (22) [Isaac & Mary Ann]; GILLELAND, Catharine (25) [George & Nancy]; white; M=16 Dec. 1875; JA Sherrill, Min. in Cald. Twsp; George Gilleland, William Gilleland, Marion Clark. 1-273.

Jacob; REES, Rosanah; M=14 Apr. 1857; GP Shuford, JP. NL.

James H. (21) [John & Elizabeth] of Alexander Co., NC; WINEBARGER, Mary C. (19) [Noah & Martha]; white; M=13 Mar. 1880; MA Holler, Meth. Min. in Hky Twsp; RN Lanier, EW Ekard, Leah Lanier. 2-9.

John S. (24) [Jonas & Sarah] of JF Twsp; WHITENER, Elizabeth (22) [Marcus & Fannie]; white; M=9 Jan. 1873; PF Smith, JP in Newt. Twsp; DM Linebarger, L. Carpenter, AF Lutz. 1-226.

Jorden [Nathaniel & n/k]; SIGMON, Agnis C. [Jesse & Adoline Irene]; M=18 Nov. 1869; EA Warlick, JP. NL.

Joseph (24); YOUNT, Rhoda (20); white; M=11 Nov. 1878; Robert Helton, Min. at Robert Helton's; GW Yount, JM Leonard, RO Ramseur.

Joshua (21) [Franklin & Anna]; MILLER, Candice B. (18) [Caleb & Susanah]; white; M=9 Aug. 1872; JH Bruns, JP in Hky Twsp; John Bolch, H. Hallman. 1-142.

BOLCH, Junius (23) [AE & Caroline]; SMITH, Harriett A. (18) [Marcus & Mahala]; white; M=24 Oct. 1880; LN Wilson, JP in Cat. Twsp; JA Robinson, NS Setzer, MJ Wilson. 2-10.

Lemuel (23); HERMAN, Amanda J. (18); white; M=n.d.; JM Smith, Luth. Min. at JM Smith's; LL Townsend, SB Waugh, SAE Bolch. NL.

Manuel; CLINE, Nancy; M=26 Feb. 1860; E. Yount, JP. NL.

Marcus H. (21) [Jacob & Roxanah]; BOLCH, Polly J. (23) [Bostain & Elmia]; white; M=1 Aug. 1872; JH Bruns, JP in Hky Tavern Twsp; A. Cline, JM Lawrence. 1-143.

N. A. [Logan & Martha Ann]; FLOWERS, Elmina [Joseph & Elizabeth] M=16 Feb. 1868; CW Herman, Esq. NL.

Perry [Elias & Catharine]; HUIT, Michael [David & Nancy]; M=14 April 1872; William H. Rockett, JP. NL.

Phillip H. (25) [Phillip & Anna] of Hky Tavern Twsp; CLINE, Adoline L. (26) [William & Lovina Turner] of Hky Tavern Twsp, white; M=9 Jan. 1873; JM Smith, Min. in Newt. Twsp; C. Henkel, JS Shell, TE Hallman. 1-227.

Polycarp (17); SHEPARD, Ellen (16); white; M=7 May 1876; Abel Barger, JP in Hky; JF Deitz, NE Sigmon, FJ Huffman. NL.

S. A. [Jonas & Soloma]; MICHAEL, Sarah R. [Peter & Hannah]; M=30 Dec. 1868; P. Burns, Esq. NL.

W. P. (22) [Joseph & Eveline]; FISHER, Caroline (18) [George & Anna]; white; M=20 Mar. 1879; JH Bruns, JP in Hky Twsp; AD Campbell, PE Fisher, Mary E. Bruns. 1-328.

William M. (22) [Anderson & Sarah]; DEITZ, Barbara E. (20) [Phillip & Harriett]; white; M=22 Feb. 1880; JH Bruns, JP in Hky; Minnie Marshall, Bettie Sigmon, Annie Kerr. 2-11.

BOLLINGER, Elbirt M. [Michael & Catharine]; HOLDER, Lura J. [Jesse & Sarah Ann]; M=13 Dec. 1871; EA Warlick, JP. 1-51.

Henry L. (30); JOHNSON, Nancy (28); white; M=18 Feb. 1874; GL Hunt, Luth. Min. at Joseph Bollinger's; Sidney Bollinger, James Bollinger, James Fry. NL.

James F. (21); FULBRIGHT, Sarah C. (20); white; M=24 Sept. 1876; GL Hunt, Luth. Min. at GL Hunt's; LA Bollinger, SA Hunt, PM Hunt. NL.

Levi A. (28); JOHNSON, Sarah E. (20); white; M=24 Sept. 1874; JC Clapp, Ref. Min. at JC Clapp's; Sidney Bollinger, A. Huffman. NL.

M. M. (18); SMITH, Alice (18); white; M=6 Jan. 1877; HA Forney, JP in Newton; Eveline Beach, AJ Helton, Eveline Helton. NL.

Sidney L. (17); MURPHY, Martha J. (16); white; M=23 Dec. 1874; JC Clapp, Ref. Min. at James Murphy's; James Murphy, Marion Starr, Joseph Murphy. NL.

W. B. [Daniel & Elizabeth]; Hoover, Elizabeth [Daniel & Jimmia]; M=5 July 1870; EP Coulter, JP. NL.

BOST, Adolphus [Andy & Caty]; GAITHER, Emeline [Eli & n/k]; M=16 July 1870; William Brooks, Min. NL.

Alexander (22) of Lincoln Co., NC; MONDAY, Esther (21); black; M=15 Sept. 1876; CW Blaylock, Min. at Greenwood; William Connor, JH Bost, TF McCaul. NL.

Alfred (22) [Burl & Rena]; REINHARDT, Rhoda (20) [n/k & Chancey Wilson]; black; M=31 Oct. 1880; EJ Harris, Min. at Snow Hill, Newton; YA Wilson, RA Johnson, C. Bost. 2-7.

Amzie; IKARD, Louisa E.; M=29 Mar. 1855; Rev. John Lantz, Min. NL.

BOST, Andrew (51); BAKER, Jane (40); black; M=19 Feb. 1877; JB
    Turner, Min. in Hky; George Feamster, Jack Phillips, Nels
    Bowman. NL.
  E. J.; DAETOS, J. C.; M=26 Sept. 1862; William L. Mehaffey, JP.
    NL.
  Ed R. (28) [Joseph M. & Anna C.] of Newton, NC; REISTER, Mattie
    E. (30) [Jonas & Winfred W. Estes] of Newton, NC; white; M=
    27 July 1880; JR Jones, Bapt. Min. in Hky Twsp; S. Tomlinson,
    DH Tuttle, H. Etta Curtis. 2-11A.
  Henry [Lalon & Jane]; REINHARDT, Ellen [Burton & Mary]; M=25
    Dec. 1871; EA Warlick, JP. NL.
  J. C.; HICKS, Julian; M=20 Dec. 1855; Henry Cline, JP. NL.
  John (24) [Moses & Patsey]; MUNDAY, Disie (19) [Isaac &
    Charlotte]; black; M=5 Aug. 1879; EJ Harris, AME Zion Min. at
    Marcus Munday's; M. Munday, RN Munday, Frank Bost. 1-330.
  John L. (23) of Hky Tavern Twsp; SMALLWOOD,, Sallie (18) of Hky
    Tavern Twsp; M=4 Sept. 1873; George Logan, Min. in Hky Tavern
    Twsp; Martin Wilfong, Fill Rowe, George Funtar. NL.
  Matthew E. (22); ALLEY, Laura (15); white; M=20 Aug. 1875; JL
    Huit, JP at Balls Creek, Cald. Twsp; GW Rabb, EG Bost, Sofa
    Wilson. NL.
  O. Perry [Joseph & Polly]; SMYER, S. Ellen [Logan & Emeline];
    M=26 Oct. 1871; JM Smith, Min. 1-52.
  Philip E. (21); HERMAN, Allace C. (19); white; M=16 Dec. 1874;
    ML Little, Luth. Min. at ML Little's; Ben F. Seagle, AF Coon,
    PW Sigmon. NL.
  Pinkney [Lalon & Jane]; REINHARDT, Ida [Edmond & Lucy]; M=25
    Jan. 1872; JL Huit, JP. NL.
  Robert H. (19); GILL, Bettie L. (19); white; M=29 Oct. 1874;
    Daniel May, Min. at Mrs. Gill's; AM Smyer, EA Gill, Lillie
    Gill. NL.
  Sidney M.; BOLCH, Lovina; M=16 Sept. 1852; HB Witherspoon, JP.
    NL.
  T. J. (24); HERMAN, Martha A. (22); white; M=10 Dec. 1874; JM
    Smith, Luth. Min. at JM Smith's; P. Cline, HS Smith, HA Kale.
    NL.
  W. R. D.; COULTER, A. A.; M=1845; Paul Cline; JA Reinhardt.
  William Perry (27) [William R. D. and Angeline] of Newt. Twsp;
    SMYRE, Delia (19) [Robert & Harriett] of Newt. Twsp; white;
    M=13 Dec. 1872; JC Clapp, Min. in Newt. Twsp; Logan Smyre,
    Daniel Rowe, Summey Coulter. 1-145.
BOSTAIN, Norman (23) of Alexander Co., NC; WILSON, Julia Ann (23);
    white; M=15 Jan. 1874; JL Huit, JP in Cald. Twsp; Logan
    Wilson, Alf Wilson, David Setzer. NL.
BOSTIAN, Omar C. (25) [David & Susan] of Alexander Co., NC; MAYS,
    Frances (21) [William & Catharine]; M=3 Nov. 1879; HA Forney,
    JP in Newton; UO Sherrill, Alfred Huffman, MA Abernathy.
    1-331.
BOSTIN, T. W.; SIGMON, M. S. A.; M=28 Mar. 1860; JB Little, JP.
    NL.
BOWMAN, Calvin (23); LAEL, Mary (20); white; M=13 Oct. 1878; PC
    Henkel, Luth. Min. at Jacob Lael's; Philo Lael, Calvin Lael,
    GP Bowman. NL.
  Daniel L. [James & Elizabeth]; SIMMONS, Alice [Franklin & Sarah]
    M=16 Nov. 1871; JM Smith, Min. 1-53.
  G. W. [John & Annie]; STARR, Harriet L. [Elam M. & Barbary]; M=
    12 May 1870; JM Smith, Min. NL.

BOWMAN, Gilbert P. (20) of Alexander Co., NC; HEFNER, Susanah C. (17); white; M=22 Jan. 1880; JM Smith, Luth. Min. at JM Smith's; CS Hefner, LC Bowman, SM Bowman. NL.
  Gilford W. (34); STARR, Nancy C. (21); white; M=9 Dec. 1877; GL Hunt, Luth. Min. at GL Hunt's; John Burns, John Bowman, W. Murphy. NL.
  J. L.; DEAL, Nisy; M=22 June 1862; PC Henkel, Min. NL.
  Jacob; BAKER, R. L.; M=26 Sept. 1855; PC Henkel, Min. NL.
  John [Daniel & Catharine]; LEMMON, Sarah Ann [Franklin & Anna]; M=17 Feb. 1870; JM Smith, Min. NL.
  John A. (21) [John J. & Anna]; HUDSON, Elizabeth V. (18) [WS & Margaret]; white; M=5 Feb. 1880; GL Hunt, Luth. Min. in Newton; LA Hudson, JM Fulbright, JA Drum. 2-14.
  Joshua; MOSER, Eliza; M=5 Aug. 1857; JB Little, JP. NL.
  Lawson; WINEBARGER, Catharine; M=14 Dec. 1853; Timothy Moser, Min. NL.
  Luther (19) [Henry & Anna]; ABERNATHY, Belza L. (14) [John & Caroline]; white; M=15 Dec. 1875; Abel Whitener, JP in Hky Twsp; DR Miller, RD Abernathy, JF Abernathy. 1-274.
  N. L. (28) [Nelson Ray & Elizabeth Ray] of Hky; HELTON, Caroline (19) [Nelson & Lawson]; black; M=11 Sept. 1880; EJ Harris, Min. in Newt. Twsp; Alfort Yount, Martin Wilfong, Ealsie Lewis. 2-13.
  Nelson [Nelson & Elizabeth Little]; JOHNSON, Ellen [Matthew & Louisa]; M=12 Oct. 1871; JH Bruns, JP. NL.
  Q. E.; PROPST, R. E.; M=25 Jan. 1866; PC Henkel, Min. NL.
  William P. (21); DEAL, Ada (17); white; M=10 Jan. 1878; PC Henkel, Luth. Min. at Silvanus Deal's; Noah Wike, LM Hoke, ML Baker. NL.
BOYD, Britton (45) [Silas & Defney] of Cald. Twsp; REINHARDT, Lizzie (30) [n/k & Mollie Reinhardt] of Cald. Twsp; black; M=4 Jan. 1873; PF Smith, JP in Newt. Twsp; JM Brown, DP Jarrett, H. Yount. 1-228.
  Franklin (26); JOHNSON, Mary A. (20); white; M=7 Sept. 1876; JL Huit, JP, Cald. Twsp; William Rabb, Joseph Johnson, Frank Smith. NL.
  Marcus; REINHARDT, Mary E.; M=22 Apr. 1852; David Crooks, Min. NL.
  R. W.; WINGATE, Phebe; M=4 June 1861; W. Carson, Min. NL.
  Thomas [Starlin Ship & Candice Boyd]; ABERNETHY, Willie [Albert Abernethy & n/k]; M=28 Feb. 1872; EA Warlick, JP. NL.
  William [Wallace & Candis]; GIBBS, Sarah Jane; M=4 Dec. 1869; EA Warlick, JP. NL.
BRADSHAW, J. B. [JT & Mary]; SIGMON, Belzie [GH & Adda]; M=5 Oct. 1869; William G. James, JP. NL.
  Thomas J.; CLIPARD, Elizabeth; M=29 Dec. 1859; JD Caldwell, JP. NL.
BRADY, F. A.; BENNICK, F. H.; M=22 Aug. 1866; DS Henkel, Min. NL.
  J. A.; MUNDY, Nancy C.; M=19 June 1860; JA Sherrill, Min. NL.
  Jonas G. (21); HEFNER, Ellen (20); white; M=11 Mar. 1877; JM Smith, Luth. Min. at Lewis Hefner's; John Brady, Burton Hunsucker, Manuel Shook. NL.
  Noah E. (22); CLONINGER, Martha E. (21); white; M=31 Dec. 1876; JM Smith, Luth. Min. at JM Smith's; JP Hefner, SL Brady, Willie A. Smith. NL.

BRIDGES, Hosea W. (31); WILKIE, Sarah (22); white; M=29 Jan. 1874; JK Howell, Bapt. Min. at LE Wilkies; Virginia C. Howell, Lovina E. Wilkie. NL.

Wallie (23); CLONINGER, Meriah (25); black; M=24 Feb. 1877; JB Turner, Min. in Hky; HC Denny, GW Feimster, George Ramsour. NL.

BRINKLEY, Daniel; BOWMAN, Susan; M=10 Jan. 1861; PC Henkel, Min. NL.

BRITTON, Adolphus Monroe (23); REINHARDT, Frances (15); white; M=7 Sept. 1876; Jacob Mosteller, JP, Bandys Twsp; JF Hudson, Jonas Britton. NL.

BROOKS, Jason (20) [William & Nancy]; NAIL, Isabella (22) [Smith Howard & Susan Nail]; black; M=11 May 1879; CV Vanderburg, Min. at Henry Nail's in Cat. Twsp; Peter Lowrance, Tom Lowrance, William Brooks. 1-332.

BROTHERTON, Hiram (48) [James & Margaret] of Lincoln Co., NC; HONEYCUTT, Rebecah A. (35) [---crcely? Bumgardner]; white; M=22 Dec. 1875; JA Sherrill, Min. in Mt Crk Twsp; WE Allen, William Howard, AE Sigmon. 1-275.

J. H. (22) [William & Martha] of Lincoln Co., NC; LITTON, M. E. (20) [Isaac & Theney]; white; M=24 Dec. 1879; JA Sherrill, Min. in Mt Crk Twsp; HD Howard. 1-334.

James F. Alex (21) of Lincoln Co., NC; HOWARD, Juliann (26) of Lincoln Co., NC; white; M=22 July 1875; JA Sherrill, Min. at JA Sherrill's; BW Howard, OM Howard, AL Cherry. NL.

BROWN, Alfred (21); WHITE, Mattie (21); black; M=3 Aug. 1876; Anderson Border, Bapt. Min. at Alf Sherrill's; Alf Sherrill, Charley ?, Mas Sherrill. NL.

Anderson A. (56); FORNEY, Sarah C. (48); white; M=1 Mar. 1877; JC Hartsell, Min. at Mrs. Forney's; AA Hoover, Kate L. Hoover, Mary Robinson. NL.

Andrew E. [Joseph & Catherine]; LITTEN, Candes [William & Eliza]; M=4 Dec. 1867; JA Sherrill, Min. NL.

Avery (21) [Franklin & Roxanah]; BAKER, Victoria (21) [n/k & Louisa Goodman]; white; M=8 Aug. 1880; JA Sherrill, Min. in Cat. Twsp; Rufus Linebarger, Abbie Jones. 2-17.

Calvin; ISAACS, Lovina; M=8 Nov. 1857; JB Little, JP. NL.

Elbert Lorenzo (22); KALE, Elmira (20); male-black/female-yellow; M=5 Oct. 1876; William Brooks, Min. at Jeff Linebarger's; William Hooper, Isaac Hooper, Jeff Linebarger. NL.

Francis M. [Franklin & Nancy]; SHERRILL, Matty [Miles & Sally]; M=22 Sept. 1869; JA Sherrill, Min. NL.

James M. (34) of Newton, NC; WILLIAMS, Mary J. (22) of Cald. Twsp; white; M=2 Dec. 1873; JC Clapp, Ref. Min. at W. Williams'; WH Williams, RW Boyd, John Williams. NL.

James M. (21); MILLER, Rocksana (17); black; M=26 Dec. 1878; JH Bruns, JP in Hky Twsp; AW Marshall, HW Hallman, AE Rowe. NL.

John J. S. (22) [Levi & Amanda]; FRAZIER, Laura (19) [Alex & Lucinda]; white; M=7 Feb. 1873; PF Smith, JP in Newt. Twsp; WB Frazier, JB Brown, FC Smith. 1-229.

R. Hosea (21); DAY, Rachel A. (23); white; M=10 Feb. 1874; SC Brown, JP in Hamilton Twsp; A. Bradburn, I. Turner, James Robinson. NL.

Ruffin; CARPENTER, Francis L.; M=1 Jan. 1852; HB Witherspoon, JP. NL.

S. C. [Joseph & Catherine]; DAY, Margaret [Osburn & Sarah]; M=16 Dec. 1868; JA Sherrill, Min. NL.

BROWN, William E. [Buckner & Elizabeth]; ELLER, Jane M. [Perry & Ann]; M=27 Sept. 1868; EL Sherrill. NL.

BRUNER, Josephas; KALE, Lucinda; M=2 June 1858; JM Lowrance, JP. NL.

  Ruben W. (21) [RM & MC]; BOLCH, Mary M. (21) [Logan & MA]; white; M=13 May 1880; MA Bolch, Luth. Min. in Hky Twsp; NA Bolch, MC Bolch, EM Bolch. 2-18.

BUMGARNER, A. L.; WAGNER, J. M.; M=6 Sept. 1864; M. Barger, JP. NL.

  A. P.; KIRKSEY, Margaret; M=7 Oct. 1851; Lyman Woodfort, JP. NL.

  Alfred; ABERNATHY, Barbara; M=8 Mar. 1852; Lyman Woodfort, JP. NL.

  Andrew (21) [Miles & Millie Ann]; SIGMON, Polly (19) [Lawson & Melinda]; white; M=28 Mar. 1880; LH Wilson, JP in Newt. Twsp; CH Deal, MW Cloninger, Noah Setzer. 2-16.

  David; CARTER, Sarah; M=19 June 1859; JW Gabriel, JP. NL.

  Eli; CLINE, Emeline; M=24 Apr. 1856; Henry Cline, JP. NL.

  Franklin (23); AUSTIN, Mattie (21); white; M=24 Mar. 1876; JL Huit, JP in Cald. Twsp; JT Huit, Jane Carpenter, Adolphus Bumgarner. NL.

  J. M.; BUMGARNER, Mary C.; M=19 Feb. 1857; Jonas Bost, JP. NL.

  John; STOWE, Kesiah; M=12 Apr. 1866; JD Caldwell, JP. NL.

  John S. (22); PROPST, Catharine (22); white; M=1 Aug. 1875; JL Huit, JP in Cald. Twsp; WA Huit, William Propst, JT Huit. NL.

  Julius (19) [Thomas & Sarah] of Newt. Twsp; ELDRIDGE, Camila (26) [Amon & Malinda] of Cald. Twsp; white; M=18 Mar. 1873; PF Smith, JP, Newt. Twsp; MC Walter, JF Rabb, JHA Yount. 1-230.

  Perry (22) [Arum & Eliza]; JONES, Lovinia (23) [James & Caroline]; white; M=24 July 1879; LN Wilson, JP in Cat. Twsp; NE Harbeson, JC Bost, ML Bost. 1-335.

  Pinckney [Aron & Eliza]; PAINTER, Harriet [John & Mary]; M=23 Dec. 1869; JL Huit, JP. NL.

  Pinkney (20); BUMGARNER, Catherine (15); white; M=4 Mar. 1875; JL Huitt, JP in Cald. Twsp; Thomas Bumgarner, Daniel Abernathy, Charles Parker. NL.

  Robert L. (21); MILLER, F. S. (25); white; M=6 Sept. 1877; PF Smith, JP in Newton; HJ Bolch, DA Bumgarner, Ellis Spencer. NL.

  Sidney; CLODFELTER, Sarah P.; M=26 Jan. 1860; H. Cline, JP. NL.

  Sidney A.; BUMGARNER, Susan; M=16 Mar. 1858; JD Caldwell, JP. NL.

  Thomas; SIMMONS, A. M.; M=27 May 1866; DA Little, JP. NL.

  Thomas L. (28); ABERNATHY, Rebecca D. (27); white; M=15 Nov. 1876; HA Forney, JP in Newt. Twsp; John P. Abernathy, JT Hewitt, TA Cline. NL.

  W. P. (26); HOLLER, Candice (22); white; M=4 Oct. 1876; JL Huit, JP in Cald. Twsp; JE Hollar, Sarah Huitt, Christine Huitt. NL.

BURKE, Johnson; LINK, Catharine; M=31 Oct. 1860; JD Caldwell, JP. NL.

BURNS, Hosea (23); MOSTELLER, Sarah E. (26); white; M=7 Nov. 1878; JH Bruns, JP in Hky; JS Tomlinson, RP Miller, DR Huffman. NL.

BURNS, J. F.; PROPST (PROBST), Patsy; M=30 Aug. 1860; PC Henkel, Min. NL.

J. H. [Frederick & Dorato]; WILFONG, M. E. [CA & Cathrine]; M=14 Apr. 1869; Elijah Allison, Min. NL.

John (60); SIGMON, Polly Ann (34); white; M=21 Feb. 1875; PF Smith, JP in Newt. Twsp; DM Linebarger, JA Witherspoon, MG Witherspoon. NL.

Phillip [Martin & Nancy]; RAMSEY, Mary E. [David & Christina]; M=8 Aug. 1867; JM Smith, Min. NL.

William [Eli & Elizabeth]; WHISENANT, Hulda [Adam & Dolly]; M=9 July 1871; JW Bandy, JP. 1-55.

BURRIS, George W. [Ezekiel & Mary]; EADES, Catharine [Isaac & Priscilla]; M=5 Jan. 1871; JM Smith, Min. 1-56.

John [Ezekiel Burris]; CLINE, Camila. No other information listed. NL.

John (26) of Newt. Twsp; STARR, Martha (19); white; M=16 Oct. 1873; MA Throneburg, JP in Newt. Twsp; A. Burris, JA Fry, MFS Throneburg. NL.

BURTON, Robert (21) of Lincoln Co., NC; McCORKLE, Jane (17); black; M=8 Mar. 1876; John E. Champlin, Min. at Branchford McCorkle's; David Battie, John Sherrill, William Sherrill. NL.

BUTLER, Rev. Thomas; RENDLEMAN, C. J.; M=19 Nov. 1856; Rev. GW Welker, Min. NL.

BYERS, Henry; BUMGARNER, Jemima; M=28 June 1866; JD Caldwell, JP. NL.

BYNUM, John J. [John G. & Candis]; SHERRILL, Jane J. [Fielding & Purlina Turner]; M=22 Dec. 1869; JA Sherrill, Min. NL.

Pink [Moses Sherrill & Tabitha Bynum]; BOYD, Mary [Simon & Mary]; M=9 July 1871; IE Cansler, Min. 1-57.

CAIN, John W. (32); BEVER, Lucy (18); black; M=27 June 1878; John A. Foil, Ref. Min. at Mrs. Lantz's; Ema Clapp, Nancy Lantz, EJ Lantz. NL.

CALAWAY, J. T.; PAINTER, Mary J. E.; M=21 Jan. 1866; Jepthue Clark Min. NL.

CALDWELL, Avery P. (17); PEARSON, Barbara E. (18); white; M=18 Sept. 1878; WC Caldwell, JP in Cald. Twsp; WC Williams, Ellen Cline, EE Williams. NL.

Elijah [Grem & Mariah Cathey]; SHERRILL, Ellar M. [Abraham & Delilah Ann]; M=24 Dec. 1868; JA Sherrill, Min. NL.

Gilbert [John & Margaret]; WALDEN, S. Harriet [Louisa]; M=16 Aug. 1867; JD Caldwell, Esq. NL.

H. H.; SUMMITT, B. M. S.; M=19 May 1861; JD Caldwell, JP. NL.

Henderson; ABERNATHY, Miery; M=16 Feb. 1854; Henry Cline, JP. NL.

J. D.; ABERNATHY, Martha A.; M=1 Sept. 1853; Henry Cline, JP. NL.

J. E. A. [Frank & Mary]; SHELTON, Martha Ann [DW & Paulina]; M=27 Dec. 1867; JA Sherrill, Min. NL.

James B. (20); PATTERSON, C. A. M. (19); white; M=24 Jan. 1878; WC Caldwell, JP in Cald. Twsp; WW Laney, JP Bollinger, NE Laney. NL.

James R. (19); WILLIAMS, Susan (23); white; M=6 Mar. 1877; JL Huit, JP in Cald. Twsp; William Caldwell, Marion Clark, Hamp Clark. NL.

Lawson; TROUTMAN, Rebecca; M=15 Mar. 1857; JD Caldwell, JP. NL

CALDWELL, L. E. F. C. (20); STOCKTON, Emma E. (18) of Iredell Co., NC; white; M-11 Apr. 1877; W. Crawford, Min. at F. Caldwell's; AF Shelton, MA Shelton, IH Caldwell. NL.

CALDWELL, Rufus A. (20); BRADSHAW, Harriet S. (17); white; M=7 Aug. 1877; W. Cranford, Min. at E. Bradshaw's; WK Tewksbury, WJ Caldwell, Andrew Clippard. NL.

W. J.; WILKINSON, M. J.; M=15 Apr. 1858; JA Sherrill, Min. NL.

William David (18) [John & Margaret]; LITTEN, Nancy Emaline (16) [Elcanah & Elizabeth Painter]; white; M=21 Mar. 1875; JL Hewit, JP in Cald. Twsp; James Lineberger, David Clipard, Bill Wilkinson. 1-276.

William C.; POOL, Nancy H.; M=23 Jan. 1862; JD Caldwell, JP. NL.

CALICUTT, James (22) [JW & WA]; CORNELIUS, Fannie (21) [Esken & Peggy]; black; M=10 June 1879; MM Gabriel, JP in Mt. Crk. Twsp; BY Cornelius, JA Cornelius, VE Gabriel. 1-336.

CALLAHAN, George W.; SUMMIT, A. E.; M=8 Oct. 1865; JS Nelson, Min. NL.

CAMP, Philo [Martin & Polly]; SHOOK, Lydia [Daniel & Polly]; M=1 Apr. 1869; D. McD. Yount, JP. NL.

CAMPBELL, A. L.; FRY, Margaret; M=30 Apr. 1858; Henry Cline, JP. NL.

D. A. [James & Elizabeth]; KESIAH, Sarah Ann [M. & Elizabeth]; M=2 Feb. 1868; Miles Goodson, Esq. NL.

Ennas L.; PROPST (PROBST), B. A.; M=9 July 1859; GM Yoder, JP. NL.

John D. (64); LINK, Margaret (40); white; M=22 Mar. 1877; Rufus England, JP in Cald. Twsp; CA Fry, IAG Potts, Ambros Bolch. NL.

John W.; CAMPBELL, Rosanah; M=28 Sept. 1853; Henry Cline, JP. NL.

Milton; SUMMEROW, Rachel; M=1 Apr. 1855; H. Cline, JP. NL.

Robert F. (23) [John & Rachael]; YOUNT, Sarah J. (26) [John & Anna]; white; M=22 Dec. 1875; D. May, Min. in Newt. Twsp; GH Holler, Sidney Yount, Louisa Holler. 1-231.

Samuel D. (21) [James & Jane M.]; JONES, China (19) [Jackson & Kate]; white; M=21 Oct. 1880; HA Forney, JP in Newt. Twsp; FP Abernethy, ME Kale, WN McCoy. 2-19.

CANIPE, J. F. (23); NORWOOD, Theodocia (17); white; M=1 Nov. 1874; AJ Fox, Luth. Min. at W. Norwood's; George Smith, WH Smith, David J. Wise. NL.

CANNON, F. A. (23) of Gaston Co., NC; SHERRILL, Julia A. (19); white; M=24 Feb. 1874; JA Sherrill, Min. at Enos Sherrill's; Alex Sherrill, Frances Sherrill, Joseph Gabriel. NL.

CANSLER, Franklin (19) of Hamilton Twsp; WATTS, Matilda (20) of Cline's Twsp; yellow; M=14 Aug. 1873; William Brooks, Min.; Ephraim Abernathy, William Abernathy, Pink Thomas. NL.

G. P. [Henry & M.]; RAMSOUR, Benna [Alfred & Larie]; M=4 Jan. 1870; Daniel May, Min. NL.

G. W.; LONG, Jane E.; M=17 Sept. 1856; Landy Wood. NL.

Jesse; ANTHONY, Isabel; M=26 Nov. 1868; John Watts, Min. NL.

Moses G. (19); HUNSUCKER, Amanda (20); black; M=18 Oct. 1877; WM Brooks, Min. at Harriet Danner's; Frank Cansler, William Hooper, Elick Neill. NL.

CANUP, Abel; HETRICK, Martha Ann; M=16 Dec. 1866; D. McD. Yount, JP. NL.

CANUP, Philo [Martin & Polly]; SHOOK, Lydia [Daniel & Polly]; M=1
    Apr. 1869; D. McD. Yount, JP. NL. (See Philo CAMP also).
CARPENTER, Adolphus J. (22) of Lincoln Co., NC; MILLER, Louisa V.
    (18); white; M=14 Feb. 1878; GL Hunt, Luth. Min. at Joel
    Miller's; DH Witherspoon, RH Thomason, JN Witherspoon. NL.
  Daniel; Lutz, Sarah Ann; M=16 Sept. 1866; J. Lantz, Min. NL.
  Daniel [William & Catherine]; MOSER, Candis [George H. & Mary];
    M=23 Dec. 1868; D. McD. Yount, JP. NL.
  Elijah [Richard & Telma]; KILLIAN, Allis [James & Ann]; M=13
    Jan. 1869; George W. McLaine. NL.
  John; FRY, Eliza M.; M=25 Jan. 1852; HB Witherspoon, JP. NL.
  John F. [Henry & Elizabeth]; YODER, Rhoda E. [Abel & Elizabeth];
    M=5 June 1869; JC Clapp, Min. NL.
  John W. (23); PETRA, Mary N. (26); white; M=27 Nov. 1877; CA
    Gantt, Min. at Lawson Petra's; Lawson Petra, R. Petra, JJ
    Cansler. NL.
  Jonas; JANET, P. L.; M=15 Dec. 1853; GP Shuford, JP. NL.
  Jonas (24) of JF Twsp; SRONCE, Mary Ann (21) of JF Twsp; white;
    M=4 Dec. 1873; Robert Helton, Min. at Andrew Scronce's; Jonas
    Jarrett, Charles Scronce, Mary Jarrett. NL.
  Joshua; SHELL, E. A.; M=9 Dec. 1859; David Crooks, Min. NL.
  L. A. (20); HUIT, Ellen M. (19); white; M=1 May 1873; JC Clapp,
    Min. in Newt. Twsp; Peter Smith, Ellmore Smith, Silas Smyre.
    NL.
  Luther C. (21); ODAM, Sarah Jane (19); white; M=30 June 1878;
    William G. James, JP in Hamilton Twsp; MW Cloninger, Philo
    Hefner, Ellen Cloninger. NL.
  P. W.; YOUNT, Carmila E.; M=15 Oct. 1856; PC Hinkle, Min. NL.
  Richmond (29); YOUNT Adline (21); black; M=4 Feb. 1874; William
    Brooks, Min. at I. Pearson's; Lewis Yount, Henry James, Alex
    Cline. NL.
  Solomon; HELDERBRAND, J. S.; M=23 Feb. 1858; Rev. A. Abernathy,
    Min. NL.
  Wade A. (24) of Gaston Co., NC; SHUFORD, Annie (18) of Hamilton
    Twsp; white; M=2 Dec. 1873; JA Sherrill, Min. at AD
    Shuford's; JF Shuford, RA Wilkinson, PF Reinhardt. NL.
  Wallace [Eli & Rosa]; GIBBS, Emma; M=29 Aug. 1870; EA Warlick,
    Min. NL.
  William Pinkney (21); BRENDLE, Frances (25); white; M=1 Jan.
    1874; JW Bandy, JP in Bandy's Twsp; Nelson Bass, Pinkney
    Richey, Daniel Lantz. NL.
  William W. (33); FRAZIER, Mildred N. (19); white; M=8 Sept.
    1875; PK Little, JP in Cline's Twsp; DF Carpenter, GA Hoke,
    JB Little. NL.
CARRELL, G. W.; WILLIAMS, Margaret; M=14 July 1861; JD Caldwell,
    JP. NL.
CARTER, John C. [Caleb & Celila]; CAMPBELL, Rhoda [John B. &
    Elizabeth]; M=4 Mar. 1869; Daniel May, Min. NL.
CASH, S. B. [SH & T]; BUMGARNER, Huldah [Eliza Bumgarner]; M=10
    Oct. 1871; DL Smith, JP. 1-58.
CASHION, Leonard (32) [Burwell & Catherine] of Mecklenburg Co.,
    NC; COCHRANE, Martha V. (25) [DC & Lucinda]; white; M=8 Dec.
    1880; JB Richardson, Bapt. Min. in Cat. Twsp; LW Cochran, AB
    Carion, CD Blanton. 2-20.
CHAMBERS, Henry A. (20); ALEXANDER, Caroline (20); black; M=14
    Dec. 1876; WS Shuford, Bapt. Min. at Alex Clark's; Aaron
    Setzer, David Byers, A. Borders. NL.

CHATMAN, H. A.; LENHART, Leah A.; M=2 Mar. 1858; GM Yoder, JP. NL.

CHENAULT, W. W.; SHERRILL, R. E.; M=27 Mar. 1861; JA Sherrill, JP. NL.

CHESSER, Ephraim A.; SHERRILL, Elizabeth; M=10 Dec. 1857; Rev. Jeptha Clark, Min. NL.

CHILDERS, Daniel W. (18) [William & Sarah]; FISHER, Roxanna (23) [Benjamin & Elviery]; white; M=26 June 1861; Rev. W. Cranford, Min. in Mt. Crk Twsp; William Howard, LA Shrum, John Mitton Howard. 2-162.

  Gilbert L. [William & Patsey]; HOWARD, Mahala [n/g & Barbara Bolch]; M=16 Feb. 1871; JH Bruns, JP. 1-59.

  Henry [William & Patsey]; WILLIAMS, Mary [Joseph & Polly]; M= 19 Feb. 1871; JL Hewitt, JP. 1-60.

  Henry H. (40) [William & Martha] of Burke Co., NC; HUFFMAN, Mary Ann (35) [Martin & Elizabeth]; white; M=21 Oct. 1880; JW Mouser, JP in Hky Twsp; JL Childers, JD Miller, DA Miller. 2-21.

  L. P.; JARRETT, Sarah; M=6 Dec. 1859; GP Shuford, JP. NL.

  Thomas C. [William & Sarah]; HOWARD, Susanna [Henry & Elizabeth] M=18 Aug. 1870; JA Sherrill, Min. NL.

CHILDREIS (CHILDERS), Miles W. (34) [William & Sarah]; HONEYCUTT, Mary (35) [Andrew & Cassa]; white; M=22 Dec. 1880; JA Sherrill, Min. in Mt. Crk Twsp; John Childris, William Fisher, Henry Sherrill. 2-22.

CHRISTOPHER, Adolphus; HUFFMAN, Ceda; M=1868; No other information given.

  Adolphus [Daniel & Lucy]; SHOOK, Meriah [Adam & Catharine]; M= 15 Feb. 1872; EA Warlick, JP. 1-146.

  Ephraim; HAFER, Elizabeth; M=18 July 1853; JB Little, JP. NL.

  Henry; HUFFMAN, Malinda; M=12 Sept. 1851; JB Little, JP. NL.

  Jacob; WINEBARGER, Delila; M=20 Mar. 1859; Jesse Gantt, JP. NL.

  Larkin [David & Lovina]; SIPE, Candice [Henry & Amanda]; M=25 Jan. 1872; PF Smith, JP. 1-147.

  Lawson; MATHEWS, Elizabeth; M=27 Feb. 1850; JB Little, JP. NL.

  William [Andrew & Elizabeth]; HEFNER, Mahala [Jacob & Sarah]; M=1 Feb. 1872; PF Smith, JP. 1-148.

CLAMPET, James [Cyrus & Martha]; RHONEY, Catharine; M=1871; record missing. NL.

CLARK, D. S.; BROWN, Manerva; M=10 Oct. 1858; JB Little, JP. NL.

  David; GILLELAND, Emoline; M=27 Oct. 1852; JM Lowrance, JP. NL.

  David H. (20); STOWE, Laura E. (19); white; M=15 Mar. 1877; JL Huitt, JP in Cald. Twsp; James Howard, JT Huit, Leroy Sanders. NL.

  James Mel (32) of Iredell Co., NC; CALDWELL, Ada O. V. (23); white; M=5 May 1875; LA Lockman, JP in Mt. Crk Twsp; J. Turner, BJ Cornelius. NL.

  Jeptha; WILFONG, Sarah Ann; M=29 Oct. 1862; JD Caldwell, JP. NL.

  John W. of Iredell Co., NC; CALDWELL, Debbie (20); white; M=25 May 1876; John E. Pressly, Presby. Min. at AJ Caldwell's; Alex Clark, Wash Brawley, Percy Clark. NL.

  P. M.; COBB, Lovina F.; M=27 Jan. 1852; Lyman Woodford, JP. NL.

  William M. A. (21) [David & Emaline]; CALDWELL, Mary A. (26) [William & Elizabeth]; white; M=8 Apr. 1875; JL Hewitt, JP in Cald. Twsp; John Caldwell, TC Caldwell, Luther Campbell. 1-277.

CLAYTON, John (20) [William & Anna] of Burke Co., NC; AUSTIN,
    Mary (25) [Manuel & Mana] of Burke Co., NC; white; M=25 Dec.
    1880; Abel Whitener, JP in Hky Twsp; Eliza Whitener, Hampton
    Whitener, E. Whitener. 2-23.
CLEMONS, Alexander [Henry & Ada]; HENDERSON, Emma [Sokes & Rutha];
    M=18 Apr. 1872; EA Warlick, JP. NL.
CLEMMER, E. P.; SIGMON, Lucinda; M=17 Nov. 1853; Henry Cline, JP.
    NL.
CLEMOR, Jonas; SIGMON, Mahala; M=4 Oct. 1855; Henry Cline, JP. NL.
CLIFTON, Thomas C. (21) of SC; YOUNT, Ellen E. (18); white; M=18
    Mar. 1875; PF Smith, JP in Newt. Twsp; JJ Clifton, DP
    Jarrett, WE Yount. NL.
CLINARD, Andrew L. (25); SULLIVAN, Bettie (20); white; M=30 Aug.
    1876; CW Herman, JP in Conover, NC; Alex McRary, WE Hallman,
    E. Blain. NL.
  Francis A. (22); JONES, Gertrude E. (19); white; M=7 June 1876;
    Edward N. Joyner, Episcopal Min. in Hky; AE Gibbs, JW Jones,
    John N. Bohaman. NL.
CLINE, A.; CHAPMAN, Elizabeth; M=4 Feb. 1860; G. Huffman, JP. NL.
  Abe J. [Jessee & Margaret]; RINK, Eliza [George & Elizabeth]; M=
    18 Sept. 1861; JH Bruns. 1-61.
  Alfred [Ephraim & Mary]; MILLER, Ceda [Joel & Elizabeth]; M=5
    Feb. 1868; JH Bruns, Esq. NL.
  Alfred K. (31); SETZER, L. Alice (23); white; M=7 Mar. 1877;
    William G. James, JP in Hamilton Twsp; EM Young, James P.
    Setzer, Jane S. James. NL.
  Ambrose; TURNER, Adaline S.; M=24 Aug. 1863; E. Yount, JP. NL.
  Calvin; FISH, Rebecca; M=11 July 1858; JW Gabriel, JP. NL.
  Charles A. (19); STARR, Sarah (18); white; M=27 Apr. 1876; JC
    Clapp, Ref. Min. at Abel Starr's; Eli Starr, Abel Starr,
    Perry Fry. NL.
  Cicero; SETTLEMYRE, Rhody; M=18 Dec. 1861; E. Yount, JP. NL.
  Coleman M. [Pinkney & Catharine]; HASS, Meriah [Simon & Anna];
    M=30 Nov. 1870; GL Hewitt, JP. 1-9.
  Coleman M. [Franklin & Salina]; HOP, Catharine [Simon & Anna];
    M=20 Nov. 1871; JL Huit, JP. NL.
  Coleman M. [Pinkney & Catharine]; HOP, Meriah [Simon & Anna];
    M=30 Nov. 1871; JL Huit, JP. NL.
  D. W.; DEAL, Adoline; M=28 Dec. 1855; JB Little, JP. NL.
  Darus; CONRAD, Adoline; M=12 Aug. 1858; John Kent, JP. NL.
  E. E.; RADER, Lima; M=12 Nov. 1857; William L. Mehaffey, JP. NL
  Eli P. R.; SETTLEMYER, Ellen C.; M=16 June 1864; M. Barger, JP.
    NL.
  Elkana; MILLER, Rosanah; M=1 Sept. 1859; E. Yount, JP. NL.
  Francis M.; ABERNATHY, Caroline; M=11 Mar. 1852; Philip Burns,
    JP. NL.
  George; HEFNER, Mary Ann; M=16 June 1863; M. Barger, JP. NL.
  Gilbert (25); TOWNSEND, Fridona E. (20); white; M=11 Oct. 1877;
    GL Hunt, Luth. Min. at Jesse Propst's; DE Link, DP Yount,
    Amanda E. Cline. NL.
  J.; GANT, Sina J.; M=13 Sept. 1855; Eli E. Deal, JP. NL.
  J. R. [Jonas & EC]; SHERRILL, Laura [Henderson & Mehafey]; M=
    9 Sept. 1869; JA Sherrill, Min. NL.
  J. Patrick [Elijah & Elizabeth]; ROWE, Lizzie [Daniel & Eliza-
    beth]; M=30 Jan. 1868; PC Henkel, Min. NL.

CLINE, James (21); FISH, Nannie I. (21); white; M=21 Oct. 1877; WA Hewitt, JP in Cald. Twsp; MM Cline, Franklin Boyd, Marcus Huit. NL.

James (29); REINHARDT, Sarah (20); black; M=17 Feb. 1875; NE Sigmon, JP in Cline's Twsp; John Herman, Ephraim Reinhardt, John Reinhardt. NL.

James E. (22); DAWTHITTE, Ella A. (20); white; M=6 Feb. 1879; JD Carpenter, Min. in Hky; AW Marshall, WH Ramsour, WF Tomlinson. NL.

Jason J. (23); MILLER, Candace (22); white; M=14 May 1874; JM Smith, Luth. Min. at JT Miller's; Marcus Cline, Adolphus Harmon. NL.

Jesse [Jacob & Polly]; YOUNT, Anna R. [John & Elizabeth]; M=23 Sept. 1869; EA Warlick, JP. NL.

John; DRUM, Roxanah [David & Martha]; M=13 Feb. 1872; JA Sherrill, Min. NL.

John P. (27); CLINE, Mary Jane (18); white; M=13 Aug. 1876; AL Yount, Luth. Min. at Daniel Cline's; Miles Wike, Timothy Cline, Noah Wike. NL.

John R. (21) of Hky Tav. Twsp; LINK, Sarah E. (22) of Hky Tav. Twsp; white; M=10 Apr. 1873; JM Smith, Luth. Min. in Hky Tav. Twsp; Aaron Sigmon, WT Cline, Jesse Hawn. NL.

John R. (24) of Burke Co., NC; LINK, Charity E. (18); white; M=1 Nov. 1876; Abel Whitener, JP in Hky; AJ Whitener, PS Ward, PM Whitener. NL.

Jonathan; SETTLEMYER, Angeline; M=2 Jan. 1862; M. Barger, JP. NL.

Joseph T. [Joseph & Ruphena]; HARRISON, Mahala [Marcus & Lydia]; M=24 Dec. 1871; GL Hunt, Min. 1-62.

L. H. G.; MILLER, Ruphena; M=7 Sept. 1854; ER Shuford, JP. NL.

L. J. (30); ECKARD, T. S. (20); white; M=11 Oct. 1877; PC Henkel, Luth. Min. at Solomon Eckard's; PC Hawn, DE Hawn. NL.

Laben Wilson [Paul & Lolina]; HOOVER, Sarah; M=1871; record missing. NL.

Logan [Aaron or Amon & Linnie]; SIGMON, Angelene [Sesse & Ada]; M=14 Feb. 1872; JH Bruns, JP. NL.

M. L.; BOST, Laura N.; M=1 Nov. 1855; PC Henkle, Min. NL.
M. N.; BARRINGER, Lina; M=12 Oct. 1854; A. Ray, JP. NL.
Maxwell; BARGER, Dinah; M=23 Nov. 1862; E. Yount, JP. NL.
Noah; BOLCH, Sophiah; M=10 Feb. 1857; Jonas Bost, JP. NL.
Pinkney; SUMMITT, Catharine; M=7 Aug. 1855; ER Shuford, JP. NL.

Reubin F. [Mathias & Mary]; LINEBERGER, Susan [MH & Elizabeth]; M=21 Dec. 1870; JM Smith, Min. 1-11.

Robert B. [Jonas & Caroline]; SHERRILL, Laura [Elam & Nancy]; M=6 Oct. 1870; Daniel May, Min. 1=10.

Rufus; FLOWERS, H. R.; M=16 Mar. 1858; John Kent, JP. NL.
Rufus; SIGMON, Harriet; M=31 July 1859; E. Yount, JP. NL.

Sylvanus (28) [Joseph & Ruphenia Huffman] of Newt. Twsp; LINK, Elizabeth (17) [Ephraim & Eliza] of Newt. Twsp; white; M=19 Dec. 1872; JM Smith, Min. in Newt. Twsp; DS Fry, PH Bolch, ME Fry. 1-149.

William; ROWE, Rosabella; M=24 Feb. 1859; John Lantz, Min. NL.
William A. (38); BOLCH, Elizabeth (16); white; M=18 Nov. 1875; JH Bruns, JP in Hky; James B. Beard, JL Lyerly. NL.

William P. (27) [Eli D. & Eliza R.]; BOST, Julia C. (25) [Joseph & Mary]; white; M=16 May 1880; AJ Fox, Min. in Newton; DL Rowe, RH Cline, Ale Fox. 2-24.

CLIPARD, David (26) [Andrew & Rebecca]; STOWE, Harriet C. (18) [Franklin & Minda]; white; M=4 Aug. 1874; JA Sherrill, Min. in Mt. Crk Twsp; TO Robinson, WM Linebarger. 1-261.

Marcus; STINE, Elizabeth; M=22 Oct. 1857; JD Caldwell, JP. NL.

CLIPPARD, Andrew (23) [Andrew & Rebecca]; LINK, Olive L. (25) [Caleb & Rhoda F.]; white; M=7 Dec. 1879; WC Caldwell, JP in Cald. Twsp; EM Lynch, Elbert Litten, Luther B. Clippard. 1-337.

Rufus W. (55) of Lincoln Co., NC; CLIPPARD, Nancy J. (24); white; M=12 May 1878; WC Caldwell, JP in Cald. Twsp; NE Laney, JP Armstrong, JT Jones. NL.

CLODFELTER, Elias; DEAL, Nancy; M=11 Aug. 1857; Joshua Wilson, JP. NL.

CLONINGER, Arachibald C. (23); McCASLIN, Margaret Ella (17); white; M=23 Sept. 1875; Rufus England, JP in Cald. Twsp; WT Cline, Ambrose Bolch, JF Rudisill. NL.

Miles W. (21); SIGMON, Anna (20); white; M=20 May 1875; PF Smith, JP, Newton; C. Setzer, H. Mooney, S. Lymon. NL.

Monroe; RABB, Margaret; M=4 Feb. 1864; JLA Yount, JP. NL.

Perry C. (22) [Noah & Paline]; BUMGARNER, Jane (21) [Emeline & n/g]; white; M=5 May 1880; JA Whitener, JP in JF Twsp; HP Rudisill, VMS Blackburn, BA Whitener. 2-25.

S. C. (24); WINKLER, Andy (19); white; M=28 Oct. 1876; Abel Barger, JP in Hky; GP Seabock, GC Turner, LA Seabock. NL.

Thomas P. [Thomas & Sarah]; SETTLEMYER, Mary M. [Hallman & Mary]; M=14 Sept. 1871; TL Smith, JP. 1-63.

COBB, Rufus; ABERNATHY, Sophia; M=20 July 1862; JW Gabriel, JP. NL.

COCHRAN, John L. [DC & Lucinda]; SHERRILL, Dorcas S. [Elisha & Betsey]; John B. Marsh, Min. No date. NL.

L. W.; REINHARDT, M. I.; M=30 Jan. 1861; J. Lantz, Min. NL.

CODY, John; ELLIOTT, Mary C.; M=27 Oct. 1859; PJ Pitts, JP. NL.

COFFEY, Henry N.; COCHRAN, Louisa S.; M=28 Oct. 1862; RH Moody. NL.

COLEY, G. D.; CLODFELTER, Catharine; M=27 Apr. 1866; JS Nelson, Min. NL.

CONNER, C. F. [Electus & Elizabeth]; POPE, Anna M. [Aaron & Elizabeth]; M=29 mar. 1871; GJ Wilkie, Min. 1-64.

Charles; SHERRILL, Mary J.; M=16 Dec. 1856; H. Asbury, Min. NL.

Henry W.; BOSTON, R. M.; M=6 Jan. 1858; Jesse Gantt, JP. NL.

William (19) [Jim & Harriet]; CORNELIUS, Jane (17) [M. & Caroline]; black; M=27 Jan. 1876; CW Blaylock, Min. in Mt. Crk Twsp; JC Bynum, FL Bost, James Long. 1-311.

CONNOR, Marion (35) [James Shuford & Sallie Hunsucker]; SIGMON, Susie (35) [Nelson Ray & Emma Little]; black; M=16 Apr. 1879; Wilum Brooks, Min. at Edman Hunsucker's; Pink Smith, Miliday Hunsucker, ? Hunsucker. 1-338.

CONRAD, John F. [Logan & Elizabeth]; STARR, Cary M. [JC & Malinda] M=4 Nov. 1869; MA Throneburg, JP. NL.

COOK, Ellis L. (19) of Burke Co., NC; MILLER, Amanda (18); white; M=10 Jan. 1878; Abel Whitener, JP in Hky; Charley Watson, BF Arney, MD Arney. NL.

F. G. (20); SIGMON, Sarah E. (19); white; M=5 Feb. 1874; JA Sherrill, Min. at JA Sherrill's; JA Sigmon, WA Loftin, WE Allen. NL.

Jacob [Abel & Eliza]; SIGMON, Susan [Abel & Elizabeth]; M=16 Apr. 1872; Abel Whitener, JP. NL.

James [Albert & Selina]; McKINZIE, Juliett [Robert & Emaline]; M=4 Apr. 1872; JA Sherrill, Min. NL.

James M. (27); DRUM, Martha J. (22); white; M=6 Feb. 1879; SC Brown, JP at TF Drum's; WL Saunders, MT Saunders, LJ Drum. NL.

L. O.; HASS, Barbara; M=23 Sept. 1855; Philip Burns, JP. NL.

COONS, Jacob; BOWMAN, Mary; M=28 Feb. 1859; JB Little, JP. NL.

Marcus M. (27) [Henry & Elizabeth]; EKERD, Candace C. (19) [Solomon & Priscilla]; white; M=5 Aug. 1880; JM Smith, Luth. Min. in Hky Twsp; JS Coons, SA Huffman, PC Coons. 2-26.

CORKILL, William M. [Thomas & Catharine]; McCOY, Julia A. [John & Sallie]; white; M=28 Jan. 1868; Elijah Allison, Min. NL.

CORNELIUS, Benjamin F. (25); SHERRILL, Mary (19); white; M=20 Mar. 1878; GM Ivey, Min. at CN Sherrill's; Adam P. Robinson, JH Cornelius, JC Sherrill. NL.

James B.; SHERRILL, Ann E.; M=7 Aug. 1859; Rev. H. Asbury. NL.

John; ABERNATHY, Susan; M=24 Feb. 1853; Jacob Hill, Min. NL.

William [Henderson & Mary]; SHERRILL, Louise [Robert & Mary]; M=23 Mar. 1870; JA Sherrill, Min. at JA Sherrill's. NL.

William O.; SHERRILL, E. E.; M=13 Sept. 1861; JA Sherrill, JP. NL.

CORPENING, John E. (23) of Burke Co., NC; RAMSOUR, Fannie B. (19) white; M=4 May 1876; JH Shuford, Min. at Elcanah Ramsour's; EF Ramsour, RA Abernathy, HE Ramsour. NL.

CORRELL, Hugh McClain (18) [George & Margaret]; POOL, Anna Matilda (18) [James N. & Mary]; white; M=11 May 1880; WC Caldwell, JP in Cald. Twsp; Pinkney Keever, EM Fish, NAE Wilkinson. 2-27.

COSTNER, Franklin (21); EKARD, Isabell (20); black; M=24 May 1877; JM Smith, Luth. Min. at JM Smith's; WA Smith, PB Smith, HA Kale. NL.

  Henry F. (21); NEIL, Arrenia (22); black; M=8 Aug. 1875; CW Blaylock, Min. at King Long's; Alex Neil, Peter Moore, Game Powell. NL.

COULTER, D. Monroe [Eli & Harriett C.]; Yount, Sarah E. [David & Liney]; M=8 Sept. 1870; JC Clapp, Min. 1-12.

  Isaac (25); SHORES, Amelia (19); black; M=25 Dec. 1876; JB Turner in Hky; Abe McCorkle, Martin Wilfong, Eli Shores. NL.

  John H. (27); PITTS, Laura E. (20); white; M=10 Feb. 1874; J. Ingold, Min. at PJ Pitt's; LH Shuford, FB Moore, TM Abernathy. NL.

  John S. [Eli & Harriet C.]; HERMAN, Saponia A. [Franklin L. & OM]; M=23 Feb. 1871; JM Smith, Min. 1-65.

  Merida (21); RAMSOUR, Harriet (18); black; M=14 Feb. 1879; EJ Harris, Min. in Newton; RA Wilfong, Stephen Graham, Julius Graham? NL.

COVINGTON, B.; ABERNATHY, L.; M=9 Sept. 1866; D. Hamilton, JP. NL.

COX, Henry C.; SRONCE, Janie O.; M=2 Sept. 1862; Rev. AR Benick, Min. NL.

CRAIG(E), George W. (36) of Hky Tav. Twsp; STANSILL, Jannia (31) of Rowan Co., NC; white; M=28 Oct. 1873; PF Smith, JP in Newton; TC Graham, GW Rockett, HA Lowrance. NL.

CRANFORD, W. Manley (20) [Wilson & Martha]; CALDWELL, Lizey S.(20) [Phillip & Sarah]; white; M=18 Mar. 1880; JA Sherrill, Min. in Cald. Twsp; Charles L. McCaul, LA Killian, Jay Beatty. 2-28.

CRAWFORD, Felix Q. [Robert M. & Margaret E.]; WHITENER, Sarah [Moses & Mary]; M=16 May 1872; Robert Helton, Min. 1-150.

CROCKLETON, Hamilton (53) [Jack Sherrill & Fanny]; HILL, Anna Rebecah (46) [George Little & Camila Conner]; black; M=9 Oct. 1875; Wallace Shuford, Bapt. Min. in Mt. Crk Twsp; Asquire Cornelius, Harris, Burton, George Hall. 1-278.

CROSON, H. H. [Thomas S. & Eliza J.]; COBB, Emma [Henry & Nancy]; M=16 Jan. 1868; John Watts, Min. NL.

CROUSE, J. L.; SUMMIT, Sarah J.; M=22 July 1862; JD Caldwell, JP. NL.

  L. R. [David & Mary]; LITTLE, Mary [George & Nancy]; M=24 Mar. 1870; Miles Goodson, JP. NL.

  Robert; ABERNETHY, Rebecca D.; M=13 Jan. 1862; JD Caldwell, JP. NL.

CROWELL, Champion (21) [Governor & Lucy]; Packet, Mary (18) [Ed & Clarasay Shuford]; black; M=24 Apr. 1879; AB Jennings, Min. in Hky Twsp; Frank Crowell, HE Deny, Mike Colmon. 1-339.

  Frank (22); McDOWELL, Mollie (21); black; M=13 Jan. 1875; JH Bruns, JP in Hky; Champ Crowell, EUD Wilfong. NL.

CUMAN, Jacob; HUIT, Ann; M=13 Jan. 1853; H. Cline, JP. NL.

CURTIS, A. F.; CARKERHAM, J. F.; M=7 Apr. 1853; GJ Wilkie, JP. NL.

DAGENHARDT, Henry V. (18) [Henry & Catharine]; NANCE, Julia (18) [William & Martha]; white; M=22 Feb. 1880; Robert Helton, Min. in JF Twsp; JW Helton, RJ Helton, AD Whitener. 2-29.

Robert L. (19); WEAVER, Sarah E. (21); white; M=21 June 1874; AC Corpening, JP in JF Twsp; JC Corpening, AE Corpening. NL.

Rufus (28) of Alexander Co., NC; GOBLE, Martha A. (28); white; M=27 Dec. 1874; James Kerley, Bapt. Min. at Lewis Goble's; TJ Christopher, Cosban Goble, Emanuel Goble. NL.

Wilbern S. (28) of Alexander Co., NC; STINE, Malinda C. (22); white; M=29 Mar. 1877; SC Brown, JP in Hamilton Twsp; EL Brown, A. Brown, RD Stine. NL.

DAGENHART, Martin L. (22); NANCE, Frances R. (21); white; M=22 Sept. 1878; Robert Helton, Min. at Mrs. Nance's; Wiley Nance, Frank Nance, William Nance. NL.

DALEY, George W. (32) [WA & Anna]; HALE, Miriam (41) [William & Henrietta]; white; M=29 Jan. 1880; HA Forney, JP in Newt. Twsp; LN Wilson, EJ Forney, Sarah Forney. 2-30.

DANNER, Henry S. (22) [Alexander & Susanah R.]; BOSTIAN, Frances G. (17) [Wallace & Lucinda]; white; M=28 Aug. 1879; QM Smith, JP in Cline's Twsp; MP White, DL Ervin, Lewis Danner. 1-340.

Hosea A. (26) [Alex & Susan]; WILKIE, Ellen (25) [George P. & Ann]; white; M=23 Dec. 1875; JK Howell, Bapt. Min. at GJ Wilkie's; Virginia C. Howell, Mattie E. Wilkie, Emily R. Howell. 1-279.

DAVIDSON, Leonados (50); MILLER, Ada M. (29); white; M=3 Nov. 1878; PK Little, JP in Cline's Twsp; MM Smith, L. Throneburg, EF Jennings. NL.

DAVIS, H. A. [Clase & Annie]; WINEBARGER, Louisa [Conrad & Susan]; M=5 Mar. 1870; JH Bruns, JP. NL.

J. W. (22); May, C. Ada (17); white; M=15 July 1874; VA Sharp, Meth. Min. in Newton; Charles Little, John Kenith, YE May. NL.

John C. (30) [Milton & Margaret]; WHITENER, Eliza (30) [Eli & Sallie]; white; M=12 Mar. 1879; Abel Whitener, JP in Hky Twsp; EL Whitener, AM Hawn, LS Whitener. 1-341.

William; MARTIN, Susan; M=24 Feb. 1856; A. Abernathy, Min. NL.

William D. (25) [Joseph & Pheba Herman] of Hky Tav. Twsp; DELLINGER, Eliza (22) [Jons Dellinger & Lina] of Hky Tav. Twsp; white; M=23 Jan. 1873; J. Ingold, Min. in Hky Tav. Twsp; Pink Dellinger, Anna Dellinger, Salley Dellinger. 1-232.

DEAL, A.; CLINE, B. S.; M=16 Aug. 1865; D. McD. Yount, JP. NL.

Adam (18); HOLLER, Sarah (21); white; M=31 May 1877; CW Herman, JP in Newt. Twsp; Irene Herman, Ada Herman, Julian M. Seats. NL.

Alfred W. [Levi & Harriet L.]; HERMAN, Harriet L. [George & Lidia]; M=27 Dec. 1869; EA Warlick, JP. NL.

Amsie (20); FRY, Jinney (19); white; M=21 Dec. 1876; HA Forney, JP in Newt. Twsp; EP Deal, JC Deal, John E. Thornton. NL.

Camy; SETZER, Susan; M=24 Nov. 1852; William L. Mehaffey, JP. NL.

Franklin; Longcryer, Delila; M=19 Aug. 1851; William L. Mehaffey, JP. NL.

George; McGee, Adoline; M=22 Aug. 1858; William L. Mehaffey, JP. NL.

Goan; SETZER, Phebe; M=3 Oct. 1852; William L. Mehaffey, JP. NL.

Henry [George & Mary]; SIGMON, Rachael [George, Sr. & Betty]; M=14 Feb. 1869; PC Hinckle, Min. NL.

Henry (25) of Newt. Twsp; FRY, Caroline (22) of Newt. Twsp; white; M=11 Sept. 1873; PF Smith, JP in Newt. Twsp; G. Setzer, William Morrison, CAR Setzer. NL.

Jacob; KILLIAN, Adeline; M=22 Dec. 1859; PJ Pitts, JP. NL.

Jefferson C. (20); SIGMON, Jinnie (17); white; M=20 Apr. 1876; HA Forney, JP in Newt. Twsp; MW Cloninger, EP Deal, Noah Setzer. NL.

John S. [Hosea & Mira]; DEAL, Eliza E. [Henry & Rebecah]; M=1 Feb. 1872; EA Warlick, JP. 1-151.

Lemuel; SMITH, Catherine; M=25 Mar. 1860; E. Yount, JP. NL.

N. S.; GREEN, Jane; M=25 Feb. 1855; WL Mehaffey, JP. NL.

Perry (21); HUIT, Lucy Jane (21); white; M-13 June 1875; PK Little, JP in Cline's Twsp; William W. Carpenter, JC Huit, Samuel Sigmon. NL.

Reubin; SMITH, Ovina; M=18 Dec. 1851; Eli E. Deal, JP. NL.

Robert H. (20) of Cald. Twsp; BARRINGER, Mary Jane (16) of Cald. Twsp; M=24 July 1873; JL Huit, JP at JL Huit's; Robert Cloninger, Mark Huit, WA Huit. NL.

Soloman; PHELPS, Nancy; M=28 Nov. 1866; D. McD. Yount, JP. NL.

Sylvanus M. [Eli E. & Eliza]; WILSON, Jinny C. [MM & CE]; M=17 Nov. 1868; PC Hinckle, Min. NL.

Wilbern P. (21); WINEBARGER, Candace (21); white; M=3 Oct. 1878; PC Henkel, Luth. Min. at Silas Winebarger's; QL Little, SW Winebarger, Silas Winebarger. NL.

DEATON, Rufus [Billy & Charlotte Griffin]; McGINNIS, Lydia [John & Sally]; M=24 Aug. 1869; JM Brown, JP. NL.

DEITZ, C. L.; REITZEL, Lucinda C.; M=4 Mar. 1858; JB Little, JP. NL.

Emanuel M. (21) [Phillip & Harriet]; HEFNER, Donie E. (21) [John & Rhoda]; white; M=19 Dec. 1880; CT Sigmon, JP, Cline's Twsp; Rufus R. Reitzel, WM Hefner. 2-31.

H. C.; CARPENTER, Martha A.; M=23 Apr. 1861; E. Yount, JP. NL.

J. L.; WHISNANT, S. E.; M=4 Mar. 1866; Alex Abernathy, Min. NL.

Julius (21) of Hky Tav. Twsp; HUFFMAN, Delia S. (21) of Cline's Twsp; M=28 May 1872; JH Bruns, JP in Hky Tav. Twsp; Noah Killian, Freeman J. Huffman, Noah Lefong. NL.

Solamon [Phillip & Harriet]; DAGERHEART, Cacean [Henry & Catharine]; M=7 Mar. 1872; EA Warlick, JP. 1-152.

Washington M. [Phillip H. & Harriet]; PROPST, Susan J. [Riley & n/g]; M=28 Mar. 1872; Abel Whitener, JP. NL.

DELLINGER, Adolphus (25) [Mike & Rachael Cline]; STAMEY, Ellen (30) of Cald. Twsp; black; M=1 Sept. 1872; PF Smith, JP in Newt. Twsp; JK Smith, LC Smith, L. Bond. 1-153.

Franklin J. (22); ROWE, Ellen (18); white; M=14 Oct. 1874; JM Smith, Luth. Min. at Noah Rowe's; Fred Smith, Laura Smith, Calvin Sigmon. NL.

DELLINGER, G. M.; SIGMON, Catharine G.; M=20 Feb. 1855; JB Little, JP. NL.
  J. H.; LOWRANCE, Melinda; M=17 Jan. 1861; JHA Yount, JP. NL.
  John C. (22); FOX, Barbara C. (19); white; M=3 May 1877; JC Hartsell, Min. in Newton; Joshua Drum, RE Bost, Socratus Benfield. NL.
  Jonas (20); ISENHOUR, Harriett (19); white; M=31 Jan. 1878; QM Smith, JP in Cline's Twsp; Daniel Isenhour, DW Cline, JC Dellinger. NL.
  Robert [Joseph & Barbara]; CARPENTER, Barbara [Eli & Rose]; M=5 Jan. 1871; William H. Rockett, JP. NL.
  Sherman; WINEBARGER, Rachel; M=25 Oct. 1852; JB Little, JP. NL.
  William (21); SHOOK, Orpha E. (20); white; M=5 Sept. 1876; GL Hunt, Luth. Min. at GL Hunt's; NC Sigmon, MC Sigmon, JS Sigmon. NL.
  William P. [Jacob & Sarah]; ANTHONY, Ann [Paul & Magdalene]; M=13 Dec. 1870; JC Clapp, Min. NL.
DEWY, James T. (21) of Caldwell; SHUFORD, Lettie (21); black; M=17 Jan. 1878; Robert Helton, Min. at Robert Helton's; ED Ramsour, T. Ramsour, Frances ?. NL.
DICKSON, Fredrick [John and Ann Moore]; GROSS, Nancy J. [Henry & n/k]; M=25 Jan. 1868; Thad Fry, Col. Min. NL.
  John A. (24) of Morganton, NC; GIBBS, Annie (23); white; M=3 July 1877; RB Anderson, Presby. Min. at GM Gibb's; JJ Pearson, JM Walker, JM Walker, Jr. NL.
DOUGLAS, E. L. [James & Rose]; FRY, E. T. [Andrew & Holly]; M=5 Mar. 1870; Miles Goodson, JP. NL.
DOURITY, Marcus A. [John & Manenry]; WILLS, Matty; M=17 Feb. 1869; PC Hinkle, Min. NL.
DOWNS, Benjamin F. (26) [Charles & Lydia]; LITTLE, Louiza M. (18) [Daniel A. & EA]; white; M=6 Jan. 1876; JH West, Bapt. Min. in Cline's Twsp; DA Little, EA Little, JB Little. 1-312.
DRUM, Albert J. (21); SIMMONS, Margaret (19); white; M=14 Feb. 1878; JH Bruns, JP in Hky; JS Tomlinson, WF Tomlinson, WA Bowls. NL.
  David; SHOOK, Sarah; M=11 Apr. 1862; J. Lentz, JP. NL.
  Filden W. (20); McGee, Eliza (21); white; M=24 Dec. 1874; GW Cansler, JP in Hamilton Twsp; JD Little, JW Blackwelder, Walter Sherrill. NL.
  Francis M. (20); LOFTIN, Mary (19); white; M=18 Aug. 1875; GW Cansler, JP in Hamilton Twsp; Walter Sherrill, Jacob Abernathy, A. Cook. NL.
  Franklin (50) [John & Barbara]; VANHORN, Nancy (43) [Elias & Elizabeth Lutz]; white; M=9 Jan. 1876; AJ Fox, Min. in JF Twsp; MM Wilson, ES Coulter, JB Lutes. 1-313.
  Hosea [Peter & Rhoda]; HEFNER, Lucy [Noah & Sallie]; M=24 Mar. 1868; JB Little, Esq. NL.
  James M.; CLARK, Rebecca P.; M=8 Apr. 1866; JD Caldwell, JP. NL.
  John P.; CLINE, R. E.; M=28 Apr. 1861; JD Caldwell, JP. NL.
  John P. (22) [Rufus L. & Mary M.]; CALDWELL, Rhoda M. (18) [David & Fannie]; white; M=16 Oct. 1879; WC Caldwell, JP in Cald. Twsp; WW Laney, Abel Caldwell, Joseph Caldwell. 1-342.

Joshua [John & Barbary]; FOX, Mag [David & Ann]; M=11 May 1870; WG James, JP. NL.

Miles; BOWMAN, Harriet E.; M=3 Jan. 1856; JB Little, JP. NL.

Perry Davidson (19) [JP & Rutha E.]; SUMMIT, Margaret Ellen (20) [JL & Perlina]; white; M=16 Sept. 1880; WC Caldwell, JP in Cald. Twsp; JJ Caldwell, Elizabeth Caldwell, Naomi E. Summit. 2-33.

Phillip L. [David & Martha]; SIGMON, Espy M.; M=1871; no other information.

Pinkney A. (24) [Monroe & Catharine]; MICHEL, Mary Julia E. (16) [Ambros & Cynthia]; white; M=20 Jan. 1876; Rufus England, JP in Cald. Twsp; AJ Seagle, Ann Drum, Alex L. Keener. 1-314.

Pinkney D. [David & Martha]; CALDWELL, Fannie E. [Phillip & Sarah]; M=31 Dec. 1871; JA Sherrill, Min. 1-66.

Rufus; TURBYFILL, Mary; M=11 Dec. 1856; JD Caldwell, JP. NL.

Rufus L. [David & Martha]; CALDWELL, Nancy; M-1871; no other information.

William A. [Phillip & Elizabeth]; WILKINSON, Nancy C. [Thomas & Elizabeth]; M=30 Apr. 1868; JA Sherrill, Min. NL.

William C. [David & Martha]; LINEBARGER, Sarah A. [Mike & Isabella]; M=25 Nov. 1868; JA Sherrill, Min. NL.

William H.; CALDWELL, Margaret R.; M=11 Apr. 1860; JD Caldwell, JP. NL.

DUNCAN, Thomas (21); WINEBARGER, Susan (22); white; M=28 May 1874; GL Hunt, Min. at GL Hunt's; WH Herman, Dora Miller, Sarah Kee.

EADES, Joel [Isaac & Priscilla]; REESE, Sarah [Lewe & Anna]; M=21 Dec. 1871; GL Hunt, Min. 1-67.

EADS, Joel (35); BALL, Mary (21); white; M=24 Sept. 1878; JB Richardson, Bapt. Min. at George Borough's house; TH Ervin, WL Moore, JA Killian. NL.

Ransome; HEFNER, Salinda E.; M=19 Oct. 1864; GH Moser, JP. NL.

ECKARD, Daniel; FRY, V. B.; M=16 Dec. 1862; James H. Rowe, JP. NL.

Daniel B.; HUFFMAN, Emoline E.; M=18 June 1858; John Kent, JP. NL.

Emanuel (25); SIMMONS, Rhoda S. (19); white; M=8 July 1875; JM Smith, Luth. Min. in Hky; PL Miller, Elcanah Ekard, GA Bolch. NL.

George; DELLINGER, Anna; M=10 Nov. 1856; CW Herman, JP. NL.

Guilford R. [Solomon & Priscilla]; STINE, Harriet B. [John & Sarah]; M=16 May 1872; JM Smith, Min. 1-154.

Logan Pinkney (28); MILLIGAN, Sarah (27); white; M=22 Feb. 1875; JA Sherrill, Min. at Mrs. Milligan's; John Sherrill, MA Abernathy, WL Sherrill. NL.

Rufus; HERMAN, Martha C.; M=13 Jan. 1859; William L. Mehaffey, JP. NL.

Simon; BOOVY, M. J.; M=14 Apr. 1861; PC Henkel, Min. NL.

Wesley D. (35); DRUM, Camila (19); white; M=8 Sept. 1878; JM Smith, Luth. Min. at JM Smith's; WA Smith, Manerva Herman, Harriet S. Smith. NL.

ECKERT, Morgan [George & Mary]; HOFFMAN, Sarah Ann [Jackson & Mary M.]; M=17 Mar. 1869; PC Hinkle, Min. NL.

EDWARDS, B. Perry (39) of Mt. Crk Twsp; LITTEN, Sarah S. (31) of
  Mt. Crk Twsp; white; M=29 July 1873; JA Sherrill, Min.;
  William G. Fisher, GP Ekerd, ML Sherrill. NL.
 Elbert [Bradford & Emeline McCorkle]; Long, Ceda [Lewis &
  Hannah]; M=21 Nov. 1869; William Burke, Min. NL.
 Henderson; DAVIS, Malinda; M=13 Dec. 1864; D. Hamilton, JP. NL.
 Howard; ABERNATHY, Abigail; M=9 Nov. 1856; John Lantz, Min. NL.
 J. S.; SHERRILL, Mary L.; M=1 May 1856; H. Asbury, Min. NL.
 James L. (63) of Cald. Twsp; BANDY, Martha Ellenor (35) of Cald.
  Twsp; white; M=3 Aug. 1873; JL Huit, JP in the bride's home;
  WA Huit, Eliza Kirksy. NL.
 John (21); EDWARDS, Martha Ann (19); white; M=29 June 1876; SC
  Brown, JP in Hamilton Twsp; JMS Edwards, Lewis Holdsclaw, TF
  Bradburn. NL.
 Miles; ALLEN, Sarah S.; M=20 Oct. 1861; JW Gabriel, JP. NL.
 Spencer; SIGMON, Martha; M=2 Jan. 1860; JW Gabriel, JP. NL.
EKARD, Abel S. [David & Elizabeth]; WAGNER, Mahala [William Herman
  & Elizabeth]; M=15 Dec. 1867; PC Henkel, Min. NL.
 Elkanah (25) of Cline's Twsp; SIGMON, Sarah Ann (22) of Cline's
  Twsp; M=13 May 1873; JM Smith, Luth. Min. in Cline's Twsp;
  PE Isenhour, Emanuel Eckard, Alf Sigmon. NL.
 John G. (21); WHITE, Fannie E. (17); white; M=6 Feb. 1879; PC
  Henkel, Min. at PC Henkel's; DE Wagner, AM Ekard, PC Ekard.
  NL.
 Marcus E. (22); HUFFMAN, Camila (22); white; M=4 May 1876; JM
  Smith, Luth. Min. at Jackson Huffman's; EL Whitener, ME
  Ekard, JP Huffman. NL.
 Poly C. (25) [David & Elizabeth C.]; SIGMON, Ferdona S. (18)
  [AN & OM]; white; M=22 Oct. 1879; PC Henkel, Luth. Min. in
  Newt. Twsp; John G. Ekard, LM Reitzel, AS Ekard. 1-343.
 W. D. E.; HUFFMAN, Polly R.; M=1 Nov. 1865; Thomas Little, JP.
  NL.
 Wesley (21) [William & Barbara]; of Alexander Co., NC; HEFNER,
  Isabel (15) [David & Sally]; white; M=1 May 1879; JH Bruns,
  JP in Hky Twsp; Lula C. Beard, JS Tomlinson, Pattie C. Roy-
  ster. 1-344.
EKERD, Eli D. (23); Fry, Martha E. (24); white; M=23 Dec. 1874; JM
  Smith, Luth. Min. at Solomon Fry's; PC Hawn, MA Setzer, AY
  Sigmon. NL.
ELDRIDGE, Jasper; CLINE, Sarah; M=27 Apr. 1864; LN Wilson, JP.
  NL.
ELLIS, John [Steven & Susan]; GAITHER, Euphemia R. [Lebentions? &
  Rebecca]; M=24 Nov. 1870; JM Smith, Min. 1-14.
 William H. (40); CROWELL, Mildred (34); white; M=21 Nov. 1877;
  George M. Gibbs, Min. at AW Marshall's; HD Abernathy, TB
  Alexander, AW Marshall. NL.
ENGLAND, N. B. [Milton & Julia]; ROBINSON, Sarah Ann [Manuel &
  Mary]; M=29 Sept. 1868; James Pastell, Min. NL.
ENNIS, John [Jeremiah & Caroline]; FISH, Lina [Uriah & Mary]; M=5
  Sept. 1869; AB Ervine, Min. NL.
EPPS, John A. (39) [James & Polly]; DEAL, Ellen P. (23) [Franklin
  & Delila]; white; M=25 Sept. 1879; GL Hunt, Luth. Min. in
  Newton; SW Sigmon, WB Winters, JB Barringer. 1-345.

ERNEY, Franklin; SHERRILL, Martha; M=21 Oct. 1866; Adam Miller, Min. NL.

ERVIN, George (22); MOSTELLER, Martha Ann (20); black; M=18 Jan. 1877; Edmond N. Joyner, Min. in Hky; Mary E. Joyner, Lizzie & Samuel Kelly. NL.

ERWIN, Maxwell E. (23); BARGER, Fannie (15); white; M=29 Mar. 1877; JH Bruns, JP in Hky; David Pitts, Simeon Barger, MS Arney. NL.

EVANS, Richard (25); RING, Ellen (20) [Eliza Ring-mother]; black; M=12 Apr. 1879; Abel Whitener, JP in Hky Twsp; PL Morgan, Addison Morgan, MJ Morgan. 1-346.

EVENS, J. W.; POPE, Nancy; M=19 Mar. 1856; TJ Hamilton, JP. NL.

FAUCETTE, Edward W. [JR & Catharine]; BOST, Ella [AL & Senora]; M=31 Oct. 1871; Jesse Rankin, Min. 1-68.

FEIMSTER, George W. (34); ROBINSON, Margaret (30); black; M=28 Dec. 1876; JB Turner, Min. in Hky; Jack Phillips, Robert Smyer, Nelson Bowman. NL.

FIELDS, Thomas E. (30); WILSON, Lillie C. (19); white; M=23 Nov. 1875; JC Hartzell, Min. at HS Wilson's; JA Shuford, HD Abernathy, Charles E. Graham. NL.

FINCANNON, J. W. [Jacob & Juda]; WIKE, Catherine A. [David & Delilia]; M=30 Dec. 1869; EA Warlick, JP. NL.

FINGER, Calvin (19); MOSTELLER, Hildy (18); black; M=14 Dec. 1876; Jacob Mosteller, JP in Bandys Twsp; Steven Warlick, Allen Whitener. NL.

D. F. [John & Lena]; KEENER, Sarah [Daniel & Mariah]; M=13 Oct. 1867; H. Cline, Esq. NL.

Daniel A. (26) of Cald. Twsp; FRY, Lucy E. (22) of Newt. Twsp; white; M=18 Sept. 1874; JW Williams, JP in Cald. Twsp; WJ Finger, Mary J. Frye, Malinda L. Reese. NL.

Franklin; IKERD, Polly; M=19 Sept. 1852; P. Burns, JP. NL.

Hugh [Steven Brevane & Sarah Finger]; ANTHONY, Manday [Ceyon Ramsour & Fanny Anthony]; M=24 July 1870; TF Wilfong, JP. NL.

John (24) of Lincoln Co., NC; ROBINSON, Harriet (17) of JF Twsp; black; M=2 Aug. 1873; EP Coulter, JP in JF Twsp; Wesley Hoyle, Monroe Coulter, Caleb Robinson. NL

Lalon [Lalon Bost & Charlothy Shuford]; ENGLAND, Catherine [James Ramsour & Milly England]; M=26 Sept. 1869; EA Warlick, JP. NL.

William J. (21); FRY, Mary J. (20); white; M=20 Aug. 1874; JL Huit, JP in Cald. Twsp; GW Rabb, Sarah Rabb, Mikeal Keener. NL.

FISH, Brisan; POOL, Elvery C.; M=20 Jan. 1856; Jeptha Clark, Min. NL.

Sidney; BRIDGES, Mary; M=19 Sept. 1852; JM Lowrance, JP. NL.

FISHER, Carry; WALDEN, Sepram; M=2 Jan. 1859; Jeptha Clark, Min. NL.

F. M. [Isaac & Anna]; HARVAL, C. C. [Thomas & Susan]; M=12 Aug. 1869; T. Caldwell, JP. NL.

Joel H.; SANDERS, Willie A.; M=9 Sept. 1866; LM Berry, JP. NL.

N. H. [Benjamin & Sarah]; COOK, M. E.; M=27 Aug. 1869; JA Sherrill, Min. NL.

N. J.; ECKARD, Eliza; M=19 May 1861; E. Yount, JP. NL.

FISHER, Pinkney C. (21); JONES, Mary Jane (21); white; M=3 Jan. 1878; JH Bruns, JP in Hky; John Barger, F. Cline, George Wilson. NL.
  William G.; LITTLE, Elisebeth; M=2 Feb. 1862; JW Gabriel, JP. NL.
  William H.; BRIDGES, Nancy M.; M=13 Dec. 1866; Alex J. Cansler, Min. NL.
  William J. [David-father]; HOWARD, Nancy E.; M=1871; record missing. NL.
  William Sidney (23) of Hamilton Twsp; SHERRILL, Catharine (20) of Cat. Twsp; white; M=21 Dec. 1873; SC Brown, JP in Hamilton Twsp; Pink S. Powell, AB Bradburn, AE Brown. NL.
FLANEGAN, Luther [Jacob & Nancy Lefevers]; HAWN, Mary [John & Sallie Yoder]; M=23 Feb. 1868; GM Yoder, Esq. NL.
FLOWERS, Adam; HERMAN, Ruby L.; M=18 Jan. 1854; E. Yount, JP. NL.
  Alexander (20); ROSEMAN, Mita (17); black; M=27 Jan. 1879; PK Little, JP at the Register's Office; R. Yoder, Alex Cline, Lee Sims. NL.
  Burgess G. [Cyrus & Elizabeth]; SEITZ, Jane E. [Abel & Catharine Seitz]; M=16 Nov. 1869; PC Hinckle, Min. NL.
  Calvin (24); CLINE, Margaret (17); black; M=31 Dec. 1877; PK Little, JP, Cline's Twsp; Alex Cline, EP Bolch, SP Bolch. NL.
  John; BOLCH, Amy; M=2 June 1863; E. Yount, JP. NL.
  John H. (26) [Thomas J. & Mary A.]; DRUM, N. Callie (18) [David & Martha]; white; M=22 Jan. 1880; JA Sherrill, Min. in Mt. Crk Twsp; GW ?, PF Bandy, GP Sherrill. 2-34.
  Joseph V. (22); REESE, Jane (23); white; M=10 Jan. 1878; GL Hunt, Luth. Min. at Henry Bollinger's; Henry Bollinger, Elbert Bollinger, James Hicks. NL.
  Nicholas (20); PUNCH, Laura (24); white; M=30 Mar. 1879; HA Forney, Min. in Newton; Mamie Graham, Etta Haynes, John Campbell. NL.
FLOYD, Marion [Commadore & Vanus]; MOSTELLER, Mina [n/k & Susan Mosteller]; M=29 Dec. 1867; AJ Whitener, Esq. NL.
FOARD, Robert O. (26) [Osburn G. & Anna]; GAITHER, Laura M. (22) [David B. & Mary]; white; M=27 Feb. 1873; RB Anderson, Min. in Newt. Twsp; RA Bost, JD Little. 1-233.
FORD, Frederic L. (24) [OG & Elizabeth]; HUDSON, Mary F. (24) [Franklin & Katie]; white; M=25 Mar. 1880; WL Little, Luth. Min. in Bandy's Twsp; Robert O. Foard, Hubert A. Canup, Robert W. Hinson. 2-35.
  William A.; SHERRILL, Ruth; M=9 Nov. 1859; Logan A. Wilson, JP. NL.
FORNEY, Albert (24) of Rutherford Co., NC; DAVIS, Mary Sue (22); white; M=3 Dec. 1873; FJ Murdock, Catholic Priest in Newton; SM Finger, GW Michal, John L. McDowell. NL.
  J. J. [Marcus L. & Louise]; BOST, Sarah [Jacob & Mary]; M=Mar. 1868; EA Warlick, Esq. NL.
  M. L.; ROBINSON, S. C.; M=10 Mar. 1858; John Lantz, Min. NL.
FOX, Adolphus; HEFNER, Camila; M=24 Dec. 1862; E. Heterick, JP. NL.

FOX, Rev. D. E.; HENKLE, S. C.; M-17 Mar. 1863; Rev. Timothy Moser, Min. NL.
  David P. (29) of Missouri; HERMAN, Linnie E. (25); white; M=25 Jan. 1877; JC Clapp, Ref. Min. at George Herman's; ML Hoke, WH Herman, HJ Reitzel. NL.
  George (19); HUFFMAN, Harriett (22); white; M=10 Jan. 1878; JM Smith, JP in Cline's Twsp; Cain Mathis, Socrates Benfield, Jeff Pope. NL.
  James (19) [Hugh & Sallie]; HUFFMAN, Catharine L. (18) [Miles & Sallie]; white; M=9 Sept. 1880; PFW Stamey, Min. at Meth. Parsonage in Newton; George Fox, Ellis Huffman, Candace Reitzel. 2-36.
  John; HUIT, Susan C.; M=17 Aug. 1865; PC Henkel, Min. NL.
  Joseph (23) of Cald. Twsp; DEAL, Jane (17); white; M=27 Dec. 1874; JM Smith, Luth. Min. at P. Deal's; Robert Deal, JM ?, Madie M. Miller. NL.
  Marcus; HETERICK, Emma; M=10 Dec. 1857; JB Little, JP. NL.
  Noah (27); Odom, Anna A. (24); white; M=21 Oct. 1875; PK Little, JP in Cline's Twsp at Susan Shook's; Adam Shook, JB Little, William Fox. NL.
  William (25); BOST, Laura (15); white; M=22 July 1875; PK Little, JP in Cline's Twsp; John Fox, David Fox, Joshua Drum. NL.
FRAYSURE, H. Y.; LOWRANCE, M. A.; M=19 Sept. 1852; John Lantz, Min. NL.
FRAZIER, Cyrus J. [Hugh & Sarah]; SMYER, Genela [John & Elizabeth]; M-9 Jan. 1872; JC Clapp, Min. 1-155.
  William Bruce (22) [Alexander & Lucinda] of Cline's Twsp; DEAL, Mary Jane (23) [Miles & Rosa] of Newt. Twsp; white; M=Oct. 1872; PF Smith, JP in Newt. Twsp; CH Sipe, JK Smith, HG Hoke. 1-156.
FREEZE, William, Jr. [William & Hannah]; WITHERSPOON, Ruannah O. [Nelson & Malinda]; M=13 Oct. 1867; Miles Goodson, Esq. NL.
FRIDAY, John A. (22) [Samuel & Esther]; ROBINSON, Jane (22) [Junius & Nancy]; black; M=14 Sept. 1880; Robert Helton, Min. in JF Twsp; RP Helton, JR Lontoy?, MC Smith. 2-37.
FRY, A. D. (26) [Calvin & Sarah]; DEITZ, Caroline (21) [Feadart? & Lucinda]; white; M=23 Sept. 1880; J. Ingold, Ref. Min. in Hky Twsp; AB Killian, JC Fry, LL Dietz. 2-38.
  Alfred H. (21); BOLCH, Susan E. (22); white; M=8 Sept. 1878; JH Bruns, JP in Hky; EE Herman, HM Hallman, JE Throneburg. NL.
  Buck [Sam & Nancy]; WHITENER, Laura [Sam & Lily]; M=15 Aug. 1867; RA Cobb, Esq. NL.
  Calvin; DELLINGER, Sarah; M=11 Apr. 1853; Henry Cline, JP. NL.
  David S. (25); MILLER, Mary M. (22); white; M=22 Dec. 1874; JM Smith, Luth. Min. at Joel Miller's; MA Setzer, PC Hawn, ME Ekerd. NL.
  David W.; REITZEL, Hance C.; M=11 Nov. 1866; DS Henkel, Min. NL.
  Enos Grover (26) [John & Amanda]; DRUM, Gillie (19) [Franklin & n/g]; white; M=21 Dec. 1873; Daniel May in Newt. Twsp; MM Wilson, CE Wilson, RC Sigmon. 1-234.
  Eph. N.; MARTIN, Sophronia; M=28 Aug. 1852; ER Shuford, JP. NL.

FRY, Frederick L. [John & Catherine]; FRY, Allice V. [Moses & Leah]; M=8 Sept. 1870; JC Clapp, Min. 1-15.
  Hansen S.; INGOLD, M. B.; M=25 June 1857; PC Hinkle, Min. NL.
  J. A.; SIGMON, Larisa E.; M=9 Apr. 1857; Adam Miller, Min. NL.
  J. D. (19) [Marcus & Margaret]; ABEE, Martha L. (20) [Ephraim & LR]; white; M=20 Aug. 1880; JH Bruns, JP in Hky; AC Link, Leroy R. Whitener, AD Blair. 2-39.
  J. E. (62) [Phillip & n/g]; FINGER, Mary Jane (36) [Daniel & n/g]; white; M=11 Sept. 1880; JC Clapp, Ref. Min. in Newton; MB Fry, JR Gaither, George Setzer. 2-40.
  J. P.; SHERRILL, Mahala; M=23 June 1859; JA Lowrance, JP. NL.
  Jacob; CLIPPARD, L. C.; M=22 Oct. 1865; Philip Burns, JP. NL.
  James C. (22); WHITENER, S. Jane (20); white; M=8 Sept. 1878; JA Foil, Ref. Min. at JA Foil's; PJ Rowe, LA Cline, SC Foil. NL.
  James H. (21) [Moses & Leah]; ABERNATHY, Elizabeth (21) [Wilford & Polly]; white; M=21 Aug. 1874; JC Clapp, Min. in Newt. Twsp; Fred Fry, Marion Starr, Terry Thronburg. 1-262.
  Joseph A. [Abel & Elizabeth]; BLACKBURN, Georgia Ann [Lizzie-mother]; M=9 Jan. 1868; J. Ingold, Min. NL.
  Marcus; BARGER, Margaret C.; M=23 Oct. 1862; P. Burns, JP. NL.
  Moses [Jacob & Elizabeth]; BOWMAN, Harriett S. [Daniel & Mary]; M=20 Nov. 1870; EA Warlick, JP. 1-16.
  Noah (19) [NH & Caty]; SMYRE, Frances (20) [Logan & Emeline]; white; M=26 Feb. 1873; PF Smith, JP in Newt. Twsp; PE Fry, L. Smyre, John D. Smyre. 1-235.
  Perry (22) of Hamilton Twsp; FRY, Nancy S. (19) of Hamilton Twsp; white; M=20 Feb. 1873; TJ Hamilton in Hamilton Twsp; Lock Kale, John W. Hamilton, LW Abernethy. NL.
  Perry E. (25) [Nilly & Catharine]; PROPST, Mary J. (20) [Frank & Julia Huitt]; white; M=11 May 1879; JM Smith, Luth. Min. in Newt. Twsp; GW Setzer, Jerome Bolick, JY Propst. 1-347.
  Pink (22); GIBBS, Elizabeth (18); black; M=3 Jan. 1878; CW Vanderburk, Min. at Aaron Bost's; Aaron Bost, Alf Wood, John Cane. NL.
  Robert M. (23); RINEHARDT, Martha (23); white; M=17 Sept. 1874; Robert Helton, Min. at Eliza Reinhardt's; JM Leonard, GL Reinhardt, Lawson ?. NL.
  Rufus [Rufus Turner & Nancy Sherrill]; HUNSUCKER, Mary [Levi & Nancy Arwood]; M=22 Jan. 1868; EA Warlick, Esq. NL.
  Sam [Buck and Milly Whitener]; GRAHAM, Mariah; M=12 Apr. 1868; EA Warlick, Esq. NL.
  William P. (25); BOST, Emma Jane (23); white; M=24 Sept. 1874; JC Clapp, Ref. Min. at Abe Miller's; Perry Bost, Logan Conrad, Phillip Bost. NL.
  William P. (28); RADER, Martha J. (18); white; M=10 Nov. 1878; GL Hunt, Luth. Min. at GL Hunt's; SM Starr, WF Rader, George E. Coulter. NL.
FULBRIGHT, Iben (23) [HF & BH]; HOLLAR, C. C. (23) [AM & RM]; white; M=18 Feb. 1880; PK Little, JP in Cline's Twsp; AS Holler, CE Little, WL Fulbright. 2-41.
  Jacob (26); LINN, Missouri C. (17); white; M=6 Apr. 1876; Jacob Mosteller, JP in Bandys Twsp; MC Fulbright, LS Fulbright. NL.

FULBRIGHT, Jonas M. (29) [John & Nancy]; POOVEY, Sallie M. (19) [Marcus & Margaret]; white; M=19 Feb. 1880; GL Hunt, Luth. Min. in Newt. Twsp; EA Chapman, John H. Sigmon, JN Fulbright. 2-42.
  Joseph; HUFFMAN, Lavina; M=10 Dec. 1861; JB Little, JP. NL.
  Joseph (52); HEFFNER, Anna (30); white; M=23 Aug. 1875; PK Little, JP in Cline's Twsp; PE Deal, Jacob Huffman, D. McD. Little. NL.
  [There is another entry for Joseph Fulbright (52) that is almost identical to the above entry, with the exception of the marriage date. The second entry states 23 Aug. 1876.]
  Lawrence A. (23); FRY, Laura (24); white; M=9 Mar. 1875; GW Cansler, JP in Hamilton Twsp; QM Little, HA Danner, Theodore Bridges. NL.
  Logan S. (22); MURPHY, Mary (20); white; M=24 Feb. 1875; JC Clapp, Ref. Min. at James Murphy's; James Murphy, Marion Fulbright, Marion Starr. NL.
  Peter A. (28); NORWOOD, Sarah (23); white; M=27 Dec. 1877; AJ Fox, Luth. Min. at William Norwood's; FS Norwood, Pink Fulbright, William W. Norwood. NL.
  William S. [Rhoda-mother]; DRUM, Rebecah [John J. & Barbara]; M=9 Feb. 1871; William G. James, JP. 1-69.
GABRIEL, A. A.; MILLIGAN, Lizzie; M-28 Feb. 1866; JA Sherrill, Min. NL.
  Connor (41) [Andrew Loftin & Ellis Gabriel]; Munday, Fanny (21) [Monroe & Jane Beatty]; black; M=9 Sept. 1880; OW ?, JP in Mt. Crk Twsp; Miles Beatty. 2-43.
  David P. [Thornton Lockman & Susan Gabriel]; BEATTY, Susan [Herman Cornelius & Ester Beatty]; M=1869; F. Caldwell, JP. NL.
  Edmond (25); WHITENER, Harriet (18); black; M=10 Feb. 1878; MM Gabriel, JP in Mt. Crk Twsp; Brad McCaul, Alex Houston, James Shuford. NL.
  Harison S. [JW & Harriett]; JONES, Fannie L. [Allen & Jane]; M=23 Nov. 1870; JA Sherrill, Min. 1-17.
  Jacob [Joseph & Rebecca]; SHERRILL, Ann E. [Smith & Malissa]; M=1 Dec. 1870; JA Sherrill, Min. 1-18.
  Joseph W. (19); BEATTY, Florence E. (17); white; M=17 Mar. 1875; JA Sherrill, Min. at JA Sherrill's; Abel Jones, WL Ree, John W. Ekard. NL.
  M. M.; SHERRILL, N. E.; M=19 Sept. 1865; JA Sherrill, Min. NL.
  Miles (30) - black; SHERRILL, Mary J.; M=Dec. 1873; Isaac Wells; Frank Bost, John Bost, Miles Gabriel. NL.
  William P.; PARKS, Amanda; M=5 Oct. 1863; JA Sherrill, Min. NL.
GAITHER, Junius P.; FRY, Minnie J.; M=1871; record missing.
  Wiley (21); WALLACE, Nancy (20); black; M=6 May 1877; JB Turner, Min. in Hky; Tate Sigmon, Bert Belmont, Frank Crowell. NL.
GAMBLE, Henry (30) [Wade & Rosa]; WHITENER, Adaline (18) [Welby & Lucinda]; black; M=15 Dec. 1875; JW Gabriel, JP in Mt. Crk Twsp; LT Gabriel, Callie Gabriel, A. Gabriel. 1-280.
GANT, A. L.; REITZEL, S. L.; M=18 May 1857; PC Hinkle, Min. NL.
  John (28); LEE, Elizabeth (17); white; M=25 May 1876; JL Huit, JP, Cald. Twsp; Levi Bandy, M. Lee, Susan Marshall. NL.

GANT, Theophilus; WITHERSPOON, Elizabeth; M=30 Nov. 1856; William L. Mehaffey, JP. NL.
GANTT, E.; POPE, S. E.; M=7 Jan. 1856; GJ Wilkie, Min. NL.
  F. M.; HEFNER, Roxanna; M=9 Aug. 1866; GJ Wilkie. NL.
  I. I. [Willis & Mary]; WIKE, Tolly [Miles & Salley]; M=8 Aug. 1870; JL Hewit. 1-19.
  J. J. [Miles & Sally]; WIKE, Polly; M=8 Aug. 1870; JA Sherrill, Min. NL.
  J. L.; SHERRILL, Elizabeth; M=11 Mar. 1858; JW Gabriel, JP. NL.
  Joseph N.; WARLICK, Francis; M=11 Sept. 1855; J. Finger, Min. NL.
GARLAND, F. R.; DEITZ, Celia; M=30 Sept. 1858; Moses Barger, JP. NL.
GARRET, A. L.; REITZEL, S. L.; M=18 May 1857; PC Henkle, Min. NL.
GARVER, John H.; REECE, Linny; M=8 Aug. 1865; Eli Starr, JP. NL.
GIBBS, Benjamin (21); KILLIAN, Dora (18); black; M=31 Jan. 1878; Rufus England, JP in Cald. Twsp; DA Ramsour, George Shull, HC Cloninger. NL.
  Charles (19); COULTER, Sallie (18); black; M=2 Sept. 1877; Rufus England, JP in Cald. Twsp; Robert L. Bolch, Alex L. Keener, AC Cloninger. NL.
  James [George & Casanah]; CONLEY, Lon [David & Nancy Wilson]; M=1 Feb. 1872; JH Bruns, JP. NL.
  Jonas [Joseph Brown & Fanny Gibbs]; WIKE, Michael [Sam & Hannah]; M=27 Feb. 1870; EA Warlick, JP. NL.
  Samuel (43) of Newt. Twsp; WILSON, Delph (35) of Hky Tav. Twsp; black; M=27 Aug. 1873; Daniel May, Min. in Newton; AJ Helton, JW Beard, Daniel Detter. NL.
  Thomas [Richard & Rutha]; ENGLAND, Lydia Ann [Fanny-mother]; black; M=25 Dec. 1870; EA Warlick, JP. 1-20.
GIBSON, J. M.; BOLCH, Susanah; M=3 July 1853; William L. Mehaffey, JP. NL.
  J. W.; WIKE, Linna R.; M=28 Mar. 1866; DE Fox, Min. NL.
GILBERT, George Ellis (23) of Caldwell; LANIER, Agnes Susan (32) white; M=6 June 1877; MA Holler, Min. at Susan Lanier's; Donah Lanier, James H. Bolick, Darius Lanier. NL.
  J. H.; SIGMON, Malinda; M=13 Jan. 1861; Adam Miller, Min. NL.
GILLELAND, Daniel [Thomas & Mary]; HARBESON, Caroline [Tisey & Polly]; M=8 Mar. 1870; EA Warlick, JP. NL.
  E. Casper (23) [Thomas & Mary]; BRADBURN, Mary (24) [Thomas & Elizabeth]; white; M=1 Jan. 1873; JA Sherrill, Min. in Hamilton Twsp; SC Brown, MA Holsclaw, JC Pain. 1-236.
  H. A.; LOWRANCE, Sarah M.; M=2 Jan. 1849; Isaac Oxford, Min. NL.
  H. A. [George & Nancy]; PUNCH, Sarah [Joel & Ann]; M=5 Mar. 1871; JA Sherrill, Min. 1-70.
GIRVAN, Charles L. [Richard & Nancy]; HOUSTON, Mary A. [Franklin & Mary Caldwell]; M=5 Oct. 1868; JW Gabriel, JP. NL.
GLASGO, Thomas (21) of Bandys Twsp; JOHNSON, Harriet (23) of Bandys Twsp; white; M=26 Mar. 1873; JW Bandy, JP in Bandys Twsp; R. Allen, Francis ?, Rich Johnston. NL.
  Zach [Thomas & Polly]; ALLRAN, Mary [James Nantz & Elizabeth]; M=4 July 1871; JW Bandy, JP. 1-71.

GOLDEN, Thomas (22); WARD, Laura (21) [Wilson & Fannie]; black; M=28 Aug. 1879; CW Blaylock, Min. in Hky Twsp; AN Bowman, Wilson Ward. 1-348.

GOLDSMITH, William W. (34); LITTLEJOHN, Emily (21); white; M=12 June 1876; Lemon Shell, Min. at the Courthouse in Newton; JM Brown, FA Bost, MO Sherrill. NL.

GOODMAN, Columbus; BANDY, Dovey; M=23 July 1861; Jonas Bost, JP. NL.

    Martin; JONES, Louisa; M=16 Jan. 1862; JM Lowrance, JP. NL.

GOODNIGHT, Joseph (28) of Lincoln Co., NC; RHONEY, Harriett (19); white; M=24 July 1873; JW Bandy, JP in Bandys Twsp; FE Broval, JE Gregory, Rixh Johnson. NL.

GOODSON, Ezell Jenkins (21) [Jerry & Malinda] of Gaston Co., NC; HOWARD, Dovey (18) [William & Jane]; white; M=18 Mar. 1880; JA Sherrill, Min. in Mt. Crk Twsp; James Howard, MW Cranford, FO Robinson. 2-44.

    Martin Luther (21) [Milton & Martha] of Lincoln Co., NC; WILKINSON, Susan Rebecca (18) [Wesly & Elizabeth]; white; M=18 Mar. 1880; JA Sherrill, Min. in Cald. Twsp; RM Beal, LA Killian, MA Wilkinson. 2-45.

GRAHAM, Benton S. (21); HEFNER, Candice (20); white; M=12 Dec. 1877; CW Herman, JP in Newton; Emaline Herman, Elisha Herman, Elizabeth Hefner. NL.

    Jacob; Starnes, Betty; M=1869; no other information.

    Stephen [Henry & Rachel Cowan]; Reinhardt, Julia [Rufus & Mina]; M=26 July 1868' EA Warlick, JP. NL.

GRAY, John (22) yellow [Joseph & Mariah]; HUIT, Sarah (18) black [William & Camilla]; M=18 Apr. 1875; Sandy Carter, Meth. Min. in Newt. Twsp; Lydia Carter, David Wilson, Samuel Kale. 1-281.

GREENWADE, Washington (30); JENNINGS, Mattie K. (16); white; M=28 June 1875; JH Bruns, JP in Hky; AC Link, JF Murrill, Hugh Southerland. NL.

GRICE, Francis M. (20) [William & Frankie]; MARTIN, Mary J. (23) [Laben & Caroline]; white; M=13 Jan. 1875; Simeon C. Brown, Hamilton Twsp; James H. Lee, RW McCombs, NB Lee. 1-282.

    Francis M. (24) [William Loften & Frankey Grice]; WILKINSON, Ada Senora (24) [John M. & Eliza]; white; M=4 Sept. 1879; WC Caldwell, JP; NE Laney, WM Keever, WW Laney. 1-349.

    James M.; ABERNATHY, Sarah Ann; M=23 Mar. 1862; JD Caldwell, JP. NL.

    John W. [John & Sarah Williamson]; COVINGTON, Charity C. [John & Lucy]; M=23 Dec. 1869; Absa Sherrill, JP. NL.

GRIER, Francis M. (20) [William & Frankie]; MARTIN, Mary J. (23) [Laben & Caroline]; white; M=13 Jan. 1875; Simeon C. Brown in Hamilton Twsp; NB Lee, James H. Lee, RW McCombs. 1-282. [See Francis M. Grice above].

GRIFFIN, Isaac (25); HOP, Malinda (22); white; M=28 Apr. 1874; JL Huit, JP in Cald. Twsp; NN Caldwell, HA Hewitt, Calvin Williams. NL.

    Nicholas M. (20) [NM & Harriett]; LANIER, Sallie T. (20) [Camilus & Harriet]; white; M=23 Dec. 1875; JC Hartsell, Meth. Min. in Hky Twsp; FA Clinard, UD Abernethy, Charles E. Graham. 1-283.

GROSS, Allen (22) of Hky Tav. Twsp; CONLEY, Candace (19) of Newton Twsp; black; M=4 Dec. 1873; Peter F. Smith, JP in Newt. Twsp; Zeke Robinson, Henry Smyre, Turner Gross. NL.

Allen (19); DUCK, Martha (19); black; M=31 Jan. 1877; JB Turner, Min. in Hky, NC; Abel McCorkle, Henry McCorkle. NL.

Daniel; LINK, Susan; M=7 Feb. 1865; AJ Whitener, JP. NL.

GUNN, John (26); JAMES, Maggie (18); black; M=6 Oct. 1878; Robert Smith, Min. in Hky; Lee Lutz, George Feamster, Wilson Ward. NL.

HAGAR, Clemmline [Henry & Lillian]; DRUM, Sarah Ann [Daniel & Jane]; M=10 Mar. 1868; JA Sherrill, Min. NL.

Thomas; SHERRILL, Sarah; M=9 Feb. 1860; William Long, JP. NL.

HAIMAN, Hiram [Mathias & Annie]; DEITZ, Polly S. [Israel & Annie]; M=20 Oct. 1869; EA Warlick, JP. NL.

HALL, Hugh M. (40) [Joseph & Darcus] of Iredell Co., NC; WILSON, Mary A. (36) [John Dickson & n/g]; white; M=1 Oct. 1872; EP Coulter, JP in JF Twsp; Ottis L. Lowe, Thomas Lee Lowe, Willie Ellen Lowe. 1-157.

Humphry; PAINTER, Sarah F.; M=2 Aug. 1861; JD Caldwell, JP. NL.

HALLMAN, Ephraim; KILLIAN, Sophina; M=3 Feb. 1852; William L. Mehaffey, JP. NL.

Laban [Daniel & Sarah]; BOLCH, Nancy E.; record missing.

Noah W. [Laban & AM]; BRINKLEY, Jane [William & n/k]; M=7 Apr. 1870; JC Clapp, Min. NL.

William E. (21); BOST, Sarah A. (18); white; M=28 May 1874; GL Hunt, Luth. Min. at GL Hunt's; WH Herman, Dora Miller, Sarah Kee. NL.

William F. (23) [Henry & Anna]; WAGNER, Lovinia (22) [William & Rachel]; white; M=9 Sept. 1880; DC Huffman, Luth. Min. in Cline's Twsp; SL Austin, DE Seabock, EE Miller. 2-46.

HAMPTON, J. F.; HETERICK, Polly; M=27 Jan. 1859; PC Henkel, Min. NL.

HANNAH, John; LITTLE, Rebecca; M=12 Mar. 1859; William Long, JP. NL.

HARBINSON, A. S.; BOLCH, Patsey; M=10 Jan. 1858; EE Deal, JP. NL.

Israel (20); HARWELL, Nancy (21); white; M=1 Sept. 1876; JC Clapp, Ref. Min. at Brown Guthrie's; Abe Miller, JM Brown, John Plonk. NL.

Jonas A. (21) of Newt. Twsp; WHITENER, Martha E. (24) of Newt. Twsp; white; M=25 Sept. 1873; GL Hunt, Luth. Min. at GL Hunt's; PM Hunt, PM Harbinson, Gilbert Cline. NL.

HARMAN, James (21) [Ephraim & Anna]; JONES, Allice (21) [Jackson & Katie]; white; M=21 Aug. 1870; PC Henkel, Luth. Min. in Newt. Twsp; IJ Wagner, ? Eckard, Charles H. Henkel. 1-355.

Stephen (20); STAMEY, Bettie (19); black; M=25 Dec. 1878?; AB Jennings, Min. at Willey Gaither's; B. Wilson, A. Jennings, Willy Gaither. NL.

HARRIS, Augustus (26); BOST, Elizabeth (27); black; M=24 Dec. 1874; Edward Harris, Min. at E. Bost's; Lucus Phelps, Linda Carter, Albert Abernathy. NL.

H. L. (29) of Mecklenburg Co., NC; BARGER, Flora M. (20); white; M=29 Dec. 1874; JH Bruns, JP in Hky; Ruben Barger, C. Sigmon, Bettie Sigmon. NL.

HARRISON, Henry; WATTS, Mary; M=6 Mar. 1860; IN Wilson, JP. NL.

HART, Isaac; MOORE, Lydia; M=28 Dec. 1863; M. Barger, JP. NL.
  Riley R.; SEITZ, Emeline; M=16 Feb. 1864; JR Ellis, JP. NL.
HARTZOE, Eli; HUFFMAN, Elizabeth; M=6 July 1858; GJ Wilkie, JP.
    NL.
  Jacob; WIKE, Scady; M=13 Nov. 1859; William L. Mehaffey, JP.
    NL.
HARTZOGE, Abel C.; CLINE, Harriet J.; M-10 Apr. 1866; Rev. JS
    Wilson, Min. NL.
HARVELL, Frances [Hardaway & Sarah]; ABERNATHY, Caroline [John &
    Polly]; M=8 Dec. 1867; EL Sherrill, Esq. NL.
HARWELL, A.W. [n/k & Mallisa]; HAGER, Julian E. [John & Julian];
    M=10 Aug. 1870; JA Sherrill, Min. NL.
  Avery H. (22); STAMPER, Martha J. (23); white; M=5 Feb. 1879;
    SC Brown, JP, at Nancy Stamper's; MY Bynum, DB Coomton, EB
    Brown. NL.
  Elbert; TURBYFILD, Carmela; M=26 Dec. 1851; Hosea Linebarger,
    JP. NL.
  Elbert [n/k & Sarah Harwell]; PARKER, Jane [Thomas & n/k]; M=22
    Nov. 1868; JA Sherrill, Min. NL.
  Henderson (25); SHERRILL, Julie E. (18); white; M=19 Mar. 1874;
    JW Pevitt, Min. at Jacob Sherrill's; SJ Whitener, FEH Beatty,
    WR Harwell. NL.
  J. Horace (23) [Hardaway & Sallie]; FLEMING, Martha (29) [Osburn
    & Sullie]; white; M=22 Aug. 1880; GW Ivey, Min. at Pisgah
    Church; HH Harwell, FG McCorkle, WR Harvell. 2-47.
  James L. [Nelson & Mary]; MILLIGAN, Jane C. [Alexander &
    Cornelia]; M=10 Nov. 1868; BG Jones, Min. NL.
  James T. (29) [Nelson & Mary]; SHERRILL, Margaret E. (28) [Enus
    & Ruaner]; white; M=28 Nov. 1872; JA Sherrill, Min., Mt. Crk
    Twsp; JW Sherrill, CF Abernethy, IF Abernethy. 1-158.
  John; HARWELL, Susan P.; M=30 Sept. 1852; HH Linebarger, JP.
    NL.
  John [Nat & Catherine]; REYNOLDS, Theresa Ann (29) [Harvy &
    Mary]; white; M-20 Aug. 1872; JA Sherrill, Min. at Balls
    Creek Campground; WB Sherrill, John Sherrill, David H.
    Parker. 1-159.
  M.J. [John H. & Mary]; SHERRILL, Lovina [GW & Martha]; M=12 Feb.
    1871; JA Sherrill, Min. 1-72.
  R.A. [John H. & Mary]; BURTON, E.E. [Calvin & Sarah]; M=11 June
    1872; JA Sherrill, Min. 1-160.
HASS, Daniel (60); CLINE, Clarinita (33); white; M=26 Jan. 1875;
    GL Hunt, Luth. Min. at GL Hunt's; NC Hunt, SA Hunt, Rebecca
    Carpenter. NL.
  David H. (31); FRY, Mary (22); white; M=30 Dec. 1877; JM Smith,
    Luth. Min. at JO Fry's; MM Huit, GW Rabb, M. Sigmon. NL.
  Henry; HEFNER, Kesiah; M=3 Oct. 1866; EA Warlick, JP. NL.
  J.A.; FISHER; Thelethia; M=22 Sept. 1865; JA Sherrill, Min. NL.
  John A. (36); SIGMON, Mary J. (26); white; M=28 Dec. 1876; JM
    Smith, Luth. Min. at Monroe Sigmon's; LE Sigmon, JF Sigmon,
    JH Sigmon. NL.
HATLEY, Rufus P. (22) [Josiah & Susan]; SEABOCK, Mary T. (24)
    [George & Ceda]; white; M=11 Dec. 1880; JW Mouser, JP, Hky
    Twsp; P. Seabock, George E. Bollinger, George P. Seabock. 2-
    48.

HAWKINS, Miles H. (21) [Willis & Mary] of Gaston Co., NC; ABERNATHY, Nancy P. (22) [Monroe & Margaret]; white; M=10 Apr. 1879; E. England, JP., Cald. Twsp; CH Deal, WS Hallman, PA Drum. 1-350.

HAWN, Abner; RINCH, Mary C.; M=25 ? 1855; E. Yount, JP. NL.

Amyia A.; YODER, Mary M.; M=9 Nov. 1856; AJ Fox, Min. NL.

C.L.; JARRETT, E.J.; M=1 Dec. 1866; AJ Fox, Min. NL.

E.L.; WARD, Rhoda; M=22 Mar. 1866; John Lantz, Min. NL.

Henry; WHITENER, Anna P.; M=3 Mar. 1864; M. Barger, JP. NL.

Jacob P. (23); TRAVIS, Fannie (21); white; M=11 Mar. 1877; GL Hunt, Luth. Min. at GL Hunt's; SH Hunt, LM Hunt, LE Hunt. NL.

James Knox Polk (24) of JP Twsp; DEITZ, Martha (23); white; M=29 Nov. 1873; Abel Barger, JP, Hky Tav. Twsp; Lazarus Deitz, Sarah Killian. NL.

John A. (25) [John & Elizabeth]; SIGMON, Lucinda S. (20) [Logan & Bettie Ann]; white; M=20 Apr. 1879; JH Bruns, JP, Hky; WM Hawn, JP Whitener, JS Tomlinson. 1-351.

John L. [Daniel & Anna]; MOORE, Jinney S. [Joseph A. & Sarah]; M=17 Feb. 1869; FL Abernathy, Min. NL.

Jonas; KILLIAN, Permira; M=26 June 1854; E. Yount, JP. NL.

Joseph [David & Susan]; THOMASON, Emeline [John & Harriet]; M=20 Sept. 1868; EA Warlick, JP. NL.

Joseph; MOUSER, Rosanah C.; M=29 Oct. 1857; E. Yount, JP. NL.

Lawson J. (21); HAWN, Elnore (18); white; M=13 Apr. 1876; Abel Barger, JP, Hky Twsp; JR Hawn, Marcus Barger, John M. Barger. NL.

Noah; YOUNT, Mary M.; M=4 Dec. 1852; E. Yount, JP. NL.

Polycarp C. (26); HEWIT, Emma (19); white; M=4 July 1878; PC Henkel, Luth. Min. at MM Huit's; Silas Smyer, JM Arnt, Jerome Bolick. NL.

Wesley M. (21) [Joseph & Caroline]; HAWN, Barbara Jane (25) [John & Elizabeth]; white; M=3 July 1880; JH Bruns, JP, Hky; BP Bas, MY Flanigan, DH Witherspoon. 2-49.

HAYNES, G.M.; GROSS, Sarah; M=1 Jan. 1861; RL Abernathy, Min. NL.

John (20) [n/k & Mary Conly]; RUSH, Patsey (19) [n/k & Sally Rush] of Lincolnton, Lincoln Co., NC; black; M=2 Aug. 1872; George McClain, Min., Newton; Robert Smyer, Alfred Abernathy, George Haynes. 1-161.

HEAVENER, John J. (28) of Newton Twsp; Sigmon, Ellen K. (18) of Newton Twsp; white; M=9 Dec. 1873; JM Smith, Luth. Min. at Mary Sigmon's; Andrew Lagle, CL Heavener, Andrew Boggs. NL.

HEDGEPETH, John; CLODFELTER, Francis S.; M=26 Jan. 1854; Joshua Wilson, JP. NL.

HEDRICK, Andrew (40) [Jacob & Unity] of Lincoln Co., NC; WARLICK, Minitz M. (30) [David & Rachel]; white; M=2 Dec. 1880; Robert Helton, Min., JF Twsp; Jn Gantt, DL Warlick, John D. Hoover. 2-50.

Daniel (23); HUFFMAN, Delila (25); white; M=7 Sept. 1876; PK Little, JP, Cline's Twsp; CE Little, Marion Moser, Saliar Huffman. NL.

Franklin M. (22); MOUSER, Harriet B. (21); white; M=15 Oct. 1874; NE Sigmon, JP, Cline's Twsp; John Mouser, JC Mouser, Polly Hedrick. NL.

HEDRICK, James L. [Eusalus & Linnie]; MOSER, Annie [Jacob & Barbara]; M=4 Jan. 1872; William H. Rockett, JP. 1-162.
 Quintis A. [David & Malinda]; SIGMON, Sarah [Henry & Ada]; M=10 Nov. 1871; CT Sigmon, JP. 1-73.
 William S. (42) [Peter & Fanny]; HUFFMAN, Salina (40); white; M=28 Oct. 1880; PK Little, JP, Cline's Twsp; JB Sigmon, ML Sigmon, Gerand Bolch. 2-51.
HEFFNER, Jacob W. (23) [Noah & Sarah] of Cline's Twsp; SHOOK, Catharine (22) [Adam & Catharine] of Cline's Twsp; white; M=27 Feb. 1873; PF Smith, JP, Newt. Twsp; JA Eppes, MG Rowe, D. Shook. 1-237.
 Poley [Hiram & AC]; MILLER, Volara L. [Ephraim & Amey]; M=21 Feb. 1871; JM Smith, Min. 1-74.
 William M. (22); Pope, Ella (24); white; M=1 Oct. 1874; PF Smith, JP, Newton; JM Wilson, WE Yount, Isaac Griffin. NL.
HEFNER, Adolphus (21) [Miles & Polly]; ABERNATHY, Alice (19) [Milton & n/g]; M=8 Feb. 1880; JM Smith, Luth. Min., Cline's Twsp; CH Henkel, GA Brady, JE Brady. 2-52.
 Ambrose (40); HEFNER, Caroline (35); white; M=26 Feb. 1876; Calvin T. Sigmon, JP, Cline's Twsp; Levi Hefner, Elia Hefner, MR Hefner. NL.
 Andrew (21) [Solomon & Sarah] of JF Twsp; JARRETT, Mary M.A. (17) [Jacob & Mary] of JF Twsp; white; M=12 Dec. 1872; AJ Fox, Min. in JF Twsp; PA Killian, DJ Shuford, AG Corpening. 1-163.
 B.C. [Jacob & Luigne]; DRUM, A.M. [John D. & Barbara]; M=25 Aug. 1869; William G. James, JP. NL.
 C.R.; Hoke, Eliza M.; M=10 Nov. 1855; JB Little, JP. NL.
 Calvin (22) [Devault & Polly A.]; HUFFMAN, Senelda E. (19) [Nelson & Rhoda]; white; M=5 June 1879; JM Smith, Luth. Min. at Nelson Huffman's in Hky; DM Huffman, NL Miller, JP Huffman. 1-352.
 Daniel; SHELL, Melinda; M=26 Sept. 1851; Eli E. Deal, JP. NL.
 Daniel (21) [George & Rachel]; SIGMON, Bell (18) [Logan & Sailie]; white; M=28 Dec. 1879; PK Little, JP in Cline's Twsp; JB Sigmon, Alfred Hefner, MS Benfield. 1-353.
 David F. (24); BAKER, Florence (18); white; M=14 Feb. 1878; PC Henkel, Luth. Min. at Dorothy Baker's; WP Bowman, TM Hoke, Jacob Bowman. NL.
 Devalt; HUFFMAN, Polly A.; M=8 Aug. 1852; Timothy Moser, Min. NL.
 Elias (76); STARNES, Lovina (33); white; M=7 Sept. 1876; AH Shuford, JP, Newton; WL Edwards, JE Hendrix, LS Hefner. NL.
 George; HEFNER, Ruanah; M=1 Dec. 1858; PC Henkel, Min. NL.
 H.; BOLCH, C.M.; M=17 Nov. 1864; E. Yount, JP. NL.
 Hosea (22); HEFNER, Emaline (22); white; M-3 Dec. 1874; JM Smith, Luth. Min. at D. Hefner's; SD Little, CS Hefner, A. Winebarger. NL.
 J.W.; MILLER, R.M.; M-17 Aug. 1865; William H. Rocket, JP. NL.
 John; KAYLOR, Rhoda; M=29 May 1853; H. Ingold, JP. NL.
 Josiah A. (19); KILLIAN, Julia E. (19); white; M=6 ? 1874; PF Smith, JP, Newt. Twsp; JHA Yount, James E. Bowlin, FW McCorkle. NL.
 L.S.; EKARD, Susan; M=6 Mar. 1864; PC Henkel, Min. NL.

HEFNER, Levi [Henry & Susannah]; PATTON, Mary R. [n/k & Barbara]; M=13 Aug. 1867; JH Rowe, Esq. NL.
    Levi (24) [John & Rhoda]; BAKER, Ellen (27) [Henry & Anna]; white; M=28 Aug. 1870; JM Smith, Luth. Min. in Cline's Twsp; AA Reitzel, JA Hoke, AE Sipe. 1-354.
    Lewis (36) of Newton Twsp; DEAL, Linnie (45) of Newton Twsp; white; M=11 Sept. 1873; PF Smith, JP in Newton Twsp; Henry Deal, George W. Whitener, Harriet Deal. NL.
    Marcus; CLINE, Kesiah; M=4 Mar. 1855; H. Ingold, JP. NL.
    Michael; SPENCER, Elizabeth; M=26 Aug. 1858; John Kent, JP. NL.
    Peter; HEFNER, Sarah; M=6 Feb. 1853; Timothy Moser, Min. NL.
    Pinkney [Peter & Lucy]; HEFNER, Susanah [Daniel & Barbara]; M=17 Dec. 1871; CT Sigmon, JP. 1-75.
    S.; BOLCH, C.M.; M=17 Nov. 1864; E. Yount, JP. 1-1.
    Sylvana [Daniel & Barbara]; WHITE, Malinda [Andrew Herman & Lewyar Herman]; M=20 May 1869; PC Hinckle, Min. NL.
    William; HERMAN, Sally; M=22 Jan. 1853; CW Herman, JP. NL.
HELDERBRAND, Daniel; ABERNATHY, Martha; M=21 Dec. 1854; Helderbrand, JP. NL.
HELDERMAN, A.J.; HILL, Rachel; M=25 Oct. 1860; JW Gabriel, JP. NL.
HELTON, Abel A. (21) [Solomon & Rosa]; CLINE, Mary C. (19) [Franklin & Rhoda]; white; M=11 Feb. 1880; JH Bruns, JP, in Hky Twsp; John M. Barger, Sam Campbell, Andrew Helton. 2-53.
    Clingman (21) of Hky Tav. Twsp; CLINE, Rhoda E. (19) of Hky Tav. Twsp; white; M=11 Sept. 1873; J. Ingold, Ref. Min. at Franklin Clines; Rhoda Cline, Franklin Cline. NL.
    John W. [Robert & Epsey]; SHUFORD, Roda C. [Daniel & Ruamia]; no other information given. From old index. NL.
    Robert [Robert & Nancy]; SMITH, Harriett [Jerry & Sarah]; M=14 Oct. 1869; John Watts, Min. NL.
    Robert J. [Robert & Espa]; SHUFORD, Isabel [George P. & Eliza]; M=13 Feb. 1872; J. Ingold, Min. 1-164.
    William; ABERNATHY, Sarah A.; M=12 Mar. 1862; JP Shuford, JP. NL.
    William; KILLIAN, Martha Ann; M=5 Nov. 1863; J. Lewis Smithdeal, Min. NL.
HENKEL, Solan (21); ICENHOUR, Emma (19); white; M-23 Dec. 1871; JM Smith, Luth. Min. at Joe Isenhours; CK Henkel, BA Hunsucker, JP Hefner. NL.
HENKLE, Charles H. (30); BRADDY,, Laura (18); white; M=1 Nov. 1877; JM Smith, Luth. Min. at Albert Braddy's; SL Henkel, CR Henkle, JP Hevener. NL.
HENSON, John [John & Charlotte]; WILLIAMS, Jane [Joseph & Polly]; M=14 Sept. 1871; JL Hewitt, JP. 1-77.

HERMAN, Abel; KENT, Phebe; M=13 Feb. 1853; E. Yount, JP. NL.
   Adolphus [Elijah & Rhoda]; MILLER, Margaret E. [David E. & Mary M.]; M=25 Dec. 1870; JM Smith, Min. 1-21.
   Benjamin; DOCKERT, Nancy; M=1 Nov. 1857; E. Yount, JP. NL.
   Charles H. [CD & Mariah]; ABERNATHY, Jane E. [Turner & Julia]; M=6 Jan. 1869; James A. Garvan, JP. NL.
   Elijah (22); MILLER, Louisa S. (20); white; M=11 Jan. 1877; Abel Rance, JP in Hky; BD Herman, CL Herman. NL.
   Elkanah; SETZER, Mahala; M=11 ? 1851; no other information given. NL.
   Ephard (21); RINK, Jane (20); white; M=31 Jan. 1878; JH Bruns, JP in Hky; SW Herman, SR Rink, FE Herman. NL.
   Ephraim; HERMAN, Mary A.; M=2 Mar. 1856; E. Yount, JP. NL.
   Frederick; BARGER, Rhoda; M=27 Sept. 1866; James H. Rowe, JP. NL.
   George D.; HOOVER, M.J.; M=30 Oct. 1859; CW Herman, JP. NL.
   George W. (26); RINK, Frances E. (23); white; M=21 Dec. 1876; Abel Barger, JP in Hky; BD Herman, CL Herman, EE Herman. NL.
   H.A.; HERMAN, Emeline; M=20 Feb. 1861; PC Henkel, Min. NL.
   Hosea M. (22) [Henry & Mary] of Newt. Twsp; SHELL, Fannie (20) [Ephraim & Ann] of Newt. Twsp; white; M=25 Dec. 1872; JM Smith, Min. in Newt. Twsp; JS Shell, NA Cline, HS Smith. 1-165.
   J.C. (27); LAEL, Eliza (27); white; M=10 Dec. 1874; JC Clapp, Ref. Min. at JC Clapp's; CM Bolch, CE Killian, AW Deal. NL.
   James [Henry & Mary]; GREEN, Amanda M. [OC & Ceda]; M=6 Nov. 1867; WL Mehaffey. NL.
   Joseph F. (24); GANT, Sue F. (15); white; M=7 May 1874; Daniel May, Min. at Jesse L. Gant's; MO Sherrill, LR Sherrill. NL.
   M.C.; CLONINGER, Carmilla; M=17 Aug. 1854; Eli E. Deal, JP. NL.
   Moses (66); LONGCRIER, Lydia (50); white; M=7 Apr. 1878; JM Smith, Luth. Min. at Elias Longcrier's; MS Deal, Elias Longcrier, T. Longcrier. NL.
   N.M. [Richard Kellar & Lucy Kellar]; JAMES, Sally [Simon & Rachel]; M=21 Feb. 1869; JA Person, JP. NL.
   Peter D.; BOLINGER, Martha; M=5 Oct. 1856; JW Pruitt, Min. NL.
   Philo G. (24); HERMAN, Irene (23); white; M=15 Nov. 1877; JC Clapp, Ref. Min. at CW Herman's; ML Hoke, Fides Herman, Adol Herman. NL.
HETERICK, John; HOUSTIN, Margaret; M=17 Nov. 1859; Hiram Hefner, JP. NL.
   John H.; BOLCH, Manerva; M=21 Oct. 1855; PC Hinkle, Min. NL.
HETRICK, Alfred H.; EKARD, Martha E.; M=20 July 1865; PC Henkel, Min. NL.
   Anderson; JOHNSON, Elizabeth; M=30 Sept. 1855; H. Ingold, JP. NL.
   Levi; NULL, Louisa; M=19 Nov. 1854; Timothy Moser, Min. NL.
HEWITT, M.W. (50) [Joseph & Linney]; ABERNATHY, Sarah Jane (30) [Miles C. & Nancy]; white; M=4 Jan. 1880; LN Wilson, JP in Cald. Twsp; WA Hewitt, JT Huitt, JL Hewitt. 2-67.
   William A. (18) [Elcainey & Mahala]; JONES, Laura Annette (18) [Milton & Jane]; white; M=11 Nov. 1880; WC Caldwell, JP in Cald. Twsp; AS Alley, Rufus Linebarger, M. Aries Edwards. 2-54.
HICKS, J.J.; FINGER, Martha E.; M=10 June 1856; John Lantz, Min. NL.

HICKS, J.J. [WW & Catherine]; FINGER, S.J. [Peter & Catherine]; M=16 Jan. 1870; EA Warlick, JP. NL.
  James M. (23) [JJ & Susan Cline]; HARTSOE, Dovey G. (17) [Eli & Mira]; white; M=23 Dec. 1880; HA Forney, JP in Newt. Twsp; E. Huffman, SL Hartsoe, Frances Hartsoe. 2-55.
  Levi; CARTER, Clementine; M=28 Aug. 1859; JW Gabriel, JP. NL.
  Nicholas F. (31) [Charles P. & Margaret]; SAYNE, Roxanna J. (19) [Joseph & Eliza]; white; M=1 Sept. 1879; WF Hull, Bapt. Min. in Bandys Twsp; JM Mull, George Morgan. 1-356.
HIDER, William; DEITZ, Eliza; M=10 Jan. 1865; Thomas Little, JP. NL.
HILDEBRAN, Jacob A. (24) of Burke Co., NC; ABEE, Sarah (22); white; M=4 Sept. 1873; William Abernathy, Bapt. Min. at Ephraim Abee's; E. Abee, WP Martin, JA Abee. NL.
HILDEBRAND, Christoper of Burke Co., NC; JOHNSON, Mattie (21); white; M=3 Feb. 1878; GW Wilkie, Bapt. Min. at Sally Johnson's; AS Layel, Dock Huffman, Julius Britton. NL.
  James (30) of Burke Co., NC; ANGEL, Caroline (19); black; M=21 Mar. 1877; AG Corpening, JP in JF Twsp; Ben Robinson, Lewis Robinson. NL.
  P.M. [Conrad & Catherine]; HOOVER, Sarah A. [GT & Eliza Shuford]; M=23 Dec. 1869; JC Clapp, Min. NL.
HILEMAN, A.F. [John & Margaret]; DETTER, L.C. [David & Harriett]; M=2 Dec. 1869; JC Clapp, Min. NL.
HILL, Cyrus (23) of Iredell Co., NC; SHERRILL, Martha (21); black; M=Apr., 1875; William Brooks, Min. at William Brooks'; Mark Sherrill, JA Abernathy, Emma McVerlas. NL.
  Isaac L. (37); KELLY, F. Ellen (33); white; M=23 Nov. 1876; JA Sherrill, Min. at JA Sherrill's; WE Allen, JF Howard, GP Sherrill. NL.
  Isaac L. (43) [Thomas & Letty]; LINEBARGER, Mary M. (32) [Jehu & Caroline Alen]; white; M=8 Aug. 1880; JA Sherrill, Min. in Mt. Crk Twsp; GP Sherrill, WE Allen, ? Sigmon. 2-56.
  J.E.; WILSON, M.L.; M=4 Sept. 1866; HJ Fox, Min. NL.
  L.H.; WHITENER, Mary; M=5 Apr. 1859; Joseph Parker, Min. NL.
HILTERBRAN, P.M.; SMYRE, C.A.; M=15 Apr. 1858; PC Hinkel, Min. NL.
HINSON, Sidney D. (28) [William & Sarah] of Lincoln Co., NC; SUMMEROW, Dorah E. (22) [Noah & Ann] of Lincoln Co., NC; white; M=21 Nov. 1875; JA Foil, Min. in Newt. Twsp; SM Finger, Henrietta C. Lantz, Emma J. Lantz. 1-284.
HINTON, Robert W. (25) [MF & Elizabeth] of Jackson Co., GA; HAYNES, Mary Etta (18) [GM & Sallie]; white; M=31 May 1880; PFW Stamey, Min. in Newt. Twsp; OG Loom, WE Yount, MO Sherrill. 2-57.
HITTERBRAND, P.M. [Conrad & Catherine]; HOOVER, Sarah A. [GT Shuford & Eliza Shuford]; M=23 Dec. 1869; JC Clapp, Min. NL.
HOBBS, John; FRY, Mahala; M-7 Oct. 1860; PJ Pitts, JP. NL.
HOKE, David; SMITH, Susan; M=8 June 1854; Timothy Moser, Min. NL.
  F.A.; DEAL, Julian; M=15 Mar. 1860; JB Little, JP. NL.
  Franklin J. (30) [John E. & Nancy J.] of Rutherford Co., NC; HULL, M.N. Alice (21) [MF & mary J.]; white; M=2 Nov. 1880; PFW Stamey, Min. in Newton; Logan Smyre, JF Bolick, MS Sherrill. 2-58.
  George A.; CARPENTER, Sarah Ann; M=27 June 1861; JB Little, JP. NL.

HOKE, Henry L. (21) of Newt. Twsp; BROWN, Patsey (18) of Cline's Twsp; white; M=14 Aug. 1873; PF Smith, JP in Newton; Pink Brown, Fannie Hoke, Knox Smith. NL.
  John D.; FRY, Linny E.; M=1 Oct. 1864; PC Henkel, Min. NL.
  Joseph (24); RAMSOUR, Mary (18); black; M=27 Feb. 1876; JB Turner, Min. in Hky; N. Bowman, George Feamster, Martin Wilfong. NL.
  Joseph (24); RAIN, Cora Ann (21); black; M=24 Nov. 1877; JB Turner, Min. in Hky; GW Feamster, Birt Bellemore, Bill Johnson. NL.
  Martin S. [Fred & Catharine]; HERMAN, Sallie L. [n/k & Mary M. Herman]; M=1 July 1868; PC Henkel, Min. NL.
  Monroe; SIGMON, Susan; M=19 Dec. 1853; JB Little, JP. NL.
  P.C. [John & Nancy]; ICENHOUR, Belzy S. [Abel & Nancy]; M=12 Sept. 1867; PC Henkel, Min. NL.
  Q.J. [Daniel & ME]; Yount, Catharine [Franklin & Amanda]; M=29 Dec. 1870; WG James, JP. NL.
  Thomas M. (21); BOWMAN, Sarah C. (20); white; M=10 Nov. 1878; CW Herman, JP in Newton; Jacob Bowman, John Hoke, Polly Bowman. NL.
HOLDBROOKS, E.B. [JC & Jane]; HAMILTON, Sarah J. [n/g & Lovina S. Turner]; M=19 Jan. 1868; SN Wilson, Esq. NL.
HOLDER, Elias (21); SETTLEMYRE, Alice (19); white; M=14 Mar. 1878; GL Hunt, Luth. Min. at GL Hunt's; Ellen Mehaffey, LM Hunt, Jane Mehaffey. NL.
  Jesse David [David & Violet]; NAUGLE, Nancy [Frederick Killian & n/k] M=13 Oct. 1868; EA Warlick, JP. NL.
HOLDSCLAW, Alexander [Lewis & Martha]; BROWN, Mary J. [n/k & Kelly Brown]; M=5 Dec. 1867; D. Hamilton, Esq. NL.
  Rufus (21) [Wesley & Minda]; ROSEMAN, Martha (19) [Alley & Jane]; black; M=22 May 1879; William W. James, JP at Alley Roseman's; Pearse Herman, Alexander Cline, Cain Widenburg. 1-357.
HOLLAR, Daniel L. [Andrew & Lovina]; HARMAN, Malinda [Elijah & Rhoda]; M=29 Nov. 1868; PC Hinkle, Min. NL.
  Eli S. [Franklin & Catharine]; HEFFNER, Harriet [Miles & Mary]; M=29 Dec. 1870; William G. James, JP. 1-22.
  Elisha; MILLER, Mary Ann; M=21 Feb. 1856; E. Yount, JP. NL.
  George W.; BISHENER, Louisa; M=31 Dec. 1857; Jonas Bost, JP. NL.
  Jacob; DEAL, Susanah; M=2 Jan. 1853; E. Huffman, JP. NL.
  Joseph [Peter & Margaret]; HUFFMAN, Abigail [Joseph & Mary]; M=15 Feb. 1872; PF Smith, JP. 1-166.
  M.C.; SEITZ, Leah; M=24 May 1857; PL Rowe, JP. NL.
  Paul; SEITZ, Cath; M=28 Mar. 1861; M. Barger, JP. NL.
HOLLER, A.D.; MILLER, Martha C.; M=20 Aug. 1865; DS Henkel, Min. NL.
  A.J. (25) [John & Catharine]; LITTLE, Alverda (19) [Daniel & Nancy]; white; M=18 Apr. 1880; PFW Stamey, Min. in Cat. Twsp; RO Lourance, Talia S. Shook, FD Leonard. 2-59.
  Alfred L. [Absolm & Rhoda]; ISAACS, Munervy [Jacob & Manervy]; M=22 Dec. 1868; D. McD. Yount, JP. NL.
  George W.S. (28); SETZER, Martha (22); white; M=10 Sept. 1878; PK Little, JP in Cline's Twsp; CF Sipe, CH Sipe, MC Setzer. NL.

HOLLER, Jefferson (22) [Peter & Margaret]; POPE, Alice (21) [Daniel & Mira]; white; 12 Feb. 1880; CT Sigmon, JP in Cline's Twsp; AJ Stine, JC Reitzel. 2-60.

John E. of Cline's Twsp; HOLLER, Dora J. of Cline's Twsp (19); white; M=1877?; William H. Rockett, JP in Cline's Twsp; Burl Huffman, Harriet Isenhour, Mat Rockett. NL.

Jonas [Franklin & Catherine]; CHRISTOPHER, Catherine [Daniel & Lucy]; M=20 Apr. 1870; WG James, JP. NL.

Lawson (21); LAEL, Catharine (25); white; M=2 Jan. 1877; CT Sigmon, JP in Cline's Twsp; Noah Lael, Henry Lael, Jeff Holler. NL.

Lawson M. (22) [Lawson & Anna]; EKARD, Ellen B. (23) [David & Elizabeth]; white; M=23 Oct. 1879; PC Henkel, Luth. Min. in Newt. Twsp; JM Smith, RA Yoder, IP Spencer. 1-358.

Marcus (22); HARMAN, Elanora (22); white; M-15 Dec. 1878; JM Smith, Luth. Min. at Elijah Herman's; RF Smith, LJ Bost, Daniel Holler. NL.

William L. (29) [John & Catharine]; YOUNT, Florance (21) [Cain & Diannah]; white; M=25 Dec. 1879; PF Smith, JP in Newt. Twsp; CH Sipe, IF Mingus, MC Herman. 1-359.

HOLLYBURTON, Thomas (24); CARPENTER, Hannah (25); black; M=3 Jan. 1878; Edwin W. Joyner, Min. in Hky; John L. Bost, Champion Crowell, Henry White. NL.

HONEYCUTT, McDaniel (22); KILLIAN, Clarinda A. (18); white; M=25 Oct. 1877; PC Henkle, Luth. Min. at PC Henkle's; JP Cline, George A. Brady, JF Hunsucker. NL.

Solomon (53) [James & Malissie] of Alexander Co., NC; POOVEY, Elizabeth (33) [Joseph & Mary]; white; M=18 Mar. 1880; JH Bruns, JP in Hky Twsp; JL Lyerly, Hal Feltes, WC Morrison. 2-68.

HOOD, G.W. [Jacob & Tellisie]; SPEAGLE, Harriet J. [Solomon & Susan]; M=4 Jan. 1870; JW Bandy, JP. NL.

William (27); HELMS, Sarah (21); white; M=17 Nov. 1879; Jacob Mosteller, JP at Mosteller Factory; GP Clay, TS Michaels. NL.

HOOPER, Isaac; RAMSAUR, Barbara Ann; M=22 May 1867; HA Lowrance, JP. NL.

Isaah (19); HUNSUCKER, Violet (18); black; M=7 June 1876; PK Little, JP at PK Little's in Cline's Twsp; Susan Cowen, JE Little, McD Little. NL.

HOOVER, C.A. (55) [Phillip & Mary] of Mecklenburg Co., NC; HOOVER, Barbara E. (48) [Jacob & Mary M.]; white; M=24 Sept. 1879; JC Clapp, Min. in JF Twsp; AA Hoover, JS Shuford, Leroy R. Whitener. 1-360.

Daniel; BOLCH, Laura E.; M=27 June 1858; Joseph Parker, Min. NL.

Jacob; CALDWELL, Martha; M=24 Apr. 1851; H. Asbury, Min. NL.

Leo (22); LEATHERMAN, Isabella (23); white; M=25 Jan. 1877; JA Foil, Ref. Min. in Newton; PA Killian, Reuben Setzer, SC Foil. NL.

Monroe; CALDWELL, Mella H.; M=5 June 1851; Henry Asbury, Min. NL.

HOUK, Coleman; MORETZ, Susan; M=11 Dec. 1854; E. Yount, JP. NL.

Sidney D. [Harrison & Sarah Ann]; TURNER, Martha S. [William & Lovina]; M=28 Dec. 1871; EA Warlick, JP. 1-78.

HOUSER, Elam [Levi & Elizabeth]; YODER, Anna C. [Able & Elizabeth]; M=4 Oct. 1868; John Watts, Min. NL.
HOUSTON, J.M.; COONS, Elizabeth; M=10 Aug. 1866; JB Little, JP. NL.
  Robert Bruce B. (34) [Joel B. & Elizabeth L.M.] of Hamilton Twsp; SETZER, Jennie (22) [George & Catharine] of Newton; white; M=14 Nov. 1872; JC Clapp, Min. in Newt. Twsp; LM Rudisill, ML McCorkle, George Setzer. 1-167.
  Daniel N. (21) [Franklin & Ann]; Isenhour, Sallie H. (21) [John & Margaret]; white; M=30 Dec. 1880; PC Henkel, Luth. Min. in Cline's Twsp; AJ Eisenhour, JI Spinks, GW Icenhower. 2-61.
  Hugh (23); SHUFORD, Etta; black; M=21 Mar. 1878; SC Brown, JP in Hamilton Twsp; MJ Brown, James Callicut, EL Houston. NL.
  Sidney A. [Joel B. & Mahala]; FRY, Jane C. [Joseph & Emely]; M=3 Oct. 1869; Daniel May, Min. NL.
  William N. [Robert & Mahala]; ISENHOUR, Rachel [David & Eliza C.]; M=20 Dec. 1870; William H. Rockett, JP. 1-23.
HOVIS, Melkiah; FRY, Sally C.; M=18 Dec. 1866; Henry Cline, JP. NL.
  Rufus; KEENER, Susan; M=23 Apr. 1863; JD Caldwell, JP. NL
HOWARD, Allen M. (26); LITTLE, Elizabeth F.E. (22) of Lincoln Co., NC; white; M=31 Aug. 1876; JA Sherrill, Min. at JA Sherrill's; JL Hills, BW Howard, HO Proctor. NL.
  Andrew (21); REED, Lovena (19); black; M=20 Sept. 1877; JA Sherrill, Min. at JA Sherrill's; LA Rudisill, ML Sherrill, Mrs. L. Sherrill. NL.
  Edmond (22); GABRIEL, Fannie (21); white; M=10 June 1874; JA Sherrill, Min. at GW Gabriel's; AE Sherrill, MM Gabriel, John W. Gabriel. NL.
  James (20); BRIDGES, Ellon; black; M=16 Oct. 1877; William Brooks, Min. at Alfred Bridges'; Albert Brown, Henry Linebarger, Robert Linebarger. NL.
  James L. [Jefferson & Eliza] of Ohio; HOLLER, Martha (19) [Alfred & Ruan] of Newton; white; M=7 Jan. 1873; GL Hunt, Min. in Newt. Twsp; CH Sipe, EB Pope, WG Yount. 1-240.
  John (26); TWEKSBURY, Carrie E. (23); white; M=16 Feb. 1879; JC Clapp, Min. at WD Tewksbury's; WR Tewksbury, PA Teweksbury, J. ?. NL.
  John M. (23) [n/k & Nancy] of Mt. Crk Twsp; ROBINSON, Rachel (18) [John S. & Epsoy] of Mt. Crk Twsp; white; M=11 Aug. 1872; JA Sherrill, Min. at Mt. Crk Twsp; GP Sherrill, GA Barkley, H. Howard. 1-168.
  Joseph A. [Allen & Elizabeth]; ROBINSON, Susan [John & Epsey]; M=1 Sept. 1870; JA Sherrill, Min. NL.
  Nelson; WILLIAMS, Mahala; M=18 Jan. 1863; E. Yount, JP. NL.
  Pinckney B.; CONNER, Harriet; M=14 Sept. 1859; Jesse Gantt, JP. NL.
  W.H.; SRONCE, Molly M.; M=5 Aug. 1857; J.W. Puett, Min. NL.
  William; ROBINSON, Jane; M=22 Jan. 1857; H. Asbury, Min. NL.
  William Pinkney (21); KALE, Ruah (22); white; M=10 Feb. 1876; JA Sherrill, Min. at A. Kale's; Pink Kale, James Howard, William Howard. NL.
HOYLE, B.W. [John & Dorothy]; SMITH, Jane; M=22 Oct. 1871; PA Whitener, Min. NL.

HOYLE, Eli (72) of Cleveland Co., NC; WISE, Elizabeth (40); white; M=5 May 1878; Solamon Hoyle, Bapt. Min. at Elizabeth Wise's; John Mull, MS Mull, Prissila Hoyle. NL.
    Israel G.; MULL, Malinda A.; M=12 Mar. 1866; Amos Helderbrand, Min. NL.
    John (25) [Burle & Jane]; FRY, Harriett (18) [Martin & Elizabeth]; white; M=1 Sept. 1880; RR Brookshiers, Min. in JF Twsp; RM Fry, JG Hoyle, ME Hoyle. 2-62.
    John W.A. (19) [JC & Mary]; WEAVER, Linnie A. (18) [Jacob & Emeline]; white; M=25 Feb. 1880; ML Little, Luth. Min. in Bandy's Twsp; Ida Ramsour, Ernest E. Hudson, Hernerie Hudson. 2-63.
    Manuel E. (23) [BW & Jane]; PROPST, Lucinda (24) [Absolom & Clara]; white; M=6 Oct. 1880; Robert Helton, Min. at JF Twsp; JA Hoyle, JG Hoyle, DG Propst. 2-63A.
    N.M.; HOWSER, Sarah; M=9 Oct. 1859; PJ Pitts, JP. NL.
    Sandy [Thomas Magbie & Hannah Hoyle]; LEWIS, Rachael [n/g & Mary Lewis]; M=31 Jan. 1871; EP Coulter, JP. NL.
    Wesley (23) [Sandy & Rachael] of Newton; ROCKET, Sarah (20) [n/g & Mima Rocket] of Newton; black; M=9 Jan. 1873; PF Smith, JP in Newt. Twsp; WE Yount, FL Herman, Frank Bolch. 1-241.
HUBBARD, Franklin (25) [David & Elizabeth]; BRITTAIN, Susan (27) [Joshua & n/g]; white; M-6 Sept. 1879; MF Hull, JP at Bandy's Twsp; CE Shull, Nancy Huffman, William Huffman. 1-361.
HUDSON, Andrew (20); CLINE, Eliza (27); white; M=10 Feb. 1875; JW Bandy, JP at Bandy's Twsp; P. Johnson, W. Pendleton, William Martin. NL.
    D.M. (27) [Daniel & Margaret]; HEDRICK, Sarah C. (20) [John C. & Margaret]; white; M=21 Sept. 1879; CT Sigmon, JP at Cline's Twsp; JF Jones, JB Ervin, MM Coons. 1-362.
    Franklin; ASHEBRANER, Catherine; M=23 Dec. 1851; George Huffman, JP. NL.
    Lawrence A. (19); STARR, Ellen (22); white; M=25 July 1878; GL Hunt, Luth. Min. at Margaret Hudson's; RA Conrad, LS Fulbright, JM Fulbright. NL.
    W.H. (30) [John & Jenny]; WEAVER, Sarah (22) [Noah & Levina]; white; M=21 Nov. 1872; JW Bandy, JP at Bandy's Twsp. 1-169.
    William S.; CLINE, Margaret E.; M=5 Mar. 1857; GJ Wilkie, JP. NL.
HUDSPETH, George (48); HARWELL, Adoline (47); white; M=8 Sept. 1877; MB Trolinger, JP in Hamilton Twsp; James Harwell, Milton Sherrill, CH Trolinger. NL.
HUFFMAN, Able B. [Eli & Nancy]; POPE, Delilia; M=1871; Record Missing. NL.
    Adolphus [Jacob & Catherine]; CANUP, Emaline [Amos & Mary]; M=10 Aug. 1871; JC Clapp, Min. NL.
    Alfred B. (25); BOLLINGER, Isabella (21); white; M=17 Feb. 1875; GL Hunt, Luth. Min. at GL Hunt's; Mary Murphy, Logan T. Fulbright, Daniel S. Coulter. NL.
    Allin; SHOOK, Malinda; M=5 Dec. 1857; JHA Yount, JP. NL.
    Ambrose; POPE, Barbara; M=9 July 1854; H. Ingold, JP. NL.
    Burle [Jacob & Susan]; HOLLER, Belzosa [Frank & Betsey]; M=23 Feb. 1868; D. McD. Yount, Esq. NL.
    Daniel; WAGNER, Catharine L.; M=9 Mar. 1864; E. Yount, JP. NL.

HUFFMAN, Daniel M. (22); SEITZ, Catharine (18); white; M=30 Sept. 1874; JM Smith, Luth. Min. in Conover; QE Teague, N. Townsend, TW Bostain. NL.

David; SHOOK, Jemima; M=31 Jan. 1858; JB Little, JP. NL.

Davidson C. (22) [Langdon & Amy]; HUNT, Nancy C.R. (17) [George L. & Sarah A.]; white; M=6 Jan. 1876; ML Carpenter, Luth. Min. in Newt. Twsp; PM Hunt, JM Huffman, AJ Carpenter. 1-315.

Davidson C. (26) [Davidson & Amy]; MILLER, Harriett M. (19) [David & Catherine]; white; M-26 Feb. 1880; JW Mouser, JP in Hky Twsp; HD Wagner, PL Miller, WP Huffman. 2-64.

Doctor R. (22); HUFFMAN, Ema E. (18) of Burke Co., NC; white; M=8 Dec. 1878; GJ Wilkie, Min. at Marcus Huffman's; IF Hudson; WB Stallings, Jonas Brittain. NL.

Elijah; SMYER, Barbara M.; M=23 Nov. 1854; E. Yount, JP. NL.

Elisha (21); DRUM, Dorothy (19); white; 23 May 1878; JC Clapp, Ref. Min. at JC Clapp's; Londa Drum, Lewis Huffman, WP Huffman. NL.

Freeman J. (21); KAYLOR, Susan D. (18); white; M=21 Sept. 1876; CT Sigmon, JP at Cline's Twsp; John A. Hoke, Jacob A. Sipe, Jacob Bowman. NL.

Gaither (22) of Burke Co., NC; WHISENHUNT, Catharine (25) of Hky Tav. Twsp; white; M=13 Nov. 1873; PF Smith, JP in Newton; NA Fry, Frank Boyd, EC Miller. NL.

Hosea F. (23) [Daniel & Nancy] of Burke Co., NC; WHISNANT, Margarett (24) [Phillip & Polly]; white; M=19 Aug. 1880; JP Styers, Bapt. Min. in Bandys Twsp; JG Huffman, Sallie L. Killian, Willian Whisnant. 2-65.

James M. (31); DAGENHART, Barbara T.E. (27); white; M=3 Feb. 1879; HA Forney, JP in Newton; A. Fulbright, DB Gaither, MA Forney. NL.

Jefferson M. (21) [Langdon & Anna M.]; HUNT, Fannie E. (18) [George L. & Sarah H.] of Newt. Twsp; white; M=19 Sept. 1872; GL Hunt, Min. in Newt. Twsp; ML Carpenter, DC Huffman, ? Kiser. 1-170.

Jeremiah; CLINE, Mahala; M=23 Dec. 1856; E. Yount, JP. NL.

John (20); LITTLE, Ellen (19); white; M=21 Dec. 1876; John M. Smith, Luth. Min. at JM Smith's; HS Smith, WA Smith, PB Smith. NL.

John P.; SPEAGLE, Fanny; M=20 Nov. 1861; G. Huffman, JP. NL.

Joseph; YOUNT, Mary S.; M=25 June 1854; H. Ingold, JP. NL.

Julius [Jasper & Mary]; TUCKER, Nancy [Samuel & Elizabeth]; M= 22 Sept. 1870; JW Bandy, JP. 1-24.

Julius (21) [Nelson & Rhoda]; MILLER, Anna Rosabell (19) [Caleb & Susan]; white; M=3 Aug. 1879; JM Smith, Luth. Min. in Newt. Twsp; HS Smith, N. Townsend, IF Townsend. 1-363.

Levi S.; MILLER, Lovina L.; M=20 Feb. 1864; William L. Mehaffey, JP. NL.

Marcus; HARTZOE, L.L.; M=10 Jan. 1861; JHA Yount, JP. NL.

Martin; CLINE, Trefena; M=22 June 1862; E. Yount, JP. NL.

Miles; MAISE, Sally; M=20 Apr. 1854; H. Ingold, JP. NL.

Noah; COULTER, Louisa; M=4 Sept. 1855; Philip Burns, JP. NL.

Rufus C. (22); MARTIN, Catharine (22); white; M=12 May 1878; Jacob Mosteller, JP in Bandy's Twsp; Rufus Hudson, JM Huffman. NL.

HUFFMAN, Solomon F. (24) [Elijah & Barbara]; HOLLER, Amanda (18) [Andrew & Lovina]; white; M=18 Sept. 1879; PC Henkel, Luth. Min. in Newt. Twsp; SE Killian, RA Bumgarner, PP Fry. 1-364.

Setthial; ECKARD, A.; M=28 Feb. 1861; E. Yount, JP. NL.

Sillis [Eli & Nancy]; BENFIELD, Mahaly [Jacob & Ruan]; M=14 Aug. 1870; William G. James, JP. 1-25.

William J. [Alfred & Polly Anderson]; HEFNER, Mary Jane; M=1871; Record Missing. NL.

William M. [Jasper & Mary]; TUCKER, Candus [Samuel & Bettie]; M=28 Jan. 1868; AJ Whitener, Esq. NL.

William P. (22) [Joseph & Mary]; DRUM, Londie (19) [Miles & Harriett]; white; M=29 Feb. 1880; PK Little, JP in Cline's Twsp; A. Killian, JS Benfield, Lewis Huffman. 2-66.

HUGGINS, Lawson A. (21); HOLLER, Caroline (27); white; M=7 Apr. 1875; Abel Whitener, JP in Hky Twsp; ML Fry, WH Atwood, LF Miller. NL.

HUGHES, Israel P.; RAY, Julia A.; M=9 Apr. 1853; J. Finger, Min. NL.

HUIT, Abel M. (26) [MH & Rhoda]; SIGMON, Sallie C. (25) [Eli & Rhoda]; white; M=11 Feb. 1875; JM Smith, Luth. Min. in Newt. Twsp; JF Smyre, PF Smith, WE Yount. 1-285.

Carry; CLINE, Mahala; M=18 May 1859; PJ Pitts, JP. NL.

Henderson (22); CLINE, Caroline (19); black; M=19 Oct. 1878; WS Shuford, Bapt. Min. at Morgan Cline's; BR Bryon, MJS Davidson, James Abernathy. NL.

J.L.; RABB, Sarah; M=24 Nov. 1866; Henry Cline, JP. NL.

Lewis; WINNBURGH, Elizabeth; M=13 Apr. 1858; Jesse Gantt, JP. NL.

Marcus (19); POOVEY, Nancy (20); white; M=19 May 1878; HA Forney, JP in Newton; CA Cline, JM Fulbright, LA Hudson. NL.

Miles (21) of Cald. Twsp; LINK, Pamphiliam (20); white; M=6 Aug. 1873; JL Huit, JP in Cald. Twsp; John Kener, JL Huit, Michael Abernathy. NL.

Noah [Moses M. & Rhoda]; LUTZ, Ellen [Jacob & Harriet]; M=20 Dec. 1870; JM Smith, Min. 1-26.

Thomas [Richmond Carpenter & Julia Huit]; JAMES, Mary [n/k & Sarah James]; M=9 Dec. 1869; BF Watts, Min. NL.

W. Adolphus (25); CLINE, Mattie (18); white; M=3 Aug. 1875; JL Huit, JP in Cald. Twsp; Noah Barringer, David Barringer, Mich Williamson. NL.

HUITT, Elcanah (21); WHITENBURG, Candace (20); black; M=22 Oct. 1876; PK Little, JP in Cline's Twsp; Jason Cowan, Sidney Hunsucker, Elvira Whitenburg. NL.

M.M. [Lewis & Margaret]; PROPST, Julia [Daniel & Catherine Smyre]; M=5 May 1870; JM Smith, Min. NL.

HULL, Silas [S. & Sarah Grop]; MCCORKLE, Eliza [Wesley Abernethy & Manervy]; M=25 Feb. 1869; James A. Garvan, JP. NL.

William P. [Silas Hull & n/k]; ICENHOUR, Froney [Levi Hunsucker & Nancy Smith]; M=20 Dec. 1868; M. Robinson, JP. NL.

William Pinkney (44); HOOVER, Emaline (25); black; M=30 Sept. 1874; Sherid Andrews, Min. at Snow Hill; Lafayett Wilson, Adolph Setzer, Yount ?. NL.

HUNICUT, Solomon (53) [James & Malissie] of Alexander Co., NC; POOVEY, Elizabeth (33) [Joseph & Mary]; white; M=18 Mar. 1880; JH Bruns, JP at Hky Twsp; JL Lyerly, Hal Feltes, WC Morrison. 2-68.

HUNSUCKER, Burton (21); CLINE, Frances (20); white; M=21 Feb. 1878; PC Henkel, Luth. Min. at Elijah Cline's; BE Smith, AM Hefner, WN Hunsucker. NL.

HUNSUCKER, Calvin; WILSON, Selia; M=14 July 1859; John Lantz, Min. NL.

Elkanah; MILLER, Sarah; M=17 Jan. 1866; GH Moser, JP. 1-4.

J.P.; SMITH, Francis A.; M=24 Apr. 1856; PC Hinkle, Min. NL.

Jacob P. (29); WITHERSPOON, Harriet (27); white; M=13 Feb. 1873; JL Hunt, JP in Hamilton Twsp; Alf Wilson, Pat Setzer, William Hunsucker. NL.

Jacob Pinkney (29) [John & Lydia] of Hamilton Twsp; WITHERSPOON, Harriet (27) [Franklin & Sarah] of Hamilton Twsp; white; M= 13 Feb. 1873; JL Hewitt, JP at Cat. Stn; Pat Setzer, Alfred Wilson, William Hunsucker. 1-238.

John F. (22); MILLER, Mary M. (18); white; M=2 Feb. 1876; JM Smith, Luth. Min. at JM Smith's; Ann Reitzel, HS Smith, Anderson Reitzel. NL.

Jonas; CLONINGER, Sarah C.; M=5 Oct. 1859; John Lantz, Min. NL.

Jonas (25); HERMAN, Clarinda (19); white; M=25 Feb. 1876; JM Smith, Luth. Min. at Camilla Herman's; MS Deal, LP Cloninger, WH Herman. NL.

L.A.; Herman, A.L.; M=26 Sept. 1861; William L. Mehaffey, JP. NL.

Levi; HUNSUCKER, Caroline; M=7 Nov. 1869; William H. Rockett, JP; acknowledgment of their marriage in South Carolina.

Marcus; WITHERSPOON, Susanah; M=18 Nov. 1856; JW Lawrance, JP. NL.

Milus; JAMES, Malinda; M=15 May 1867; HA Lowrance, JP. NL.

Silas A. (22); JAMES, Nancy (21); black; M=3 Mar. 1875; GW Cansler, JP in Hamilton Twsp; BC Yount, GWC Long, John W. Blackwelder. NL.

William Nelson (38) [Joseph & Polly] of Cline's Twsp; CLINE, Candace M. (20) [Elijah & Elizabeth] of Cline's Twsp; white; M=25 Dec. 1873; JC Clapp, Min. in Cline's Twsp; Daniel Deal, NN Hunsucker, Nelson Sigmon. 1-239.

HUNT, Hiram [David & Mary]; MULL, Adline [Richard & Lula]; M= 20 Jan. 1869; JH Brindle, Min. NL.

Peter M. (21); MILLER, Frances E. (22); white; M=8 Aug. 1875; George S. Pasour, Luth. Min. at JM Huffman's; DC Huffman, JM Huffman, TA Witherspoon. NL.

HUNTER, Alex [John & n/k]; DAVIDSON, Emeline [n/k & Mary Davidson]; M=31 Mar. 1870; F. Caldwell, JP. NL.

HUNTLEY, Virgil; LINK, Eve C.; M=22 Jan. 1861; PC Henkel, Min. NL.

ICENHOUR, John [JH & Sarah]; ECKERD, Susanna C. [Solomon & Percilla]; M=25 Dec. 1869; JM Smith, Min. NL.

IKERD, Bob [Forney Killian & Vina Rudisill]; ENGLAND, Julia [n/k & Fanny England]; M=28 Aug. 1867; H. Cline, Esq. NL.

Franklin C. [George A. & Susan]; COULTER, Martha J. [Eli & Harriet]; M=4 Jan. 1871; JC Clapp, Min. 1-79.

Willis (21); SMYER, Jane (19); black; M=28 Nov. 1878; JH Shuford, Ref. Min. in Hky; Ada Schenk, Jane Halaway, JE Hendrix. NL.

INGLE, Jacob; HOWARD, Patsey; M=4 June 1856; HH Linebarger, JP. NL.
  Levi; CARTER, M.C.; M=1 Sept. 1861; JD Caldwell, JP. NL.
  Michael; KIRKSEY, Eliza; M=29 Jan. 1862; JD Caldwell, JP. NL.
INGRAM, Fields (52) of Alexander Co., NC; WIKE, Rhoda (45); white; M=13 Sept. 1877; JC Clapp, Ref. Min. at Delila Wike's; James McRee, RC Setzer, Daniel Setzer. NL.
  John L. (20); KALE, Fannie (22); white; M=20 Sept. 1877; JA Sherrill, Min. at Lawson Kale's; JA McCombs, LG Kale, J. Blackwelder. NL.
  William D. (25) of Iredell Co., NC; LITTLE, Martha G. (23); white; M=16 Aug. 1876; PK Little, JP in Cline's Twsp; JM Smith, MD Little, Sims Little. NL.
ISAAC, John F. (18) [Levi & Anna]; HEFNER, Candace (21) [Miles & Polly]; white; M=23 Nov. 1879; PK Little, JP in Cline's Twsp; JH Hefner, D. Hefner, JH Miller. 1-365.
ISAACS, Levi; HUFFMAN, Anna; M=24 May 1860; JB Little, JP. NL.
ISANHOUR, Wilson M. (27) [JN & Sarah]; ISANHOUR, Harriett (18) [Abel & Susan]; white; M=25 Dec. 1879; PF Smith, JP in Newt. Twsp, Conover; PC Hawn, Jonas Dellinger, D. Dellinger. 1-366.
ISENHOUR, Daniel [JH & Sarah]; DEAL, Sarah A. [LA & Susan]; M=15 Nov. 1871; William H. Rockett, JP. 1-80.
  David (26); SETZER, Mary (18); white; M=8 Jan. 1879; WG James, JP in Newton; CH Sipe, GW West, Noah Barringer. NL.
  George W. (24); SPINKS, Laura A. (17); white; M=31 Jan. 1877; CW Herman, JP in Newton; A. Huffman, Jeff Cline, J. Spinks. NL.
  Jacob (65); Hunsucker, Harriet (46); white; M=7 Feb. 1878; CW Herman, JP in Newton; Noah Leffon, Burton Hunsucker, Lawson Hunsucker. NL.
  Joseph R.C. (26); HEFNER, Lucinda (22); white; M=20 Dec. 1877; CW Herman, JP in Newton; Daniel Hefner, George Isenhour, JB Bolden. NL.
  Marcus [John & Margaret]; MILLER, Elenora [Conrad & Elizabeth]; M=6 Mar. 1872; EA Warlick, JP. 1-171.
  Martin M. (18); ISENHOUR, Julia G. (25); white; M=3 Feb. 1876; JM Smith, Luth. Min. at John Isenhour's; EA Miller, JRC Isenhour, GW Isenhour. NL.
  Philo (22); STINE, Margaret C. (18); white; M=6 Oct. 1874; JM Smith, Luth. Min. at John Stine's; JM Stine, AJ Stine, David Isenhour. NL.
  Wilson M. (27) [JH & Sarah]; ISENHOUR, Harriett (18) [Abel & Susan]; white; M=25 Dec. 1879; PF Smith, JP in Newt. Twsp, Conover; PC Hawn, Jonas Dellinger, D. Dellinger. 1-366.
ISENHOWER, David; HETERICK, Eliza C.; M=3 Jan. 1853; H. Ingold, JP. NL.
ISLY, James H.; LEONARD, Sarah E.; M-21 Feb. 1860; AJ Fox, Min. NL.
IVENS, J.W.; POPE, Nancy; M=19 Mar. 1856; TJ Hamilton, JP. NL.
JAMES, Auther (21) [James & BA]; LOCKMAN, Mattie (22) [David & Elizabeth] of Lincoln Co., NC; white; M=17 Mar. 1880; MM Gabriel, JP in Mt. Crk Twsp; JE Howard, John J. Smith, JH Carswell. 2-70.

JAMES, George M. (24); WILFONG, Lucinda (19); black; M=3 May 1877; JC Clapp, Ref. Min. at JC Clapp's; Carel Clapp, Milton Clapp, Charles Clapp. NL.
  James [David & Emoline]; ELLIOTT, Mary [Lawson Smyre & Judith]; black; M=3 Aug. 1872; BF Watts, Bapt. Min. in Hamilton Twsp. 1-172.
  James G.; HOBBS, Avoline; M=30 Dec. 1856; Jonas Bost, JP. NL.
  McDuffey [Stephen & Cassey]; BOST, Ellen [Andy & Caly]; M=2 Dec. 1871; William Brooks, Min. NL.
  William; BRIDGES, Henrietta; M=29 Mar. 1864; GJ Wilkie, JP. NL.
JARRETT, Alfred [Jacob & Mary]; JARRETT, Isabell; M=1871; Record Missing. Taken from old index. NL.
  D.P.; YODER, Mary Caroline; M=4 Nov. 1866; HJ Fox, Min. NL.
  David M. (21); KESTLER, Alice (19); white; M=31 Oct. 1876; AJ Fox, Luth. Min. at John Kestler's; JJ Willas, DJ Shuford, WS Jarrett. NL.
  H.R. [Jacob & Mary]; FULBRIGHT, Susan C. [John & Lizzie]; M=12 Sept. 1867; AJ Fox, Min. NL.
  James F. [Daniel & Mahala]; HAWN, Flora E. [n/k & Annah]; M=30 July 1868; PC Henkel, Min. NL.
  John J. [Jacob & Mary]; REEPE, Margaret [Emanuel & Elizabeth]; M=5 June 1870; JC Clapp, Min. NL.
  John J. (27); YODER, Eliza (28); white; M=7 Oct. 1877; GL Hunt, Luth. Min. at GL Hunt's; GH Reep, LM Hunt, SA Huit. NL.
  John R. [Samuel & Clara]; ALBRIGHT, Sallie E. [JA Ester & W. Ester]; M=12 Mar. 1872; JC Clapp, Min. 1-173.
  Jonas (73) [John & Catherine] of JF Twsp; LITTLE, Mary (30) [Thomas & Matilda] of Bandys Twsp; white; M=26 July 1872; JW Bandy, JP in Bandys Twsp. 1-174.
  O.M. [Connie & Mehaley]; HAWN, Jane [Jesse & Amy]; M=9 Dec. 1869; AJ Fox, Min. NL.
  W.S. [Milton & Fannie]; Keever, Martha [James & Caroline]; M=16 May 1872; John W. Abernethy. 1-175.
JENKINS, William; HOKE, Mary; M=18 May 1857; John Lantz, Min. NL.
  William (20); SIGMON, Louisa (20); white; M=14 Sept. 1877; Robert Helton, Min. at Robert Helton's; Ida Helton, JH Sigmon, Henry F. Sigmon. NL.
JOHNSON, Bartlet (21) [Henry & Sarah]; HICKS, Elizabeth (21) [Charles & Margaret]; white; M=21 Nov. 1872; JW Bandy, JP in Bandys Twsp. 1-176.
  C. Perry (21); DEAL, Adoline (30); white; M=26 Jan. 1875; JC Clapp, Ref. Min. at JC Clapp's; Sarah Propst, Carell Clapp, Emma Clapp. NL.
  David [William & Elizabeth]; HUBBARD, P.M. [Matthew & Elizabeth]; M=25 Nov. 1869; Robert Helton, Min. NL.
  David (28) [Max & Sarah]; TUCKER, Missouri (18) [Dempsie & Lucy]; white; M=4 Jan. 1880; JP Styers, Bapt. Min. in Bandys Twsp; WS Burns, JB English, Samuel Tucker. 2-69.
  Eli; LOWRANCE, M.C.; M=6 Dec. 1866; GJ Wilkie, Min. NL.
  Hosea R. (23); WHISENANT, Mary (22); white; M=28 June 1876; Jacob Mosteller at Bandys Twsp; James Lynn, Sarah Linn. NL.
  John [WB & Elizabeth]; ROCKETT, Agnes E.; M=1871; Record Missing. Taken from old index. NL.

JOHNSON, John M.; SPEAGLE, Clary; M=4 July 1861; George Huffman, JP. NL.
  Pink (27); MULL, Sophronia (28); white; M=9 Sept. 1878; WF Hull, Bapt. Min. at WF Hull's; JM Hull, HP Shuford, LH Bandy. NL.
  R.W. (50); ROBINSON, Caroline (43) [George Settlemyre & Hannah]; white; M=17 Oct. 1879; JC Clapp, Ref. Min. in Hky Twsp; AW Robinson, AM Settlemyer, John T. Robinson. 1-367.
JONES, Able [Allen & Jane]; GABRIEL, Mary [Joseph & Rebecca]; M=20 Oct. 1869; JA Sherrill, Min. NL.
  Andrew L. (21); SIGMON, Alace (20); white; M-1 Sept. 1878; Robert Helton, Min. at William Jenkins; Lea Hoover, WA Yoder, SZ McCaslin. NL.
  Evelind H. (34) [Hiram & Martha Ervin]; BROWN, Catharine (34) [Franklin & Roxanah]; white; M=18 Aug. 1880; JA Sherrill, Min. at Mt. Crk Twsp; RA Gabriel, EL Ervin, RA Linebarger. 2-71.
  G.W.; SHERRILL, Susan; M=20 Nov. 1862; JW Gabriel, JP. NL.
  Isaac G. [PR & Margaret]; ALBRIGHT, Mary [Richard Wilson & EJ]; M=6 Feb. 1872; EA Warlick, JP. 1-177.
  J.F. [Hiram & Martha]; SETZER, Ann C. [Jacob & Delila]; M=11 Nov. 1867; WL Mehaffey, Min. NL.
  James [David & Emoline]; HUIT, Mary [Lawson Smyre & Judith]; black; M=1 Aug. 1872; BF Watts, Bapt. Min. in Hamilton Twsp. 1-172.
  Jim [Kinston & Patsy Wilfong]; ROBINSON, Phillis [Robert & Patence]; M=29 Feb. 1868; EA Warlick, Esq. NL.
  John Turner (21) [WE & Linnia]; CALDWELL, Elizabeth Rebecca (18) [HC & Elmiry]; white; M=29 Feb. 1880; WC Caldwell, JP in Cald. Twsp; John F. Caldwell, John P. Abernathy, Levi S. Caldwell. 2-72.
  John W. (23); JONES, Julia A. (19); white; M=24 Feb. 1875; JC Hartzell, Min. at John Jones'; TE fields, DW Turner, JE Hartsell. NL.
  M.J.; ROBINSON, M.A.; M=27 Dec. 1863; John Huit, JP. NL.
  Mitten; SHERRILL, S.J.; M=8 Nov. 1860; JM Lowrance, JP. NL.
  Nelson; LINEBARGER, Susan; M=12 Feb. 1861; JM Lowrance, JP. NL.
  Osburn (23); PUNCH, Martha E. (18) [JD & Anner]; white; M=8 Apr. 1875; JA Sherrill, Min. in Mt. Crk Twsp; JB Hoke, HA Gilleland, DC Williamson. 1-286.
  Pinckney; SIGMON, Susanah; M=7 Nov. 1860; JW Gabriel, JP. NL.
  Samuel Gregory; BANDY, Jane E.; M=21 Apr. 1866; Rev. A. Stamy, Min. NL.
  Thomas J. (23); PAINE, Rosanah (24); white; M=19 Apr. 1874; JA Sherrill, Min. at IE Paine's; IE Paine, James Paine, Dorsy Sherrill. NL.
  William; LINEBARGER, Mary; M=2 April 1856; JM Lowrance, JP. NL.
JULIAN, F.P.; TURBYFILL, Martha M.; M=25 Dec. 1860; JA Sherrill, JP. NL.
KAEL, Samuel (19); HUIT, Jane (15); black; M=17 Dec. 1874; JL Huit, JP in Cald. Twsp; Abel Huit, Wilson Smyre, Pink Hull. NL.
KAHILL, Daniel; MILLER, Rachel; M=7 Nov. 1859; E. Yount, JP. NL.
KALE, Absalam [Elisha & Sallie]; MOOSE, Susan A. [Alex C. Lackey & Elizabeth]; M=26 Dec. 1867; D. Hamilton, Esq. NL.

KALE, Albert E. (25); FRASURE, Laura (20); white; M=29 Oct. 1876; William G. James, JP in Catawba; GW Cansler, JH Trolinger, George S. Powell. NL.
  L.H.; ODEM, C.E.; M=21 Dec. 1865; LN Wilson, JP. NL.
  Lihue L. (23); STILES, Sarah (21); white; M=23 Aug. 1877; JA Sherrill, Min. at Sarah Stile's; L. Webb, LA Keever, JK Stiles. NL.
  Marcus Augustus (22) of Hamilton Twsp; BOST, Selia (20) of Hamilton Twsp; white; M=13 Nov. 1873; JL Hewitt, JP in Cald. Twsp; JF Rabb, Alex Wilson, Avery Wilson. NL.
  Palsen; FISH, Emily; M=18 Jan. 1853; JM Lowrance, JP. NL.
  Pinckney C. [Absolom & Sarah]; LOWRANCE, Catherine [N. Lowrance & Rachel]; M=16 Nov. 1869; Absey Sherrill, JP. NL.
  Polsen; FRY, Angeline; M=1 Mar. 1859; PJ Pitts, JP. NL.
  Sidney; NULL, Marthy A.; M=8 Oct. 1863; PJ Pitts, JP. NL.
KANUP, Enos [Amos & Mary]; HEFNER, Sarah Ann E.; M=1871; Record Missing. NL.
KAYLOR, Alfred; STARNES, Salina; M=5 Feb. 1864; JR Ellis, JP. NL.
  David E. [Henry & Elizabeth]; PATTENT, Sarah [Samuel & Barbara]; M=27 Feb. 1868; CW Herman, Esq. NL.
  Joseph E. (19) [Manuel & Malinda]; BOOVEY, Nira Malinda (19) [M. Boovey & Nancy]; white; M=7 Oct. 1880; GL Hunt, Luth. Min. in Newt. Twsp; FY Yount, GW Cline, FJ Huffman. 2-73.
KEENER, Alfred L. [Daniel & Meriah]; SMYER, Mary Jane [Logan & Emeline]; M=8 Dec. 1870; Daniel May, Min. 1-27.
  Alexander L. (34); MOOSE, Margaret Ann (26); white; M=12 Mar. 1874; JC Clapp, Ref. Min. at Larkin Kestler's; Henry McCaslin, Larkin Kestler, Ted H. Forney. NL.
  Daniel (37) [Mikel & Catherine] of Lincoln Co., NC; STOWE, Mary E. (19) [James F. & Minty]; white; M=25 Dec. 1872; JA Sherrill, JP in Mt. Crk Twsp; AD Hewit, JT Sanders, MA Wilkinson. 1-178.
  Daniel; BOST, Julia A.; M=30 Nov. 1864; Philip Burns, JP. NL.
  David (23) [John & Francis]; MOOSE, Barbara (22) [Andy & Eliza] of Cald. Twsp; white; M=12 Jan. 1873; JW Williams of Cald. Twsp; Ann E. Williams, Malinda T. Keener. 1-242.
  David A. (28) [John & Frances]; SETZER, Saphronia (28) [Franklin & Caroline]; white; M=14 Jan. 1880; IN Wilson, JP in Cat. Twsp; AH Wilson, YJ Setzer, SA Wike. 2-74.
  George (20); MAUNEY, Vira (22); white; M=28 Jan. 1879; R. England, JP at R. England's; RL Bolick, ML Mauney, William W. Norwood. NL.
  J. Frank [John & Francis]; Finger, Malinda [John & Lenore]; M=1 Oct. 1868; EA Warlick, JP. NL.
  Marcus; MOOSE, Margaret A.; M=14 Nov. 1875; Jonathan Clark. 1-6.
  Michael (24) [John & Frances] of Cald. Twsp; FRY, Harriett (27) [Davidson & Ann] of Newton; white; M=22 Sept. 1872; JL Hewit, JP in Cald. Twsp; Lou Fry, Franklin Keener, Barbara Keener. 1-179.
KEEVER, Aaron; DETTER, Catharine Y.; M=23 Feb. 1863; Henry Cline, JP. NL.
  Alexander (56); EDWARDS, Sallie Ann (64); white; M=15 Dec. 1878; JC Clapp, Min. at AD Shuford's; AD Shuford, Miles Edwards, MA Shuford. NL.

KEEVER, Amos (22) [n/k & Bettie Keever]; PROPST, Clara (20) [L. Wilfong & Lucy Propst]; black; Robert Helton, Min. in JF Twsp; RB Helton, James Lufday, Caroline Smith. 2-75.
   Daniel C. (21); JARRETT, Clara E. (18); white; M=18 May 1876; AJ Fox, Luth. Min. at Daniel Jarrett's; GP Jarrett, AP Keever, WS Jarret. NL.
   Franklin [Lawson & Malinda]; KILLIAN, Laura L. [Abel & Lovina]; M=5 July 1872; JH Bruns, JP in Hky Tav.; J. Keever, N. Killian. 1-180.
KEISTLER, Joseph; SHITTE, Jane E.; M=1 Mar. 1855; GP Shuford, JP. NL.
KELLER, Henry; GRIMES, Eve; M=27 Nov. 1862. NL.
   Mitchell (50) [Mitchell & Susan]; ROWE, Lucy (50); black; M=10 Sept. 1879; N. Helton, Min. in Hky Twsp; Amos Watts, W. Ward, Jones Smyer. 1-368.
   Peter; KELLER, Mira; M=12 July 1866; DA Little, JP. NL.
   Pinkney L. (21) [n/k & Mira]; HEFNER, Harriett (21) [David & Lanah]; white; M=15 Aug. 1880; CT Sigmon, JP in Cline's Twsp; JS Coons, JF Killian, PC Coons. 2-77.
   W.A. (22) of Burke Co., NC; HULL, Ella (18); white; M=18 Dec. 1879; Joseph M. Smith, Min. at Jonas Brittain's; JT Brittain, JQ Vanhorn, Jonas Brittain. NL.
KELLY, Samuel (22); MICHER, Elizabeth (26); black; M=26 July 1876; AH Shuford, JP in Hky Twsp; GW Feimster, Robert Smyre, Abel Naples. NL.
KIDDER, George W. (35) of Wilmington, NC; HILL, Florence (27) of Hky; white; M=19 Dec. 1877; Edwin W. Joyner, Min. in Hky; AE Gibbs, AC Gibbs, JM Walker. NL.
KILLIAN, Alfred L.; DRUM, Rebecca; M=20 Mar. 1860; Hiram Hefner, JP. NL.
   Andrew; LARR, Elizabeth; M=4 Dec. 1863; PC Hinkle, Min. NL.
   Caleb P. (23); SIPE, Saphronia (20); white; M=5 Sept. 1878; DC Huffman, Luth. Min. at W.M. Hider's; WE Killian, JF Killian, DH Lefevers. NL.
   Frank [Andrew & Mary Ann]; PEACOCK, Virginia W. [Daniel Brown & n/g]; M=4 Apr. 1870; Daniel May, Min. NL.
   Gabriel (21); HALLMAN, Camila (18); white; M=27 Dec. 1877; GL Hunt, Luth. Min. at JH Hallman's; JM Miller, Hanna Hallman, John T. Hallman. NL.
   Henry (21) [Jonas & Roxanah]; CLINE, Catharine (21) [Francis & n/g] of Lincoln Co., NC; white; M=6 May 1875; Robert Helton, Min. in JF Twsp; JM Leonard, IW Helton, MA Leonard. 1-287.
   Henry C. (23) [Abel & Lovinia] of Hky Tav. Twsp; GREEN, Mary Jane (18) [OC & Priscilla] of Hamilton Twsp; white; M=23 Oct. 1872; GW Callahan, Min. in Hamilton Twsp; Eli Smyer, OC Green, OC Harman. 1-181.
   J. Franklin (36), black, of Lincoln Co., NC; ARWOOD, Mary (26), yellow; M=13 July 1876; JW Pewitt, Min. at Susan McComb's; Henry Brevard, Adol Dellinger. NL.
   John (20) [Jesse & Lovina] of Hky Tav. Twsp; HAWN, Julia (18) [Noah & Magdelene] of Hky Tav. Twsp; white; M=24 Oct. 1872; JM Smith, Min. in Newton Twsp; Henry Seitz, Luther Seitz, Mrs. L. Smith. 1-182.
   Laban (28) [Thomas & Elizabeth]; MOSER, Maria (25); white; M=21 Sept. 1879; William G. James, JP in Cat. Twsp; Anna Sherrill, LA Sherrill, SL Sherrill. 1-369.

KILLIAN, Luther (19); WEAVER, Malinda (18); white; M=25 July 1877; JH Bruns, JP in Hky; CM Eddins, Mollie Elliott, Bettie Devereux. NL.

Luther [Jesse & Isabell]; LINEBARGER, Susan E. [Fred & Elizabeth]; M=15 Nov. 1868; J. Finger, Min. NL.

M.A. [Abel S. & Lovina]; MILLER, Fannie E. [Frederick & Adoline]; M=6 June 1872; EA Warlick, JP in Newton. 1-183.

Marion M. (20) [Jonas E. & Roxanna] of Hky; WEAVER, Alice (18) [David H. & Eliza] of JF Twsp; white; M=28 Mar. 1880; GM Yoder, JP in JF Twsp; CT Abernethy, CM Yoder, PR Yoder. 2-76.

Noah (22) of Cline's Twsp; HUFFMAN, Catharine M. (28) Cline's Twsp; white; M=21 Aug. 1873; JM Smith, Luth. Min. at Alfred Huffman's; JL Deitz, S. Killian, N. Leffon. NL.

Pinkney A. (23) [Elijah & Malinda]; JARRETT, Susan Jane E. (23) [Jacob & Mary]; white; M=29 Aug. 1872; JM Smith, Luth. Min. in JF Twsp; JW Propst, DP Jarrett, HR Jarrett. 1-184.

Samuel E.; FRY, Frances; M=20 Nov. 1866; PC Henkel, Min. NL.

Sylvanus (22); BAKER, Candace Angeler (17); white; M=17 Aug. 1876; JM Smith, Luth. Min. at Henry Baker's; JA Hoke, AE Sipe, ML Baker. NL.

W.F.; HOOVER, Frances; M=25 Sept. 1866; CW Herman, JP. NL.

W.L.C. (26) [SE & Isabella] of Denver, NC; WILSON, Cora (18) [WP & Arilia] of Newton; white; M=1 Jan. 1880; CM Anderson, Min. in Newt. Twsp; HP Killian, William Mundy, HD Shelton. 2-78.

William (22) [Anthony & Mary]; HUFFMAN, Julian (20) [Alfred & Malinda]; white; M-11 Feb. 1880; John T. Shell, Bapt. Min.; John T. Shell, Alfred Huffman, RE Sigmon. 2-79.

William L. [Ephraim & Mary]; BAKER, Eva [Solomon & Anna]; M=1 Oct. 1871; JC Clapp, Min. 1-81.

KING, Adolphus H. [William & Fanny]; SHELTON, Mary E. [James B. & Elizabeth]; M=24 Jan. 1872; JA Sherrill, Min. 1-185.

Jacob (26) [Lewis & Elizabeth]; BARGER, Eveline (22) [n/k & Mary Ann Barger]; white; M=18 Feb. 1879; Abel Whitener, JP in Hky Twsp; Mary Miller, Abram Miller, GA Wallace. 1-370.

KIRKSEY, J.W.; SPENCER, Emeline; M=5 July 1866; JD Caldwell, JP. NL.

William; CALDWELL, Susan; M=9 Sept. 1860; JD Caldwell, JP. NL.

KLUTZ, Levi; FRADT, Susan; M=1 Nov. 1859; John Lantz, Min. NL.

KNIPE, John M.; LINN, Patsey; M=15 Oct. 1854; G. Huffman, JP. NL.

KNOW, Robert A. (39) of Salisbury, NC; BOST, Harriet E. (42) of Newton; white; M=14 May 1873; Joe E. Neiffer, Luth. Min. in Newt. Twsp; JD Little, Robert O. Ford, Laura M. Ford. NL.

KNOX, Ephraim (26); HOUSTON, Lettie (22); black; M=9 Oct. 1873; SC Brown, JP in Hamilton Twsp; A. Sherrill, RH Brown, O. Gilleland. NL.

Hiram [David Kerr & Susan Kerr]; MCCORKLE, Dolly [Thomas Abernethy & Smithey McCorkle]; black; M=18 June 1871; F. Caldwell, JP. 1-82.

LACKEY, J.H. [John & Lena]; DRUM, Leah [Adam & Catharine]; M=20 Apr. 1868; JB Little, Esq. NL.

LAEL, A.D.; LOWRANCE, Cammilla; M=18 Oct. 1864; JHA Yount, JP. NL.

Calvin; BOST, Sophrona; M=29 Sept. 1863; JHA Yount, JP. NL.

Sylvanus (22); COONS, Mary Ann (20); white; M=29 Jan. 1874; NE Sigmon, JP in Cline's Twsp; J. Lael, EA Sigmon, Mat J. Sigmon. NL.

LAFEVERS, Daniel; BURNS, Caroline; M=5 Oct. 1854; E. Yount, JP. NL.
LAFON, Daniel W.; WEAVER, Rebecca C.S.; M=29 Mar. 1859; Hiram Hefner, JP. NL.
  Timothy; SHEPARD, Mary L.; M=12 Oct. 1865; Hiram Hefner, JP. NL.
LAIL, Calvin (27) [Jacob & Susanna]; WINEBARGER, Lorina (27) [Silas & Malinda]; white; M=6 Nov. 1879; PC Henkel, Luth. Min. in Cline's Twsp; TS Hefner, QL Little, GW Winebarger. 1-371.
  George; STARNES, Anna M.; M=23 Feb. 1857; E. Yount, JP. NL.
  George W. (21) [George & Melissa]; DIETZ, Ellen (21) [Frederick & Lucinda]; white; M=24 Aug. 1879; DC Huffman, Luth. Min. in Hky Twsp; DW Fry, SM Dietz, LL Dietz. 1-372.
  Gerard (23); COONS, Cumila (16); white; M=23 July 1875; PF Smith, JP in Newton; WH Harris, Robert O. Ford, HA Lowrance. NL.
  Levi (26); HERMAN, Mahala M. (21); white; M=28 Jan. 1875; CW Herman, JP in Newt. Twsp; Baxter Killian, Lawson Lagle, Philo G. Herman. NL.
  Levi F. (27) of Burke Co., NC; SIGMON, Sarah H. (22); white; M=20 Nov. 1875; JH Bruns, JP in Hky; Mary E. Bruns, Pink Warlick. NL.
  Noah (22) [Peter & Mary]; HOLLER, Polly Maria (22) [Peter & Peggy]; white; M=29 May 1879; CW Anderson, Meth. Min. in Newton; Dezy Holler, Emma Pruette, ME Anderson. 1-373.
LALLER, H.L.; BRIDGES, M.M.; M=26 Oct. 1865; Alex J. Cansler, Min. NL.
LANEY, Noah E. (24) [IH & Catharine]; CALDWELL, Margaret M. (19) [Lawson & Rebecca]; white; M=5 Oct. 1879; WC Caldwell, JP in Cald. Twsp; JD Caldwell, LS Caldwell, MC Laney. 1-374.
LANIER, Burton N. [Edmond & Susanna]; ECKERT, Emeline E. [Elijah & Leah Huffman]; M=7 Dec. 1869; Martin A. Holler. NL.
  Canny; LAGLE, Elizabeth; M=22 Feb. 1859; CW Herman, JP. NL.
  Cornelius G. (26); GIBBS, C. Sophia (21); white; M=28 Feb. 1877; RB Anderson, Presby. Min. in Hky; FA Clinard, John W. Bohannon, WP Reinhardt. NL.
  Jacob Setzer; FRASURE, Nancy M.; M=4 Oct. 1851; HB Witherspoon, JP. NL.
  Joseph; MULL, Eliza; M=12 Jan. 1860; George Huffman, JP. NL.
LAWRENCE, William H. [Lee & P.]; LAWRENCE, Mag E. [CM & Mary]; M=22 Dec. 1868; JM Smith, Min. NL.
LEATHERMAN, Newton A. (22); MILLER, Harriett (27); white; M=7 Nov. 1875; AG Corpening, JP in JF Twsp; Ruben Yoder, Lawson Petree, ALJ Yoder. NL.
  Solomon (23) of JF Twsp; WORKMAN, Sarah Ann (22) of JF Twsp; white; M=29 Apr. 1873; Robert Helton, Min. in JF Twsp; Daniel Keever, Maggie Keever, Sarah N. Keever. NL.
  Stewart [James & Elizabeth]; WEAVER, Susan. No other information. NL.
LEE, J. Hart (20) of Hamilton Twsp; MARTIN, Lucy Ann (20) of Cat. Twsp; white; M=18 Dec. 1873; SC Brown, JP in Hamilton Twsp; EH Jones, Thos. Wilkinson, HW Bridges. NL.
  James S.; NORWOOD, Susanah; M=22 Oct. 1857; JW Puett, Min. NL.

LEE, Osburn [William & Susannah]; DEAL, L.A. [Fred & Catherine
    Hoke]; M=15 Sept. 1869; JM Smith, Min. NL.
  Robert; MARSHALL, Mary; M=20 Feb. 1859; JA Sherrill, JP. NL.
  Robert G. [Lawson & Nelly]; MARSHALL, Sarah [William & Phebia];
    M=22 Feb. 1872; EA Warlick, JP. 1-186.
  Rufus (30) [Jesse & Nancy]; HUNSUCKER, Susan (30) [John &
    Lillie]; white; M=23 Dec. 1875; G. Cansler, JP in Hamilton
    Twsp; GC McNeill, HC Culbert. 1-288.
LEFEVERS, Daniel M. (23); MOUSER, Susan M. (21); white; M=31 Dec.
    1876; Abel Barger, JP in Hky; JT Cline, Agnes E. Barger, GM
    Barger. NL.
  William E. (21); FRY, Caroline (23); white; M=13 May 1877; R.
    England, JP in Cald. Twsp; John C. Sims, SL Huffman, Andrew
    Gilbert. NL.
LEFFON, Noah [Daniel & Ragenia]; HUFFMAN, Erpha [Alfred &
    Malinda]; M=23 Nov. 1871; TL Smith, JP. 1-83.
LENAER, Carry; LAGLE, Elizabeth; M=22 Feb. 1859; CW Herman, JP.
    NL.
LENNRE, J.L.; HERMAN, Leah; M=21 Jan. 1859; John Lantz. NL.
LENTZ, J.F.; SHUFORD, M.C.; M=16 Oct. 1858; David Crook, Min. NL.
  Jacob; LUTZ, Jane; M=23 Oct. 1863; J. Lewis Smithdeal, Min. NL.
LEONARD, D.E.; PROPST, Margaret E. (Probst); M=16 Sept. 1858; CM
    Yoder, JP. NL.
  Eli; MILLER, H.C.; M=2 Feb. 1860; AJ Fox, Min. NL.
  James M. [Daniel & Elizabeth]; FRY, Barbara M. [Martin & Eliza-
    beth]; M=16 Dec. 1868; AJ Fox, Min. NL.
  J.Y. [Eleanora & Emma]; WYANT, M.J. [DM & Salley]; M=19 Jan.
    1869; AJ Fox, Min. NL.
LESTER, Charles H. (27); TURNER, S.D. (21); white; M=24 Jan.
    1877; SC Brown, Hamilton Twsp; J. Turner, TF Bradburn, DA
    Shuford. NL.
LINCH, George [Jule & Adeline]; MCCORKLE, Elizer [Richard & Mary
    Sherrill]; black; M=1 Oct. 1870; W. Cranford, Min. 1-28.
LINEBARGER, Augustus (22); GABRIEL, Callie (18); white; M=22 Feb.
    1876; JA Sherrill, Min. at JW Gabriel's; MM Gabriel, Robert
    Shelton, AE Sherrill. NL.
  Frederick L. (52); JONES, Caroline (34); white; M=
    2 Dec. 1874; JA Sherrill, Min. at Allen Jones'; Alec Jones,
    William Wilson, HS Gabriel. NL.
  Henry D.M. (20); LITTLE, Susan (16); white; M=29 May 1875; JA
    Sherrill, Min. at John Little's; LA Killian, DW Shelton, AEF
    Thompson. NL.
  J.Y. [Frederick & Mary M.]; RHODES, C.E. [Caleb &
    Miranda]; M=22 Dec. 1868; JR Peterson, Min. NL.
  John W. [Mike & Isabella]; ALLEN, Mary M. [Jehue & Caroline];
    M=11 Aug. 1870; JA Sherrill, Min. NL.
  Robert (22); SHERRILL, Susan (18); black; M=12 July 1877;
    William Brooks, Min. at Miles Sherrill's; Miles Sherrill,
    Alex. Sherrill, Jeff Linebarger. NL.
  Worth [Hosea H. & Susan]; BEATTY, Elizabeth [Frank & Salina];
    M=4 Jan. 1871; JA Sherrill, Min. 1-84.
LINGLE, John; HUFFMAN, Catherine; M=19 Feb. 1856; E. Yount, JP.
    NL.
LINK, Caleb; WILKERSON, Sarah E.; M=8 May 1855; WC Patterson, Min.
    NL.

LINK, David E. (22); PROPST, Mary A. (18); white; M=21 Feb. 1878; JM Smith, Luth. Min. at Jesse Propst's; DP Yount, JW Propst, S. Cline. NL.
  Henry J.; SEAGLE, Mary Ann; M=5 Feb. 1851; Henry Goodman, Min. NL.
  John M.; LEONARD, Harriet A.; M=18 Mar. 1856; AJ Fox, Min. NL.
  Mitus [Henry W. & Catherine]; RAMSOUR, Henrietta [William L. & CA]; M=17 Apr. 1870; JH Bruns, JP. NL.
LINN, Jacob [John & Elizabeth]; SMITH, Susan [Areh & Manda]; M=2 Aug. 1871; JW Bandy, JP. 1-85.
  Philo R. (26); KESTLER, Eliza J. (22); white; M=17 Dec. 1876; Robert Helton, Min. at Robert Helton's; AA Linn, HD Stallins, ZB Campbell. NL.
LIPPARD, John (23) [John & Lucinda]; NORWOOD, Mary E. (18) [Robert & Sina]; white; M=8 Apr. 1880; WC Caldwell, JP in Cald. Twsp; MW Huitt, JL Hewitt, Sarah Yount. 2-80.
LITTEN, Elcany; GILLELAND, Elizabeth; M=14 Feb. 1858; J. Lawrance, JP. NL.
  J.A. [Willie & Eliza]; ALLISON, Jinnie [John & Mary]; M=8 Jan. 1869; Elijah Allison, Min. at Elijah Allison's. NL.
  Thomas [Wesley & Caroline]; KALE, Elizabeth [Lawson & Lovina]; M=5 Jan. 1870; JA Sherrill, JP. NL.
LITTLE, Alexander M. (23) [Samuel & Vasti] of Lincoln Co., NC; SHERRILL, Nancy (21) [Washington & Mattie] of Lincoln Co., NC; white; M=9 Dec. 1875; JA Sherrill, Min. in Mt. Crk Twsp; Clay Barkley, JD Lockman, GP Sherrill. 1-289.
  Columbus (21) [Coleman & Lucy]; SMYRE, Sarah (20) [Wilson & Lizzie]; black; M=18 Nov. 1880; JC Clapp, Min. in Newt. Twsp; Caleb Bost, Amanda Smyre, Lizzie Duckworth. 2-81.
  Franklin P. (21); LITTLE, Alice (16); white; M=24 Mar. 1875; PK Little, JP; AJ Payne, QL Little, SD Little. NL.
  George S. [Lewis & Delitha]; YOUNT, Elizabeth [Peter & Catharine Little]; M=21 Aug. 1867; BG Jones, Min. NL.
  Hinchal [Daniel & Catherine]; WHITE, Emaline; M=1871; Record Missing. NL.
  J.A.; ROBINSON, Anna E.; M=10 Mar. 1858; H. Asbury, Min. NL.
  Jacob L.; CLONINGER, Manerva; M=15 Feb. 1860; JB Little, JP. NL.
  James B.; ALLIN, Margaret; M=11 Apr. 1860; JW Gabriel, JP. NL.
  Jason C. (21) [Daniel & Catharine]; RECTOR, Candace (19) [John & Jimmina]; white; M=31 Dec. 1879; CT Sigmon, JP in Cline's Twsp; DS Sigmon, Jefferson Holler, William Maye. 1-375.
  Lewis (32); STINE, Mary Jane (30); white; M=28 Feb. 1878; JM Smith, Luth. Min. at John Stine's; JM Stine, JD Little, MM Witherspoon. NL.
  Marcus L. [Peter & Harriet]; HERMAN, Candace A.; M=1871; Record Missing. NL.
  Peter; HUNSUCKER, ?; M=27 Dec. 1850; JB Little, JP. NL.
  Peter K. [JB & Susan]; SMITH, Catharine E. [Marcus M. & Catharine M.]; M=16 Feb. 1871; PF Smith, JP. 1-86.
  Quintus (24) [JB & Susan]; MITCHAEL, Elizabeth (20) [Harbison & Elmira]; white; M=23 Dec. 1875; JM Smith, Luth. Min. in Newt. Twsp; JM Stine, GW Little, MM Witherspoon. 1-290.

LITTLE, Quintus M. (25) [Peter & Malinda]; POWELL, Eva L. (18) [Dr. A.M. & Fannie] of Hamilton Twsp; white; M=18 Feb. 1873; JA Sherrill, Min. in Hamilton Twsp; LH Shuford, JD Little, LA Shuford. 1-243.

  Solon C. (24); ISENHOUR, Candace (22); white; M=10 Aug. 1875; CT Sigmon, JP in Cline's Twsp; QE Pope, LA Hunsucker, GC Benfield. NL.

  Solon C. (24); ISENHOUR, Candace (22); white; M=10 Aug. 1876; CT Sigmon in Cline's Twsp; QE Pope, LH Hunsucker, CC Benfield. NL.

  Stanley (21) [Daniel & Elizabeth]; HEFFNER, Harriett (18) [Devault & Polly]; white; M=16 Dec. 1875; JM Smith, Luth. Min. in Cline's Twsp; LM Wagner, Levi Hefner, David Hefner. 1-291.

  Thomas; BOSTAIN, A.E.; M=21 Nov. 1861; William S. Mehaffey, JP. NL.

  Thomas A. (22); LONG, Martha A. (23); white; M=12 Feb. 1879; SC Brown at Thomas Long's; GF Brown, DB Harwell, JW Long. NL.

  William (23); BEATTY, Nancy (20); black; M=8 Aug. 1878; OW Asbury, JP in Mt. Crk Twsp; JF Little, HL Cornelius, HD Lineberger. NL.

LIVINSTON, John; COCHRAN, Celila; M=1870; No other information. NL.

LOCKMAN, Jones D. (21) [David & Elizabeth] of Lincoln Co., NC; JAMES, Norah (16) [James & Avoline]; white; M=30 Dec. 1873; LC Brown, JP in Hamilton Twsp; AE Brown, AB Bradburn. 1-244.

LOFTIN, Adolphus G. (20) [William & Catherine] of Lincoln Co., NC; DRUM, Rebecca M. (17) [Peter M. & Catharine]; white; M=17 Apr. 1879; R. England, JP in Cald. Twsp; MK Bost, HT Martin, MJ Finger. 1-376.

  Eldridge L. (21) of Lincoln Co., NC; MONDAY, Arther (17); white; M=22 June 1876; JW Powell, Min. at Spencer Monday's; Anna D. Tyson, Mary P. Pewitt, John A. Tyson. NL.

  James Edmon (20) [Franklin & Elizabeth] of Hamilton Twsp; MCKINSEY, Susan Rebecca Jane (20) [Robert E. & Emeline] of Hamilton Twsp; white; M=19 Dec. 1872; JA Sherrill, Min. at Mt. Crk Twsp; GP Sherrill, W. Loftin, Robert McKinsey. 1-187.

  John A. (21) of Lincoln Co., NC; BEATTY, Martha Ann; white; M= 10 Oct. 1877; JA Sherrill, Min. at Frank Beatty's; SJ Whitener, JT Cochran, WLC Killian. NL.

  William; DRUM, Catharine; M=26 Nov. 1854; Thomas Ward, JP. NL.

  William Alex (23); CRANFORD, Laura R. (20); white; M=28 Jan. 1875; JA Sherrill, Ref. Min. at William Howard's; LA Rudisill, LL Burkhead. NL.

LOGAN, William; DETTER, Mary M.; M=13 Feb. 1855; ER Shuford, JP. NL.

LONG, John W. [Thomas & Jamima]; FISHER, Faney E. [Gooding & Fanny]; M=21 Dec. 1871; JA Sherrill, Min. 1-87.

  John W. (25); FLEMING, Elizabeth J. (27); white; M=15 Dec. 1874; JA Sherrill, Min. at Arch Fleming's; Warren Monday, William Fisher, Mary A. Fleming. NL.

  Johniah [Uriah & LE]; YOUNT, Laura C. [Franklin A. & Jemima]; M= 3 Apr. 1872; JM Smith, Min. NL.

LONG, Pearson [Timothy & Winnie]; SHERRILL, Elizabeth [Richard & Rutha Rankin]; License Issued=17 June 1871. No other information. 1-88.
  William T.; FISHER, Emeline; M=2 Jan. 1862; JW Gabriel, JP. NL.
LORE, E.; LEONARD, Mary; M=27 Sept. 1860; PC Henkel, Min. NL.
LORETTS, Fayette [Miles Wilson & Emeline Loretz]; GIBBS, Jane [n/k & Cosia Gibbs]; M=11 Mar. 1868; HC Cline, Esq. NL.
LOVE, Valentine [George & Susannah]; SMITH, Martha A. [Jerry & Sarah]; M=10 Oct. 1869; Robert Helton, Min. NL.
LOURANCE, William H. [Lee & P.]; LOURENCE, Mag E. [CM & Mary]; M=22 Dec. 1868; JM Smith, Min. NL.
LOWERY, Randolph (21) [Miles Johnson & Rebecah Lowery] of Mt. Crk Twsp; LEWIS, Sarah (27) [n/k & Catherine Ring] of Newton; black; M=25 Dec. 1872; Edward Harris, Min. in Newt. Twsp; Henry Smyre, Albert Abernethy, Lucas Phelps. 1-188.
LOWRANCE, B.A.; MOODY, Mary H.; M=11 Nov. 1865; LN Wilson, JP. NL.
  C.E.; MARTIN, Anna M.; M=24 Aug. 1859; Joseph Parker, Min. NL.
  John W. [Nelson & E]; WYCOFF, Mary F.E. [Jacob & Epps]; M=18 Aug. 1871; JA Sherrill, Min. 1-89.
  Thomas (19) [Peter & Susan]; WATTS, Fanny (20); black; M=5 June 1879; William Brooks, Meth. Min.; McClean, Frank Stevenson, Frank Cansler. 1-377.
LUTZ, Alonzo F. (25); HEWITT, Amanda (19); white; M=22 Mar. 1876; JM Smith, Min. at MM Huit's; J. Bolick, JB Lutz, Moses Witherspoon. NL.
  David (23); HUFFMAN, Sarah (21); white; M=19 Mar. 1878; JC Clapp, Ref. Min. at JC Clapp's; WL Lutz, SF Nagle, Joseph M. Lutz. NL.
  Frankin; HUIT, Barbara; M=16 Dec. 1852; H. Cline, JP. NL.
  J.F.; SHUFORD, M.C.; M=16 Oct. 1858; David Crook, Min. NL.
  J.S. [Jacob & Harriet]; SETZER, Mary Ann [Reuben & Lovina]; M=25 Mar. 1868; J. Loretz, Min. NL.
  Jacob [Jacob & Mary]; ROBINSON, Ann [Jacob Bisaner & Elizabeth Heterick]; M=17 Sept. 1867; J. Loretz, Min. NL.
  James [Laban & Adoline]; DEAL, Mary Jane [John & Malinda]; M=20 Sept. 1868; EA Warlick, JP. NL.
  Lee Andrew (21) black; SMYRE, Amanda (21) yellow; M=14 Apr. 1875; Daniel May, Min. at Henry Smyre's; Pheba Bell, Albert Abernathy, Linke Phelps. NL.
  William (25) [Laban & Adline]; WHISNANT, Jane (23) [John & Pollie]; white; M=24 Apr. 1879; GL Hunt, Luth. Min. in Newt. Twsp; PE Lutz, JAM Hunt, LJE Hunt. 1-378.
LYERLY, John L. (45); WALKER, Ada G. (27); white; M=29 May 1877; Vastine Strickley, Luth. Min. in Hky; AM Peeler, E. Peeler, WH Ellis. NL.
LYNN, James; JOHNSON, Elizabeth; M=23 Sept. 1858; G. Huffman, JP. NL.
LYTTLE, Joseph N. [n/k & Mary Lytle]; SHERRILL, Julia A. [Elisha & Caroline]; M=12 Dec. 1869; JA Sherrill, Min. NL.

MACE, William; LACKEY, Susan A.; M=22 Apr. 1856; TJ Hamilton, JP.
   NL.
MAHUE, Stephen (Lewis & Milly); TURNER, Mina [Titus & Letty Sang];
   M=11 Apr. 1868; GW McCain, Min. NL.
MAIZE, G.W.; SHOOK, E.L.; M=11 Apr. 1861; PC Henkel, Min. NL.
MARLOW, W.H. [Daniel & Meriah]; ASHLEY, Genelia; M=1871; Record
   Missing. NL.
MARSHALL, Andrew W. [Gabriel & Mary J.]; WILFONG, Mildred C.
   [Henry & Dealia]; M=19 May 1870; JC Clapp, Min. NL.
MARTIN, A.F. [Latin & Caroline]; LEE, Martha [Bird & Catherine];
   M=24 Aug. 1871; JA Sherrill, Min. 1-90.
  A.F. (22) of Hamilton Twsp; MCCOMBS, Ellen (22) of Cat. Twsp;
   white; M=18 Dec. 1873; SC Brown, JP in Hamilton Twsp; John
   Gant, LP Edwards, Warren Gant. NL.
  Eli J. (21); WATSON, Mary (21); white; M=22 Aug. 1876; Abel
   Whitener, Hky; James Watson, WF Atwood. NL.
  George H.; WITHERSPOON, Emoline S.; M=25 Feb. 1858; JM
   Lowrance, JP. NL.
  Harry L. [Alfred & Caty]; BUMGARNER, Frances A. [Alex & Emma];
   M=5 Dec. 1867; H. Cline, Esq. NL.
  J.W. (22); MCCOMBS, Ida (18); white; M=23 Feb. 1879; SC Brown,
   JP at SC Brown's; FC Brown, PK Turbyfield, AC Brown. NL.
  John; WILKINSON, Nancy E.; M=2 Oct. 1853; Thomas Ward, JP.
   NL.
  William [David & Elizabeth]; HICKS, L.C.; M=1871; Record Miss-
   ing. NL.
  William P. (22) of Burke Co., NC; ABEE, Jane E. (18); white;
   M=25 Dec. 1873; HS Proctor, Min. at Ephraim Abee's; ES
   Martin, EP Martin, Ephraim Abee. NL.
  Zebedee B. (22) of Burke Co., NC; RHONEY, Martha (21); white;
   M=5 July 1874; JW Bandy, JP in Bandy's Twsp; JW Bandy, FB
   Martin, Sarah Linn. NL.
MASON, Andrew; RUDISILL, Ellena; M=4 Sept. 1851; George Huffman,
   JP. NL.
  John T. (24); HULLIT, Sarah (21); white; M=7 Jan. 1877; Jacob
   Mosteller, JP at George Smith's; Adly Huffman, JA Rudisill.
   NL.
MASSEY, Logan (18); MCCALL, Rachael (20); white; M=4 Feb. 1877;
   SC Brown, JP in Hamilton Twsp; JA Litten, MT Bynum, John D.
   McCall. NL.
  William L.; KALE, Angeline; M=28 Feb. 1858; JM Lowrance, JP.
   NL.
MATHES, Daniel [Peter & Elizabeth]; HUFFMAN, Catharine [Henry &
   Mary]; M=8 Mar. 1871; JH Bruns, JP. NL.
MATHIS, Daniel Forney (38) [John & Frankie]; BANKS, Sarah (22)
   [Harvey & Nancy]; white; 14 Sept. 1879; PK Little, JP in
   Cline's Twsp; JB Little, Susan Little, FM Smith. 1-379.
  Elcanah (21); FOX, Mary Ann (19); white; M=23 Aug. 1874;
   PK Little, JP in Cline's Twsp; JB Little, CE Little, Adam
   Shook. NL.
  John (60) [William & Elizabeth] of Cline's Twsp; SHEPARD,
   Susan (37) [Jacob & Catharine] of Cline's Twsp; white; M=9
   Jan. 1873; William H. Rockett, JP in Cline's Twsp; Daniel
   Deal, NE Sigmon, PE Isenhour. 1-245.
  Jonas [Levi & Malinda]; POPE, Candace [William & Susan];
   M=23 Nov. 1871; EA Warlick, JP. 1-92.

MATHIS, Peter (55) of Cline's Twsp; SIPE, Mary (40) of Cline's Twsp; white; M=18 Dec. 1873; NE Sigmon, JP in Cline's Twsp; Elkanah Mathis, WH Hunsucker, Mahala Winebarger. NL.
MATTHEWS, John; YOUNT, Catharine; M=27 Apr. 1864; JH Moser, JP. NL.
  Julius [Peter & Elizabeth]; MATTHEWS, D.C. [Nathan & Malisa]; M=24 Dec. 1868; D. McD. Yount, JP. NL.
MAY, Samuel Y. [David & Elizabeth]; BOLCH, Sarah; M=1871; Record Missing. NL.
MAYBERRY, Robert (23) of Alexander Co., NC; YOUNT, Susan C. (21) of Hamilton Twsp; white; M=6 Nov. 1873; AJ Fox, Luth. Min. at Frank Yount's; JN Long, JW Williams, ML Cline. NL.
MAYE, William; MILLER, Catharine; M=28 Dec. 1857; Hiram Hefner, JP. NL.
MAYHEW, Henry L. (21) [John J. & Betsie] of Iredell Co., NC; SHERRILL, Octavia E. (20) [Whit & Betsie]; white; M=17 Dec. 1879; JA Sherrill, Min. in Mt. Crk Twsp; WA Mayhew, EM Mayhew; LW Sherrill. 1-380.
MAYSE, Jack; POPE, Ophy M.; M=19 Aug. 1860; JHA Yount, JP. NL.
  Pinkney; PAGE, Louisa; M=15 May 1853; H. Ingold, JP. NL.
MCCALL, F.G. [James H. & Obediance]; HARWELL, Ann E. [John H. & Mary Ann]; M=20 Aug. 1869; CE Land, Min. NL.
  James A. [James M. & Martha]; BARKLEY, Sarah E. [Hubert & Martha]; M=6 May 1869; JA Sherrill, Min. NL.
  John C.; MODY, Lucinda; M=5 May 1857; HH Linebarger, JP. NL.
MCCASLIN, Charlie (19) [William & Isabella]; WHITENER, Mary (20) [Logan G. & Mahala]; white; M=6 Jan. 1876; Rufus England, JP in Cald. Twsp; EV Boyd, AC Cloninger, L. Whitener. 1-316.
  H.Y. [William & Susanna]; LOVE, Sally V. [Valentine & Susanna]; M=22 Sept. 1868; AJ Love, Min. NL.
  J.C.; JANET, H.A.; M=6 June 1861; AJ Fox, Min. NL.
MCCAY, A.J.; LITTEN, Lizzie; M=4 June 1863; SM Berry, Min. NL.
MCCLELLAN, Monroe (18) [Bery & Adline] of Alexander Co., NC; GAITHER, Candace (19) [Martin & Milla]; black; M=30 Oct. 1879 at Martin Gaither's; AS Alexander, A. Arton Gaither, Rev. O. Settlemyre. 1-382.
MCCOMBS, James; WILKINSON, Martha A.; M=19 Aug. 1857; JW Gabriel, JP. NL.
  Robert (22) [JJ & Roxanah]; MARTIN, Ada (15) [LF & CP]; white; M=23 Dec. 1875; JA Sherrill, Min. in Mt. Crk Twsp; Pink Sigmon, James Lineberger, PA Thompson. 1-292.
MCCORKLE, Bradford (23) [Bob & Evelin]; SCOTT, Rilla (20) [John & Jane]; black; 12 Mar. 1879; William Brooks, Min. in Hamilton Twsp; Cala Brown, Pinkney Brown, Ammiline Brown. 1-381.
  Carry [Thomas Abernathy & Cynthia McCorkle]; CLARK, Mary [William & Rosea]; M=20 Dec. 1871; F. Caldwell, JP. NL.
  Charles [Thomas & Dolly]; Shipp, Sarah [Wesley & Winnie]; black; M=20 Aug. 1867; J.W. Gabriel, Esq. NL.
  D.N.; SMITH, Rhoda S.; M=21 Feb. 1856; Lanny Wood, Min. NL.
  David (22); BEATTY, Vira (21); black; M=20 Dec. 1877; OW Asbury, JP in Mt. Crk Twsp; JO McCombs, CL McCaul, Charley Byers. NL.

MCCORKLE, Henry (22); COULTER, Laura (19); black; M=30 Nov. 1876; AG Corpening, JP in JF Twsp; Ann Corpening, Camilla Corpening, AM Corpening. NL.

Henry M. (22); BENNICK, Jane (21); black; M=18 July 1878; CW Vanderburg, Min. at Katie McCorkle's; EJ Harris, Harry Sims, Young Wilson. NL.

Levi (20) [Thomas & Dolly] of Mt. Crk Twsp; GOODE, Frances (18) of Mt. Crk Twsp; black; M=31 Dec. 1872; Isaac Wells, Min. in Mt. Crk Twsp; John Sherrill, Peter Houston, William Sherrill. 1-189.

Richard A.; HARRIS, Nancy; M=27 Sept. 1866; Jeptha Clark, Min. NL.

MCDADE, Joseph [JB & Rebecah]; LITTLE, Jinnie [Dr. Little & Lucinda Huit]; M=18 Apr. 1871; PF Smith, JP. 1-93.

MCDURGHER, John (45) of Hky Tav. Twsp; BOLCH, Sophronia (21) of Hky Tav. Twsp; white; M=30 Nov. 1873; JC Hartzell, Min. at Samuel May's; SZ May, WG Shell, WL Abernathy. NL.

MCGEE, John L. [Daniel D. Megee & Adoline Megee]; DEAL, Lymie E.; M=1871; Record Missing. NL. {See John L. Megee}.

Jonas M. (37) [Jacob & Adline] of Alexander Co., NC; BOWMAN, Candace E. (27) [Jesse & Sarah]; white; M=22 Jan. 1880; CS Hefner, LC Bowman, SM Bowman. 2-82.

Noah H. [John & Elizabeth]; GREEN, Sarah S. [OC & Ceda]; M=6 Nov. 1867; WL Mehaffey. NL.

Thomas N. [JW & Sarah A.]; JONES, Emaline [James & Caroline]; M=12 May 1872; TJ Hamilton, JP. 1-190.

William S. (22) [DD & Adline]; LOWRANCE, Ida (20) [Clinton & Harriett]; white; M=22 Dec. 1880; PK Little, JP in Cline's Twsp; AI Bandy, FW Drum, CA Connor. 2-83.

MCGINNIS, John J.; BANDY, Chantz M.; M=6 May 1863; JD Caldwell, JP. NL.

MCKAY, A.J.; LITTEN, Lizzie; M=4 June 1863; SM Berry, Min. NL.

MCKINNIS, G.A.; LOFTIN, Harriet; M=11 July 1866; GJ Wilkie, Min. NL.

MCKINZIE, David A. [Robert & Emeline]; LINCH, Sarah; M=15 Dec. 1870; Wilson Cranford, Min. 1-29.

Jonathan; CLARK, Mary L.; M=18 Apr. 1856; E. Conner, JP. NL.

William J. [Robert W. & Emeline]; STILES, Emeline [Jesse & Nancy]; M=18 Aug. 1869; JA Sherrill, Min. NL.

MCNELEY, Julius [Henry & Judy]; HOOPER, Elisa [William & Nully]; M=20 Nov. 1870; Isaac Cansler. 1-30.

MCNELY, Julius [Henry & Judy]; HOOPER, Elizer [William & Nuly]; M=20 Nov. 1871; Isaac Cansler, Min. NL.

MCREE, James (24); HOKE, Frances (21); white; M=12 Sept. 1877; JC Clapp, Ref. Min. at Clara Setzer's; JS Deal, RC Setzer, JS Deal. NL.

James P. (22); WIKE, Ellen (19); white; M=26 Aug. 1875; JM Smith, Luth. Min. at David Wike's; Silas Wike, Rhoda Wike, Daniel Setzer. NL.

Peter (22); BOST, Mary (16); black; M=25 Dec. 1878; EA Harris, Min. at EA Harris'; Calvin Woods, Adline Harris. NL.

MCRORIE, Jacob [George Stocton & Emaline]; BOGLE, Julia [Cintha Conley]; License Issued=29 June 1871; No other information. 1-94.

MEGEE, Hiram (21); BURCH, Ellen (21); white; M=29 Dec. 1874; GW
    Cansler, JP in Cat. {Hamilton Twsp}; AH Houston, JM Clark,
    MB Trollinger. NL.
  John L. [Daniel D. & Adaline]; DEAL, Lynia [Miles & Rosanah];
    M=15 June 1871; William G. Jarret, JP. 1-95.
MEHAFFEY, Joseph [Joseph & Isabella]; LUTZ, Martha [Jacob &
    Harriet]; M=6 Oct. 1870; JC Clapp, Min. 1-31.
MICHAEL, A.; FINGER, Synthia R.; M=25 Jan. 1859; AF Fox, Min. NL.
  J.L.; WEAVER, Sarah S.; M=20 Mar. 1856; Daniel E. Warlick, Min.
    NL.
MICHAL, Albert (22); ISENHOUR, Sidney Jane (22); white; M=7 Dec.
    1877; JM Smith, Luth. Min. at JM Smith's; HS Smith, WA Smith,
    PB Smith. NL.
MICHUM, Lawson; RICHEY, Sarah; M=21 July 1864; PA Whitener, Min.
    NL.
MILLER, Abel P. [Ephraim & Emma]; SMYER, Ellen M. [George W. &
    Sally E.]; M=23 Feb. 1871; JM Smith, Min. 1-96.
  Able P. [EA & ML]; BOWMAN, Frances S. [Baustin & Mary]; M=16
    Feb. 1871; JM Smith, Min. 1-97.
  Absalom [Phillip & Margaret]; BOST, Ann A. [Daniel Coulter
    & Nancy Coulter]; M=15 Sept. 1870; GL Hunt, Min. 1-32.
  Absalom; NORWOOD, Mary; M=18 Sept. 1862; M. Barger, JP. NL.
  Albert A. (29) [Coon & Julia A.]; DRUM, E. Jane (14) [S. Peter &
    Rhoda M.]; white; M=6 Apr. 1879; PK Little, JP in Cline's
    Twsp; SE Yount, MM Smith, WL Fulbright. 1-383.
  Andrew; LOFTIN, Barbara; M=18 Oct. 1860; Hiram Hefner, JP.
    NL.
  B.J.; BUMGARNER, Rhoda C.; M=11 Aug. 1860; JW Gabriel, JP. NL.
  Daniel A.; SHELL, Sarah C.; M=7 Oct. 1855; GJ Wilkie, JP.
    NL.
  David; HUNSUCKER, Catharine; M=23 Dec. 1858; PC Henkel, Min. NL.
  Emanuel W. (21) [Ambros & Amanda] of Newt. Twsp; FRY, Frances C.
    (15) [EN & ES] of Newt. Twsp; M=21 Nov. 1872; GL Hunt, Luth.
    Min. in Newt. Twsp; AI Miller, CC Martin, LC Fry. 1-191.
  Franklin; BROWN, Mary Ann; M=5 Sept. 1858; JB Little, JP. NL.
  George; BOLCH, Martha; M=27 Nov. 1859; E. Yount, JP. NL.
  J.F. [John & Jane]; SIGMON, C.E. [Aaron & Caroline]; M=14 Mar.
    1872; Abel Whitener, JP. NL.
  Jacob Conrad (51) [John & Sarah] of Cline's Twsp; LAIL, Juliann
    (43) [Henry & Margaret]; white; M=18 Aug. 1872; CF Sigmon, JP
    in Cline's Twsp; Susan Lail, Gerard Lail, Catherine Lail. 1-
    192.
  Jacob H. (21) [DA & SC]; SIGMON, Olivia C. (18) [Elkana & HE];
    white; M=3 Dec. 1879; GL Hunt, Luth. Min. in Newt. Twsp; GA
    Miller, MLS Miller, RA Bumgarner. 1-384.
  James F. (23); FRY, Frances L. (19); white; M=1 Mar. 1874; JM
    Smith, Luth. Min. at Margaret Frye's; CC Miller, WB Setzer,
    JL Miller. NL.
  James L. (21); FRY, Sarah C. (21); white; M=7 Nov. 1878; PC
    Henkle, Luth. Min. at Solomon Fry's; RH Thomason, SE Killian,
    MM Holler. NL.
  James M. (33) [Frederick & MA]; HALLMAN, Jermina C. (25) [Henry
    & Anna B.]; white; M=8 Feb. 1880; JW Mouser, JP in Hky Twsp;
    EE Miller, WG Hallman, JA Killian. 2-84.

MILLER, James Monroe (25); HALLMAN, Julie E. (21); white; M=19 Mar. 1874; GL Hunt, Luth. Min. at Henry M. Hallman's; EC Punch, WF Hallman, SE Hallman. NL.

John (25); LAEL, Mary (21); white; M=8 Jan. 1878; Charles M. Anderson, Min. in Newton; ME Anderson, Jefferson Holler, Bettie Anderson. NL.

John (86) [Jacob & Catharine]; PRICE, Emaline (32) [Israel Spencer & Bettie Ann Spencer]; M=21 Mar. 1872; JH Bruns, JP. NL.

John (29) [John & Alice] of Newt. Twsp; CLINE, Juliann C. (27) [Lawson & Eliza] of Newt. Twsp; white; M=22 Dec. 1872; MA Throneburg, JP in Newt. Twsp; A. Miller, DH Settlemyre, John Burris. 1-193.

John [Berry & Ellen]; TROUTMAN, Mary E. [Joseph & Ursley]; M=16 Oct. 1869; DL Huit, JP. NL.

John; WILKIE, L.V.; M=7 Sept. 1855; Alex Abernathy, Min. NL.

Jones [Daniel & Vina]; WILSON, Catharine [Joseph & Catharine]; M=16 Aug. 1871; AJ Fox, Min. 1-98.

Joseph (75); MILLER, Caroline (38); white; M=17 Feb. 1875; Abel Whitener, JP in Hky Twsp; SJ Whitener, Eliza Whitener, AH Whitener. NL.

Lancan (23); BROWN, Rebecca (19); white; M=9 May 1874; PK Little, JP in Cline's Twsp; CE Little, Sylvanus Benfield, Jacob Benfield. NL.

Larkin [Isaac & Elvira Gantt]; BROWN, Mat[ilda] [Levi & n/k]; M=11 Mar. 1870; William G. James, JP. NL.

Lemuel C. [Able & Jemima]; HOFFMAN, Jemima C. [Nelson & Rhoda]; M=16 Mar. 1870; JM Smith, Min. NL.

Nelson A.; WILFONG, Adoline C.; M=1 Oct. 1851; JH Crawford, Min. NL.

P.L. [Jacob & Elizabeth]; HEFNER, Abigail [Miles & Polly]; M=26 Mar. 1868; D. McD. Yount, Esq. NL.

Reuben (24); DRUM, Cynthia (20); white; M=15 Feb. 1877; JH Bruns, JP in Hky; RB Davis, AE Townsend, HH Poovy. NL.

Rufus (22) [Absalom & Leah]; CLINE, Martha S. (19) [Henry & Christina R.]; white; M=23 Nov. 1879; JW Mouser, JP in Hky Twsp; CR Cody, JM Cline, DY Seabock. 1-385.

Samuel E.; RABY, Caroline; M=7 Mar. 1858; E. Yount, JP. NL.

Wesley; DEAL, Rosanah M.; M=3 Jan. 1854; ER Shuford, JP. NL.

William A. (22) [Alex & Laura] of Cline's Twsp; SMITH, Alice (18) [Andy & Delpha] of Cline's Twsp; black; M=30 Oct. 1872; William H. Rockett, JP in Cline's Twsp; Mart. Sigmon, James Abernathy, Elcana Hunsucker. 1-194.

William E. (22) [Jacob A. & Agnes B.] of Lincoln Co., NC; WHITENER, Dora (19) [ZB & Mary]; white; M=8 Jan. 1880; JA Foil, Ref.Min. in Newt. Twsp; HA Whitener, ZB Whitener, DW Whitener. 2-85.

William L. (22); WHITE, Frances C. (19); white; M=24 Oct. 1876; AH Shuford in Hky; WP Morgan, SY May, RP Miller. NL.

William Marcus (21); BENFIELD, Sarah (21); white; M=30 Apr. 1874; PK Little, JP in Cline's Twsp; SJE Yount, CE Yount, QM Smith. NL.

MILLIGAN, Gilbert P. (21); BAKER, Julia (17); white; M=23 Dec. 1874; JK Harwell, Bapt. Min. at Henry Baker's; Walter Sherrill, Walter Hevener. NL.

MILLS, H.M.; ROBINSON, Ann M.; M=4 Feb. 1863; John Lantz, Min. NL.
  John (29) [John & Alice] of Newton Twsp; CLINE, Juliann C. (27) [Lawson & Eliza] of Newton; white; M=22 Dec. 1872; MA Throneburg, JP in Newt. Twsp; John Burris, DH Settlemyre, A. Miller. 1-193.
MINGUS, And[y]; FOX, Susan; M=25 Mar. 1860; JB Little, JP. NL.
  George; DOUGLASS, Jane; M=5 Jan. 1856; Jesse Gantt, JP. NL.
  John F. (23) [MD & MS]; HERMAN, F. Virginia (19) [Elcana & Lovina]; white; M=27 Jan. 1880; PK Little, JP in Cline's Twsp; DW Hollar, CF Sipe, NL Benfield. 2-86.
MIRES, Thomas P.; BOLCH, Emaline E.; M=24 Apr. 1860; Jonas Bost, JP. NL.
MITCHAM, John Wesley (20) [A. Aren & Dolly] of Lincoln Co., NC; PROPST, Catherine (21) [Able & Sally] of Bandys Twsp; white; M=23 Nov. 1873; JW Bandy, JP in Bandys Twsp; DA Lutz, Mary Ann Henly, Joe Dale Propst. 1-246.
MITCHEL, James S.; YOUNT, Jemima A.; M=10 Apr. 1856; PC Hinkle, Min. NL.
MITCHELL, Hosea [Aaron & Polly]; RITCHEY, Marthey [Joe & Cinda]; M=5 Aug. 1869; JCY Brendle. NL.
MONDAY, Fletcher [Jeremiah & Clara Cloe]; WARD, Mahala M. [William & Rebecca]; M=18 July 1867; JD Caldwell, Esq. NL.
  Marcus (21); SHUFORD, Susan (17); black; M=10 Apr. 1874; Isaac Wells, Min. at CE Pain's; M. Shuford, John Sherrill, Eli Sherrill. NL.
  Miles (21); CORNELIUS, Alace (18); black; M=15 Apr. 1874; Isaac Wells, Min. at Alace Cornelius'; John Bost, Frank Bost, Alf Sherrill. NL.
MOONEY, William Pinkney (24); CLINE, Candace (20); white; M=2 Feb. 1875; JC Clapp, Ref. Min. at D. Cline's; Geo. Rabb, Henry Cline, Davidson Cline. NL.
MOORE, Andrew (18) [Jacob & n/k]; HOLDSCLAW, Roxann (18); black; M=1 Dec. 1872; Isaac Wells, Min. in Mt. Crk Twsp; Jim Ward, Levi Moore. 1-195.
  H.L. (24) [Joseph H. & Sarah]; YODER, Martha A. (20) [Moses & Sarah]; white; M=28 Dec. 1879; JM Smith, Luth. Min. in JF Twsp; JF Moore, JC Yoder, LS Yoder. 1-386.
  Henry [Porter & Hannah]; BROOKS, Mary [William & Hannah]; black; M=1 Jan. 1871; George N. McClain, Min. 1-99.
  J.P.; FOX, E.M.; M=11 Dec. 1860; JD Caldwell, JP. NL.
  Leonidas J. (29) of Newberne, NC; TERRY, Bettie F. (21); white; M=21 Oct. 1875; GM Gibbs, Presby. Min. in Hky; JN Bohanan, AM Kirkland, Frank A. Clinard. NL.
  Samuel; MURPHY, Susan; M=2 Dec. 1859; JW Gabriel, JP. NL.
MOOSE, Ceredlons? M. (26) of Alexander Co., NC; LITTLE, Henrietta A.J. (18); white; M=7 Sept. 1876; JM Smith, Luth. Min. at JM Smith's; JM Sloop, E. Cline, LE Little. NL.
  D.F.; HOWARD, M.A.; M=5 Feb. 1861; J. Lantz, Min. NL.
  Daniel; DOCTOR, M.E.; M=1 Mar. 1864; Henry Cline, JP. NL.
  Daniel [George & Drusa]; BOST, Julia A. [MM Huit & Rhoda Huit]; M=25 Aug. 1867; PC Henkle, Min. NL.
  Daniel W. (25); DEAL, Harriett L. (34); white; M=19 Dec. 1876; PK Little, JP in Cline's Twsp; John Finger, Christine Finger, Rhoda Finger. NL.

MOOSE, G.R. [Martin & Elvira]; WIKE, Jemima [David & Lile]; M=28
    Jan. 1869; PC Hinckle, Min. NL.
  V.A.; WIKE, Sarah; M=27 Dec. 1865; LN Wilson, JP. NL.
MORGAN, Lafayette [Martin & Elizabeth]; DELLINGER, Margaret
    [Ephraim & Anna]; M=1 Feb. 1870; Miles Goodson, JP. NL.
MORRISON, Andrew (25) of Hky Twsp; yellow; WHITENER, Rettie (20)
    of Hky Twsp; black; M=30 Apr. 1873; JH Bruns, JP in Hky Tav.
    Twsp; EL Harion, Mary E. Bruns, WS Ramsour. NL.
MORROW, William (21); YOUNT, Elizabeth (19); white; M=14 Nov.
    1878; J. Ingold, Min. at Levi Yount's; Mal Helton, William
    Beard, Levi M. Yount. NL.
MOSE, Peter [Jacob Seller & Hannah Mose]; NAIL, Molly; M=2 Jan.
    1868; D. Hamilton, Esq. NL.
MOSER, Franklin P. (22); DEAL, Susan J. (20); white; M=18 Jan.
    1877; PK Little, JP in Cline's Twsp; A. Deal, DF Carpenter,
    HA Hoke. NL.
  J.C.; FOX, Amy; M=18 Feb. 1864; GH Moser, JP. NL.
MOSS, [George] [John & Armen]; GILLELAND, Jenelia [blank Gille-
    land & Meary]; M=19 Dec. 1867. NL.
MOSTELLER, Forney M. (24); FRY, Emma (20); white; M=8 Jan. 1874;
    Jacob Mosteller, JP in Bandy's Twsp; Rufus Mosteller, Lawson
    Mosteller. NL.
  Lawson [George & Elizabeth]; BAKER, Jane [David &
    Sallie]; M=16 Nov. 1869; Robert Helton, Min. NL.
  Levi (20); WHITENER, Bertha (21); black; M=24 Feb. 1877; Jacob
    Mosteller, JP in Bandy's Twsp; Allen Whitener, Livonia
    Shuford. NL.
MOUSER, Eli; MILLER, Catharine; M=11 Sept. 1853; CW Herman, JP.
    NL.
  John W. (27) of Hky Tav. Twsp; MILLER, Susana E. (25) of Hky
    Tav. Twsp; white; M=21 Aug. 1873; PF Smith, JP of Newt. Twsp;
    MJ Rowe, AH Hoke, Reuben Setzer. NL.
  William H. (31) of Hky Tav. Twsp; PROPST, Mary E. (21) of Hky
    Tav. Twsp; white; M=10 Apr. 1873; JM Smith, Luth. Min. in
    Hky Tav. Twsp; JW Mouser, AA Spencer, AP Miller. NL.
MULL, Andrew [Joseph & Polly]; ROBINSON, Polly [Mandy & Catherine]
    M=20 Feb. 1870; JW Bandy, JP. NL.
  John (23); MARCH, Cynthia Ann (20); black; M=18 Feb. 1877; John
    Bumgarner, Bapt. Min. at Liry Mull's; AA Tallent, MB Burton,
    John K. Tallant. NL.
  John (26); DOWNS, Margaret (23); white; M=20 Feb. 1878; JM
    Smith, Bapt. Min. at WF Hull's; AP Smith, NF Hicks, WF Hull.
    NL.
  Marion A. [William & Angeline]; HELDERBRAND, Nancy C. [IP &
    Tiny]; M=20 Apr. 1868; EA Warlick, JP. NL.
  Peter; MULL, Emoline; M=17 Oct. 1852; Amos Hilderbrand, Min.
    NL.
  Wallace B. (21) [William & Margaret] of Cleveland Co., NC; MULL,
    Barbara Alice (19) [Peter & Emeline] of Burke Co., NC; white;
    M=21 Nov. 1880; WF Hull, Bapt. Min. in Bandy's Twsp; LL Lail,
    WP Rhoney, WD Wilkie. 2-87.
MUNDAY, D.; MUNDAY, Rebeker; M=15 Jan. 1858; HH Linebarger, JP.
    NL.
MURPHEY, Frank D. [John & Elizabeth White]; HAMESLY, Catharine
    [JP & Sallie Wilson]; M=25 June 1868; PC Henkel, Min. NL.

MURPHEY, James; YOUNT, Amanda; M=17 May 1857; William L. Mehaffey, JP. NL.

MURPHY, Joseph S. (23); BOWMAN, Zenith A. (24); white; M=1 Mar. 1877; GL Hunt, Luth. Min. at GL Hunt's; LM Hunt, JM Fulbright, RH Conrad. NL.

Syirus M. (22); KEES, Sarah (18); white; M=9 July 1874; GL Hunt, Luth. Min. at Gilbert Kees; Noah Fox, MM Murphy, MJ Murphy. NL.

MURRILL, John F. [Elijah & Nancy A.]; INGOLD, Alice E. [Jeremiah & Margarett]; M=23 Nov. 1871; JC Clapp, Min. 1-100.

MURRY, Robert V. (22); SIGMON, Frances M. (21); white; M-1 Feb. 1874; PF Smith, JP in Newt. Twsp; GH Moser, GW Holler, JB McNeill. NL.

William (22) [Lambert & Elizabeth]; RABB, Harriett (20) [John & Rebecah]; white; M=22 Aug. 1872; JL Hewitt, JP in Cald. Twsp; Nancy Murry, Sarah Blankenship, William Rabb. 1-196.

NANGLE, Levi J.; MILLER, M.L.; M=6 Aug. 1861; M. Barger, JP. NL.
NANCE, Franklin (23); CONRAD, Mary (18); white; M=28 Dec. 1876; JA Foil, Ref. Min. at JC Clapp's; RF Conrad, JT Conrad, Charley Clapp. NL.
  John [William & Martha Ann]; SMITH, Emaline [Jeremiah & Sarah]; M=17 Dec. 1871; Robert Helton, Min. 1-101.
  Wiley [William & Martha Ann]; WEAVER, Martha [Henry & Nancy]; M=5 Jan. 1871; Robert Helton, Min. 1-102.
  William H. (20) [William & Martha A.]; DAGENHARDT, Missouri (18) [Henry & Katie]; white; M=6 Nov. 1879; Robert Helton, Min. in JF Twsp; TX Michel, JS Leonard, CS Reinhardt. 1-387.
NEILL, Alexander [Smith & Fanny]; POWELL, Mary [Jefferson Shuford & Johnnie Powell]; M=30 July 1869; William Brooks, Min. NL.
  George C.M.; FRAZIER, Martha A.; M=30 Oct. 1866; LN Wilson, JP. NL.
  Henry (22); SHUFORD, Catharine (20); black; M=9 Sept. 1877; William Brooks, Min. at King Long's; Alex Neill, William Hooper, Isac Hooper. NL.
  William S.; LONG, Ruth V.; M=11 Jan. 1853; Thomas Ward, JP. NL.
NEWBIN, Thomas (21) of Alexander Co., NC; CLINE, Patsey (18); black; M=6 Dec. 1877; Robert Smith, Min. at EO Elliott's; W Rasker, James Smith, John Newbin. NL.
NEWTON, David (28) [Ebenezer & Synthia]; BARGER, Rebecca (26) [John & Rachel]; white; M=27 July 1879; GL Hunt, Luth. Min. in Hky Twsp; LC Killian, CW Bolch, MJ Killian. 1-388.
  Eboneezer (21); ELLIS, Susan (20); white; M=27 Oct. 1874; JC Hartzell, Min. at JC Hartzell's; D. Wortman, LF Yount, CM White. NL.
  William M. (25) [Andrew & Mary]; WORKMAN, Sarah Ann (18) [Wyley & Margaret C.]; white; M=15 July 1879; JD Carpenter, Min. in Hky Twsp; RB Davis, Laban Queen, Franklin Newton. 1-389.
NICKSON, Munroe (22) [Archabald & Susan] of Lincoln Co., NC; GILLILAND, Jane (20) [Osbourn & Emeline]; white; M=18 Dec. 1872; JA Sherrill, Min. in Hamilton Twsp; John Gabriel, HA Gilleland, JC Sherrill. 1-197.
NORWOOD, G.W.; WILSON, Cairan; M=31 Oct. 1855; Joshua Wilson, JP. NL.
  R.C.; SETZER, Sina; M=12 July 1860; William L. Mehaffey, JP. NL.
NULL, Ambrose; HETERICK, Anna; M=20 Feb. 1853; H. Ingold, JP. NL.
  John; ROW, Catharine A.; M=3 Sept. 1854; No Other Information. M=1868 or 1869. NL.
ODELL, Thomas [John & Rebecah]; STARR, Mary Ann; M=1871; Record Missing. NL.
ODOM, Henry (21) of Hamilton Twsp; HOLLER, Susanah E. (20) of Newton Twsp; white; M=30 Sept. 1873; NE Sigmon, JP in Cline's Twsp; AJ Holler, GG Shell, William W. Carpenter. NL.
OGBURN, Charles J. (37) [James E. & Sarah H.] of Forsyth Co., NC; LINDSEY, Anna E. (24) [Robert E. & Emily]; white; M=21 Dec. 1880; CM Anderson, Min. in Hky Twsp; EL Shuford, CD Ogburn, Bettie Anderson. 2-88.
ORNT, Henry; MACE, Seana E.; M=8 Aug. 1852; Joshua Wilson, JP. NL.
OSWALT, John (27); JONES, Jane (26); white; M=23 Jan. 1878; JA Sherrill, Min. at Jane Jones'; Abel Jones, Eli Jones, TM Sherrill. NL.

PACE, John F. [Abner & Julia A.]; WOODSON, Mary F. [Obediah & Mariah]; M=19 July 1869; AJ Whitener, JP. NL.
PAIN, Coleman; ROWE, M.A.; M=25 June 1857; Rev. JH West, Min. NL.
  Isaac R.E. (22); SHERRILL, Susan L. (26); white; M=1 Aug. 1878; GW Ivey, Min. at Rock Springs; JL Pain, LW Munday, AH Sigmon. NL.
PAINE, A.B.; WILSON, Lena A.; M=15 Apr. 1858; John Lantz, Min. NL.
  John W. [Thomas C. & Sarah]; MOORE, Mary [James H. & Sarah]; M=18 Jan. 1868; GD Sherrill, Min. NL.
PAINTER, J.L.; BURKE, Martha; M=21 Dec. 1853; Thomas Ward, JP. NL.
  O.P.; BUMGARNER, S.E.; M=11 Sept. 1861; JD Caldwell, JP. NL.
PARKER, Charley; BUMGARNER, A.B.; M=11 Mar. 1866; JD Caldwell, JP. NL.
  John J. (17); LEE, Sarah (17); white; M=16 Mar. 1876; JL Huit, JP in Cald. Twsp; Marcus Beal, Robert Norwood, George Strout. NL.
  Lemuel P. (32); KEENER, Francis (22); white; M=19 Dec. 1877; HA Forney, JP in Newton; Mary Forney, Sarah Forney, Peggy Scronce. NL.
  Samuel [William & Rebecca]; KEENER, Adaline [John & Fanny]; M=1 Sept. 1867; JD Caldwell, Esq. NL.
  Samuel (20); WITHERSPOON, Eliza (21); white; M=7 Jan. 1874; JL Huit, JP in Cald. Twsp; Lemuel Parker, William A. Huit, George Arndts. NL.
PARLAND, F.R.; DEITZ, Celia; M=30 Sept. 1858; Moses Barger, JP. NL.
PATRICK, Calvin [Jefferson Turner & Sophia Turner]; CLINE, Caroline; M=22 Aug. 1869; BF Watts, Min. NL.
PATTEN, Robert; WARLICK, H.E.; M=12 May 1861; Rev. DW Warlick, Min. NL.
PATTERSON, Calvin (55) of Lincoln Co., NC; HAMILTON, Julina (44); white; M=20 Dec. 1876; SC Brown, JP in Hamilton Twsp; D. Day, BC Yount, TJ Hamilton. NL.
PEELER, David H. (55) [Barney & Sarah]; ROBINSON, Mary Ann (38) [David & Ann]; white; M=24 July 1879; CM Anderson, Min. at JF Twsp; ES Rhyne, BC Rhyne, Ellis I. Rhine. 1-390.
PENCE, Hugh A. (21); WILSON, Alace V. (21); white; M=21 June 1874; JC Clapp, Ref. Min. at EG Bost's; Frank Smyre, David Dettor, Molten Berry. NL.
PENN, Rufus (21) [John & Ruth]; STEELE, Callie (22) [Hinse & Frances]; black; M=28 Aug. 1879; CW Blaylock, Min. in Hky Twsp; AN Bowman, Wilson Ward. 1-391.
PERKINS, Henry; SETZER, Menerva; M=20 Oct. 1861; JD Caldwell, JP. NL.
PERRY, Henry H.; BOYD, Francis; M=2 Oct. 1859; E. Yount, JP. NL.
PETERSON, J.A.; HAWN, S.E.; M=1 Mar. 1866; R. Yoder, JP. NL.
  John [Samuel & Elizabeth]; MILLER, Adaline [Jonas Fry & n/g]; M=23 Aug. 1871; AJ Fox, Min. 1-103.
PETRE, M.; LEONARD, Susan; M=23 May 1861; GP Shuford, JP. NL.
PHILIPS, C.L.; HOYLE, C.L.C.; M=15 Feb. 1866; DE Warlick, Min. NL.
PITTS, Abel; HOLLAR, Elizabeth; M=7 Apr. 1857; Joseph Parker, Min. NL.
  Conrad (22); HOLLER, Prucilla (21); white; M=7 Feb. 1878; Abel Whitener, JP in Hky; Monroe Pitts, Julius Beard, William Pitts. NL.
  Daniel; BEARD, Caroline; M=15 Apr. 1860; Daniel May, Min. NL.

PITTS, David [John & Sarah]; ERVIN, Ann [Hugh & Jemina]; M=26 Dec. 1867; AL Shuford, Esq. NL.
  James M. (21); HOLLER, Melinda (18); white; M=27 Dec. 1877; Abel Whitener, JP in Hky; NE Propst, MJ Pitts, Julius Beard. NL.
  John Henry (24); INGOLD, Laura I. (19); white; M=10 Feb. 1874; J. Ingold, Ref. Min. in Hky; JH Coulter, JF Murrill, LH Shuford. NL.
  William P. (21); YOUNT, Sarah Ann J. (19); white; M=16 Nov. 1876; AH Shuford, JP in Hky; John B. Baker, WL Abernathy. NL.
PLONK, Jacob Lemuel (25); NIPPER, Elizabeth (18); white; 22 Mar. 1876; Lemuel [Lemon] Shell, Min. at AJ Nipper's; FS Smyre, SE Smyre, AJ Nipper. NL.
POOVEY, Amianal (35); CLINE, Margaret R. (25); white; M=15 May 1878; GL Hunt, Luth. Min. at Jesse Cline's; JC Poovey, Jones F. Hawn, DE Seabock. NL.
  D.S.; POOVEY, E.R.; M=31 Mar. 1861; E. Yount, JP. NL.
  Eli F. (21) [n/k & Polly Poovey]; SETZER, Jane (17) [John & Sally]; white; M=15 Aug. 1880; LH Wilson, JP in Cat. Twsp; JT Huitt, LA Harbinson, Jack Setzer. 2-89.
  Henry L. (24); CLINE, Amanda E. (20); white; M=24 Aug. 1876; HA Forney, JP in Newt. Twsp; HA Whitener, Harriet Whitener. NL.
  James M. (23); SIGMON, Julie Ann (22); white; M=22 Dec. 1878; HA Forney, JP at E. Sigmon's; Candas Sigmon, Hugh A. Pennell, Mary Sigmon. NL.
  John Zeno (19) [Miles M. & Nancy]; BOLCH, Carmila (22) [Andrew & Rosa]; white; M=21 Dec. 1879; JA Foil, Ref. Min. in Newton; JW Cecil, James A. Propst, GH Bolch. 1-329.
  Miles M.; SIGMON, Malinda; M=11 Nov. 1866; EA Warlick, JP. NL.
  Silas; FRY, Emily E.; M=27 Dec. 1859; Henry Cline, JP. NL.
  William P.; STARR, Caroline; M=8 Jan. 1857; Jonas Bost, JP. NL.
POPE, Alfred; HEFNER, Sally; M=7 Apr. 1859; JHA Yount, JP. NL.
  Alfred; LAIL, Matilda; M=15 June 1866; JB Little, JP. NL.
  Augustus (19); BENFIELD, Catherine (19); white; M=3 May 1877; JC Hartsell, Min. in Newton; IN Fox, Joshua Drum, Socrates Benfield. NL.
  Carry; ISENHOUR, Mary; M=25 Jan. 1852; JB Little, JP. NL.
  Daniel; KAYLOR, Gemima; M=28 Feb. 1852; JB Little, JP. NL.
  Davant (18) [Marcus & Vina]; THOMPSON, Bettie Ann (19) [John & Martha]; white; M=2 Oct. 1879; PK Little, JP in Cat. Twsp; CC Harvell, TA Killian, WP Huffman. 1-392.
  David; HEFNER, Sida; M=14 July 1859; Jesse Gantt, JP. NL.
  F.L.; SIGMON, E.S.; M=21 Nov. 1858; E. Conner, JP. NL.
  Franklin; HUFFMAN, Eliza; M=12 Sept. 1858; JB Little, JP. NL.
  George; SHOOK, Sarah; M=26 Apr. 1857; JB Little, JP. NL.
  Henry; SHOOK, Mattie M.; M=12 July 1860; JB Little, JP. NL.
  Henry (29) of Hky Tav. Twsp; BOLCH, Caroline (28) of Hky Tav. Twsp; white; M=16 Oct. 1873; ML Bean, JP in Hky Tav. Twsp; VE Teague, JD Bolch, GW Herman. NL.
  Jeff (20) [George & Sallie]; POPE, Belza (20) [Frank & Eliza]; white; M=14 Aug. 1879; CM Anderson, Min. in Meth. Parsonage; JC Little, Lewis Heavner, HB Anderson. 1-393.
  Lafayett; WEAVER, Eliza; M=3 Jan. 1855; AJ Whitener, JP. NL.
  Logan; MINGUS, Margaret; M=19 Aug. 1851; William L. Mehaffey JP, NL.
  Marcus; HUFFMAN, Mary L.; M=23 Sept. 1860; JHA Jarrett, JP. NL.

POPE, Milus; LAEL, Catharine; M=17 May 1866; JB Little, JP. NL.
  Quincy E. (28) [David & Jiminia]; MOSER, Laura (21) [George & Mary]; white; M=2 Dec. 1880; JM Smith, Luth. Min. in Cline's Twsp; RT Pope, MD Sigmon, EE Dellinger. 2-90.

PORTER, John R. (23) [John Porter & n/g]; BENFIELD, Sarah (23); white; M=15 Dec. 1879; JR Jones, Bapt. Min. at Hky Twsp; DE Faire, E. Faire, A.Mackey. 1-394.

POTTER, A.J.; LEE, Mary; M=1 Apr. 1866; JD Caldwell, JP. NL.

POWELL, HF [AM & Fanny E.]; HOWARD, Fanny A. [George & Sarah]; M=16 June 1868; JA Sherrill, Min. NL.
  John Enza [John & Anna]; MILLER, Sarah [Moses & Elizabeth]; M=29 June 1868; AL Shuford, Esq. NL.
  Julius (23); WILSON, Sarah (21); black; M=11 May 1873; William Brook, Min. in Hamilton Twsp; E. Abernethy, Henry Moore, Julius McConley. NL.
  Robert S. (19); SHELTON, Laura J. (18); white; M=28 Nov. 1877; JA Sherrill, Min. at Munday Spencer's; WL Sanders, EH Sherrill, John H. Loftin. NL.

PRICE, Gilbert E. (19) [Smith & Emeline]; SHEPPARD, Jane (21) [John & Sarah]; white; M=25 Sept. 1879; CT Sigmon, JP at CT Sigmon's in Cline's Twsp; AM Sigmon, Timothy Lafon, ? Hefner. 1-395.
  Israel C. (22); DRUM, Mary (24); white; M=9 Aug. 1877; Abel Barger, JP at Lemuel Miller's; Rebecca Killian, Rebecca M. Barger. NL.
  Smith; SPENCER, Amy; M=19 Aug. 1855; E. Yount, JP. NL.
  Waitsell A. (22); Parker, Alice (18) of Hamilton Twsp; white; M=26 Oct. 1873; JA Sherrill, Min. at Mrs. Parker's; TB Parker, MT Saunders, PS Powell. NL.
  William C. (25); DAY, Elizabeth (23); white; M=8 Jan. 1878; SC Brown, JP at Hamilton Twsp; JR Day, MA Holdsclaw, JA Edwards. NL.

PROCTOR, R.G.; SHELTON, S.J.; M=24 Oct. 1865; ED Thompson, Min. NL.
  S.H.; MUNDAY, Julia A.; M=14 July 1870; JA Sherrill, Min. NL.
  Samuel (21) of Lincoln Co., NC; SHERRILL, Rutha (23); white; M=1 Aug. 1878; JA Sherrill, Min. at JA Sherrill's; OM Asbury, WR Harwell, LA Rudisil. NL.

PROPST, Adolphus M. (24) [Absalom & Clarissa]; WHISENANT, Susan (21) [Philip & Polly]; white; M=23 Dec. 1875; Jacob Mosteller JP in Bandy's Twsp; C. Baker, DA Whisnant. 1-293.
  Alfred; YOUNG, Martha; M=24 Aug. 1853; Henry Cline, JP. NL.
  Avory (23); STARR, Laura (23); white; M=2 Mar. 1873; PF Smith, JP in Nwtn Twsp; Eli Starr, GW Bowman, MA Throneburg. NL.
  D. Franklin (22) [Lawson & Malinda]; WITHERSPOON, Sarah [Nelson & Malinda]; white; M=2 Apr. 1875; JL Hewit, JP in Cald. Twsp; M. Wilson, Adolphus Propst, Frank Burnes. 1-294.
  D.L.; SMYRE, Julian; M=11 June 1856; PC Hinkle, Min. NL.
  Daniel A. (26) [Lawson H. & Anna]; BRADSHAW, Alice R. (17) [Sidney & JE]; white; M=12 Oct. 1879; LC White, Meth. Min. in Bandy's Twsp; Lanzo Propst, Charles Hubbard, HW Anthony. 1-396.
  Daniel E. (24) [Jonas & Lovina]; HEFNER, Sonova A. (18) [Hiram & Ann]; white; M=16 Nov. 1879; JW Mouser, JP in Hky Twsp; WF Hallman, HG Hallman, TA Witherspoon.

PROPST, Elcanah (23) of Cald. Twsp; HARWELL, Sarah (20) of Cald. Twsp; white; M=13 Aug. 1873; JL Huit, JP in Cald. Twsp; John Gant, Walter Setzer, John Wilson. NL.

Eli (22); SHOOK, Elizabeth (20); white; M=20 Jan. 1878; JH Bruns, JP in Hky; LN Waters, JS Bobbitt, JS Marshall. NL.

Franklin [Mingo Wilfong & Lucy Propst]; ANTHONY, Catharine [Frank Coulter & Clara Anthony]; black; M=5 Jan. 1871; ST Wilfong, JP. 1-104.

George M.; PUNCH, Amanda; M=22 Dec. 1853; William L. Mehaffey, JP. NL.

George W. [John & Christenia]; HARMAN, Jane [Daniel Hoover & Sarah Hoover]; M=11 Apr. 1869; James A. Garvan, JP. NL.

Harvy [Lawson & Malinda]; GREEN, Martha [OC & Ceda]; M=30 Jan. 1868; WL Mehaffey, Esq. NL.

J.C.; PROPST, B.G.; M=1870; No Other Information Given. NL.

J.H.; ?, Manah; M=17 Aug. 1856; Jonas Bost, JP. NL.

J.S. (21) of JF Twsp; ABERNATHY, N.J. (17) of JF Twsp; white; M=14 Jan. 1873; JC Hartzell, Min. at AF Abernathy's; AC Link, Thomas E. Fields, JA Rayfield. NL.

John H. [James & Loenia]; SPENCER, Sallie [Israel & Betty Ann]; M=22 Dec. 1867; CW Herman, Esq. NL.

John W.; JANET, Catharine; M=10 Jan. 1861; AJ Fox, Min. NL.

N.E. [LH & MM]; KEENER, J.C. [Daniel & n/k]; M=10 July 1870; AJ Fox, Min. NL.

Reuben (21); YODER, Julia A. (19); white; M=18 Dec. 1876; Robert Helton, Min. at Reily Propst's; JF Propst, BF Propst, AA Propst. NL.

William (31); SHERRILL, Elizabeth (37); white; M=10 Aug. 1874; JL Huit, JP in Cald. Twsp; WA Huit, Henry Linebarger, Elcanah Propst. NL.

William; BOLCH, Susan; M=11 Oct. 1866; DS Henkel, Min. NL.

PUNCH, Adolphus (24) [Franklin & Amy] of Nwtn Twsp; MILLER, Martha Ann G. (19) [Wesley & Manerva] of Hky Tav. Twsp; white; M=1 Sept. 1872; D. May, Min. in Nwtn Twsp; Susan May, Kate May, TE May. 1-198.

Joseph L.; BOLCH, Salina E.; M=22 Oct. 1863; John Lantz, Min. NL.

RABB, George W.; ROBINSON, Sarah Ann; M=9 Oct. 1866; EA Warlick, JP. NL.

W.H. (25) [John & Rebecca]; SETZER, Kate (21) [n/k & Susan Setzer]; white; M=4 Apr. 1880; WC Caldwell, JP in Cald. Twsp; Manuel Wilson, JB Caldwell, Levi L. Caldwell. 2-91.

RABY, George W.; KILLIAN, Elizabeth; M=3 Apr. 1860; E. Yount, JP. NL.

H.A.; HARTZOE, Barbara; M=3 Dec. 1857; JHA Yount, JP. NL.

James C.; HART, Margery; M=10 Apr. 1866; Richard R. Dagnall, Min. NL.

John (25); BOLCH, Gemima (27); white; M=2 May 1878; DC Huffman, Luth. Min. at Jesse Cline's; HM Hallman, Josiah A. Poovy, John J. Abernathy. NL.

John W.; LINK, Catharine S.; M=29 July 1862; AR Benick, Min. NL.

Lawson; STAMY, Eve; M=9 Mar. 1853; A. Abernathy, Bapt. Min. NL.

W.A.; EDWARDS, Mary; M=7 Sept. 1859; Jonas Bost, JP. NL.

William [Samuel & Martha Ann]; WALKER, Adoline [John & Mary Ann] M=26 Apr. 1872; EA Warlick, JP. NL.

RABY, William; CLINE, Harriet; M=30 Oct. 1859; E. Yount, JP. NL.
  William R.; GAPET, Melinda A.; M=27 Feb. 1852; HB Wither-spoon, JP. NL.
RADER, Jonas M. [Daniel & Fanny]; STARR, Cate E. [Connor & Malinda]; M=27 Nov. 1867; DS Henkel, Min. NL.
  William P. (39); STARR, Barbra S. (24); white; M=7 Nov. 1878; GL Hunt, Luth. Min. at SM Starr's; WP Fry, WF Rader, RP Rader. NL.
RAMSEY, S.J.; HOLLAR, M.A.; M=28 Mar. 1861; PL Rowe, JP. NL.
RAMSOUR, D.W. [Alfred & Jane]; REINHARDT, Alice [Henry & Elizabeth]; M=28 Jan. 1868; John Watts, Min. NL.
  David Henry (29) [AL & EC]; YODER, Florence I. (19) [GM & Rebecca]; white; M=24 Dec. 1879; Julius H. Shuford, Ref. Min. at JM Shuford's; RW Wilson, RW Robinson, JM Shuford. NL.
  Edward (21); ABERNATHY, Fannie (19); black; M=15 June 1875; Robert Helton, Min. at Robert Helton's; JW Helton, MA Leonard, Ida Helton. NL.
  Eli (28) of Lincoln Co., NC; SHUFORD, Laura (19); white; M=25 Aug. 1875; J.H. Shuford, Ref. Min. at JM Shuford's; RW Wilson, RW Robinson, JM Shuford. NL.
  George (21) [Franklin & Jenny]; COULTER, Fanny (19) [Willis & n/g]; black; M=31 Aug. 1872; ET Coulter, JP in JF Twsp; Scot Hunter, Wesley Lewis, James Coulter. 1-199.
  Milton H. (30) [David & n/g] of Lincoln Co., NC; BLACKBURN, Rhoda (27) [Samuel & Elizabeth]; white; M=30 Jan. 1873; J. Ingold, Min. in JF Twsp; David Lore, George W. Hawn, LA Wilfong. 1-247.
  P.W. [George & Eliza]; RAMSOUR, Mollie [Elkanah & Adline]; M=4 Jan. 1871; J. Ingold, Min. 1-105.
  Rufus (21); Wilfong, Alice (18); black; M=4 Feb. 1877; William G. James, JP in Hamilton Twsp; Delila Lael, KEL Pope, Judy James. NL.
  Sidney (22); Wilfong, Chana (19); black; M=25 Mar. 1877; Robert Helton, Min. at Robert Helton's; CG Butler, Ida Helton, Zacran Helton. NL.
  Thomas [n/k & Winnie N.]; REINHARDT, Jance C. [Jack & Amy]; M=23 Dec. 1869; Jeremiah Ingold, Min. NL.
RANKIN, Will (21) [Thomas Fisher & Mary Rankin]; BURTON, Lizzie (21) [Thomas & Ruth]; black; M=28 May 1879; AB Jennings, Meth. Min. in Hky Twsp; Jane Neel, Moses Broomfield, Mike Colman. 1-399.
REA, William L. (21) [Silas & Anah] of Iredell Co., NC; SHERRILL, Cenia (20) [Enus & Ruana]; white; M=16 Apr. 1879; JA Sherrill, JP in Cat. Twsp; FA Connor, WW Sherrill, WLC Killian. 1-400.
READE, Pinckney (24) [Robert Sherrill & Mary Sherrill]; STAMEY, Lovina (19) [Manuel & Mary]; black; M=1 Jan. 1873; JA Sherrill, Min. at Mt. Crk Twsp; John M. Stowe, John Beatty, LA Rudisill. 1-248.
REAP, Daniel; WEAVER, Anna; M=12 Apr. 1860; AJ Whitener, JP. NL.
RECTOR, Brett; SHOOK, Elizabeth; M=10 Oct. 1856; JB Little, JP. NL.
  Burton; SHOOK, Leah; M=8 Jan. 1853; H. Ingold, JP. NL.
  John; POPE, Gemima; M=9 Sept. 1860; JHA Yount, JP. NL.

RECTOR, William (23) [Gilbert & Elizabeth]; WINEBARGER, Mary (24) [Silas & Malinda]; white; M=17 Oct. 1880; CT Sigmon, JP in Cline's Twsp; S. Lael, AM Sigmon, GW Winebarger. 2-92.

REEL, Hamilton (25) of Lincoln Co., NC; CLIPPARD, Lovina R. (25); white; M=25 Oct. 1876; JL Huitt, JP in Cald. Twsp; John Clipard, David Clipard, Theadore Huitt. NL.

REEP, Gilbert N. (21); DRUM, Ellen (21); white; M=26 Nov. 1876; JC Clapp, Ref. Min. at Franklin Drum's; Perry Fry, MM Wilson, Frank Drum. NL.

 Susan (sic); CALDWELL, Sarah; M=28 June 1863; David E. Warlick, Min. NL.

 W.F. (23) [John & Anna E.] of Lincoln Co., NC; LUTZ, A.E. (21) [Noah & Roseanna E.]; white; M=9 Nov. 1880; PFW Stamey, Min. at JF Twsp; AJ Lutz, ND Lutz, JR Crocker. 2-93.

REES, Aarin R.; REES, Lavina M.; M=7 Apr. 1854; CW Herman, JP. NL.

 Calvin; PUNCH, Selina; M=22 Apr. 1856; CW Herman, JP. NL.

 William; STARR, Amelia; M=26 Jan. 1857; Jonas Bost, JP. NL.

REESE, George; CLINE, Susan; M=22 Mar. 1866; EP Coulter, JP. NL.

 Martin L. (23); FULBRIGHT, Mahala (25); white; M=16 Aug. 1876; JC Clapp, Ref. Min. at JC Clapp's; Perry Fry, James Bollinger, Monroe Fulbright. NL.

REINHARDT, Alexander [Rufus & n/g]; LOVE, Allie [Daniel Love & n/g]; M=27 Dec. 1868; George W. McLaine. NL.

 Andrew; WHITENER, Sarah Ann; M=22 May 1856; DE Warlick, Min. NL.

 Calvin (25) [Ephraim & Lydia]; MOBLEY, Nellie (19) [Bryant & Julia]; black; M=4 Mar. 1875; NE Sigmon, JP in Cline's Twsp; James Cline, Miles Baker, Cebren Reinhardt. 1-295.

 Ephraim B. (22); GAMBLE, Sarah (21); white; M=6 Mar. 1877; JC Clapp, Ref. Min. at Fannie Gamble's; SV Goodson, ML McCorkle, GM Beatty. NL.

 Frank (28) [Levi & Mary A.]; COBB, Minta (22) [Rufus & Sophia]; white; M=20 Mar. 1879; Robert Helton, Min. in Bandy's Twsp; CS Reinhardt, LM Reinhardt, TS Michael. 1-401.

 George H. (23); HEFNER, Eliza J. (20); white; M=12 Sept. 1876; Robert Helton, Min. at Sol Hefner's; RM Fry, Daniel Rink, HF Sigmon. NL.

 Graham (21) [Ephraim & Lina]; ERVIN, Clara (22) [Henry & Lucinda]; black; M=21 Aug. 1879; JM Smith, Luth. Min. in Hky Twsp; C. Reinhardt, James Simpson, Henry Richerne. 1-402.

 Isaac; MICHALS, Mary M.; M=22 Jan. 1863; Philip Burns, JP. NL.

 J. Edd (23) [Franklin & Sarah] of Lincoln Co., NC; WILSON, Fannie A. (19) [Ezekiel & Sarah] of JF Twsp; white; M-16 Dec. 1873; JC Clapp, Min. in JF Twsp; Luther Boyd, Col. ML McCorkle, Frank McCorkle. 1-249.

 J.J. [Henry & Elizabeth]; SIGMON, Ellen [DJ & Lina]; M=4 May 1869; Elijah Allison, Min. NL.

 James L. (24) [Ambrose & Jane]; HEFNER, Emma F. (18) [Solomon & Saidy]; white; M=29 June 1879; Robert Helton, Min. in JF Twsp; JA Hoyle, AT Whitener, GL Reinhardt. 1-403.

 John; FULBRITE, Sarah; M=1 Aug. 1858; G. Huffman, JP. NL.

 Leban [Ephraim & Letty]; HUNSUCKER, Laura [Alan & Lena]; M=4 Oct. 1869; BF Watts, Min. NL.

 Monrow [Isaac & Elizabeth]; RUDISILL, Eliza Ann [Absolom & Lueaza]; M=8 Nov. 1871; JW Bandy, JP. NL.

REINHARDT, Pinkney M. (22); MICHAL, Eliza Ann (24); white; M=7 May 1876; Robert Helton, Min. at Eli Clay's; Eli F. Clay, LF Reinhardt, PW Bangle. NL.

REITZEL, Anderson; SIGMON, Ann; M=10 Nov. 1850; JB Little, JP. NL.

  C.G. {Christian Guido}; SHOOK, Susan; M=20 Dec. 1857; PC Hinkel, Min. NL.

  Henry J.; EKARD, Veronica B.; M=3 Oct. 1866; PC Hinkel, Min. NL.

  {Jerome Cass} [CG & Dellia]; HOLLER, {Sarah} [Peter & Margaret]; M=2 Aug. 1868; JB Little, Esq. NL.

  Leroy M. (21) [Anderson & Anna]; SIGMON, Tabitha H. (18) [Logan & Catharine]; white; M=2 Nov. 1879; CT Sigmon, JP in Cline's Twsp; BE Smith, ME Ekard, QL Little. 1-404.

REYNOLDS, John F. [Harry & Mary]; SIMS, H.A. [Brittin & Sally]; M=4 June 1869; JA Sherrill, Min. NL.

RHINE, Eli S.; WHITENER, S.C.E.; M=6 Aug. 1856; JW Puett, Min. NL.

  John; PARTIS, Lucinda N.; M=3 Aug. 1852; JP Hughes, Min. NL.

RHONEY, Franklin (23); JOHNSON, Catharine (22); white; M=31 May 1874; JW Bandy, JP in Bandy's Twsp; JM Mull, Sidney Shuford, JN Goodnight. NL.

RHYNE, Burton C. (23) [ES & Susan]; BROWN, Mary Etta (18) [AA & Rhoda C.]; white; M=3 Aug. 1880; PFW Stamey, Min. in JF Twsp; MA Rhyne, RM Roseman, AL Rhyne. 2-94.

RICHARD, Charley [Henry & Mena]; ABERNATHY, Mattie A. [John & Caroline]; M=16 Jan. 1872; EA Warlick, JP. 1-200.

RICHEY, George Pinkney (21) [Paul & Maliney] of Lincoln Co., NC; MOOSE, Mary (19) [Isaac & Polly] of Cabarrus Co., NC; white; M=28 Dec. 1873; JW Bandy, JP in Bandy's Twsp; Sidney Shuford, RF Leonard, JN Goodnight. 1-250.

  Joseph W. (20); WYANT, Sarah (21); white; M=8 July 1875; Jacob Mosteller, JP in Bandy's Twsp; Rufus Mosteller, Lovinia Mosteller. NL.

RIGGINS, Archey (29) [Allen Sinclair & Billie King]; MCCORKLE, Nancy (30); black; M=30 Sept. 1880; EJ Harris, Min. in Nwtn; Bill Baley, EE Slad, YO Wilson. 2-95.

RILEY, Andrew; HOWARD, Lucinda; 22 Nov. 1857; JD Caldwell, JP. NL.

RINCK, George F.; BOLLINGER, Polly J.; M=12 Oct. 1865; PC Henkel, Min. NL.

  Paul; MILLER, Sally M.; M=16 Dec. 1860; M. Barger, JP. NL.

RINK, Andrew; MILLER, Emoline; M=4 Dec. 1852; E. Yount, JP. NL.

  Christian F. (28) [George & Elizabeth] of Iredell Co., NC; PROPST, Phebe C. (25) [WA & Abigail]; white; 8 Dec. 1880; GL Hunt, Luth. Min. in Hky Twsp; NW Propst, AM Settlemyer, George F. Rink. 2-96.

  Christian R.; REITZELL, Lydia S.E.; M=29 Apr. 1864; E. Yount, JP. NL.

  Daniel (30) of Lincoln Co., NC; CHILDERS, Emma C. (18) of Lincoln Co., NC; white; M=2 Mar. 1879; Robert Helton, Min. at Robert Helton's; RW Kistler, JF Lentz, JT Sain. NL.

  Eli F.; SHELL, Elizabeth M.; M=18 Nov. 1863; PC Henkel, Min. NL.

RITCHEY, P.C. (27) [Jacob & Mary] of NC; SHERRILL, L.V. (19) [Sidney & Francis]; white; M=1 Jan. 1880; KC Richey, Min. in Hamilton Twsp; JA Beal, AD Bandy, Alexander Keever. 2-97.

ROBARDS, Burtin [Daniel & Lempy]; CHAMBERS, Catherine L. [Alfred & Lovina]; M=24 Jan. 1869; BF Watts, Min. NL.

ROBB, J.F.; ARNT, T.S.; M=10 Jan. 1861; Adam Miller, Min. NL.
   James P. (26); BOST, Sarah A. (21); white; M=3 Oct. 1878; JC Clapp, Ref. Min. at Abel Ikerd's; Jacob Rudisill, Frank C. Ikerd, George Rabb. NL.

ROBERTS, D.W. [JA & MC]; WARLICK, Matta A. [David E. & Rachel]; M=12 Nov. 1869; John Watts, Min. NL.
   Henry H.; ROBARDS, Annie K.; M=17 May 1864; H. Haughton, JP. NL.

ROBESON, George (21) [Jack & Adline]; NEILL, Lucy (20) [Anthony & Nearnt] black; M=10 Apr. 1879; GM Yoder, JP in JF Twsp; FA Yoder, RAL Yoder, CM Yoder. 1-405.

ROBINSON, Aarin; BLACKBURN, Mary; M=24 May 1856; DE Warlick, Min. NL.
   Andrew (55) [Morgan & Betsy]; WATTS, Sally (37) [Thomas Loftin & Margaret]; white; M=17 June 1880; WC Caldwell, JP in Cald. Twsp; JP Caldwell, LS Caldwell, JS Gwaltney. 2-98.
   Augustus [LD & Lovina]; SHOOK, Mary [Jacob & Susan]; M=22 Mar. 1868; HA Lowman, Esq. NL.
   Benjamin (22) [Joseph Gross & Peggy Robinson]; HILDEBRAND, Saphronia (22) [William & Eliza]; black; M=21 Mar. 1875; NM Hoyle, Min. in Icard Twsp, Burke Co., NC; J. Hildebrand, Sally Hildebrand, ? Hildebrand. 1-296.
   Caleb [Jacob & Hilda]; WILFONG, Harriet [Andy & Nancy]; black; M=22 Dec. 1870; EP Coulter, JP. 1-33.
   D.S.; BYSING, A.A.; M=30 May 1861; AJ Fox, Min. NL.
   F.O.; HOWARD, M.C.; M=1 Aug. 1866; JA Sherrill, Min. NL.
   Francis O. (37) [John & Cammila]; GABRIEL, Fanny (31) [Joseph & Rebecca]; white; M=11 Aug. 1880; OW Gabriel, JP in Mt. Crk Twsp; A. Jones, JW Gabriel, HS Gabriel. 2-99.
   Gabriel (21); WILSON, Mary (19); black; M-12 Apr. 1873; EP Coulter, JP in JF Twsp; CL Lowe, JS Leonard, Thomas L. Lowe. NL.
   George (21) [Jack & Adline]; HILL, Lucy (20) [Anthony & Nearnt]; black; 10 Apr. 1879; GM Yoder, JP. in JF Twsp; FA Yoder, RAL Yoder, CM Yoder. 1-405.
   Hiram (25); LITTON, Ann (19); white; M=17 Sept. 1874; LA Lockman, JP in Mt. Crk Twsp; AE Sherrill, FM Abernathy, CT Robinson. NL.
   Isaac; HICKS, Susanah; M=23 Jan. 1862; JD Caldwell, JP. NL.
   Jackson A. (35) [Andrew & Kate]; ROBINSON, Martha Eveline (23) [n/g & Margaret Burke]; white; M=22 Apr. 1880; WC Caldwell, JP in Cald. Twsp; William Gilleland, Elizabeth Painter, George Gilleland. 2-100.
   James; SHERRILL, Sarah; M=3 Oct. 1857; William Long, JP. NL.
   Jim [Jim Coulter & Eda Robinson]; REINHARDT, Ann [Rufus & Elmira]; M=14 Mar. 1868; EA Warlick, Esq. NL.
   John S. [John & Jane]; SHERRILL, Jane C. [Cepthey & Betsy]; M=26 Aug. 1869; JA Sherrill, Min. NL.
   Lawson A. (25); MOORE, Dollie (18); white; M=1 Mar. 1875; JL Hunt, JP in Cald. Twsp; JM Wilson, John Wilson, Harriet Wilson. NL.
   Lewis [Thomas & Eliza]; ANGEL, Alice [James & Eva]; M=17 June 1871; George W. McLeane. 1-107.
   Martin [Mingo Wilfong & Dorus Wilfong]; COLTER, Manga [Willis & Nancy]; M=16 Oct. 1867; EA Warlick, JP. NL.

ROBINSON, Martin M. (22) [John S. & Epsy]; LINEBERGER, Dovy (16) [FH & Elizabeth]; white; M=19 Jan. 1873; JA Sherrill, Min. in Mt. Crk Twsp; IA Killian, EA Proctor, John M. Howard. 1-251.

Miles [n/k & Phillis Coulter]; WILFONG, Bettie [Nelson & Mahala]; M=25 May 1872; JH Brown, JP. NL.

N.L. [William M. & Margaret]; LITTEN, Margaret [L. & Perthany]; M=1 July 1869; F. Caldwell, JP. NL.

Noah (21); COULTER, Sallie (18); black; M=23 Mar. 1878; EJ Harris, Min. at Snow Hill; Pink Wike, Marinda Coulter, Mott Gross. NL.

Pinckney [John S. & Epsy]; BARKLEY, Mary [Robert & Martha]; M=2 Nov. 1870; Avant, Min. 1-34.

Robert [Jack & Amy]; RUDISILL, Ann; M=24 Aug. 1867; EA Warlick, Esq. NL.

Sidney [Jacob & Heldy]; WILFONG, Julia Ann [Andy & Nancy]; M=26 Jan. 1868; EP Coulter, Esq. NL.

William (22); GABRIEL, Ada M. (17); white; M=26 Feb. 1879; JA Sherrill, Min. at Wilson Gabriel's; JA Sherrill, John W. Howard, FO Robinson. NL.

William (68); GIBBS, Cassiann (65); black; M=18 Jan. 1874; JW Williams, JP in Cald. Twsp; AE Williams, Malinda S. Keener. NL.

William (22) of JF Twsp; REINHARDT, Margaret (21) of Lincoln Co., NC; black; M=11 Sept. 1873; AG Corpening, JP in JF Twsp; AB Hoyle, JC Corpening. NL.

William [Thomas & Eliza]; DAVIS, Violett [Wesly Davis & n/g]; black; M=10 Oct. 1871; AG Corpening, JP. 1-108.

William R.; SHERRILL, Martha; M=28 Aug. 1861; JW Gabriel, JP. NL.

Willis [Ephraim & Fanny]; LOWE, Mary [Willis Coulter & Nancy]; M=31 July 1869; James A. Garvan, JP. NL.

ROCKET, E.M.; ROCKET, Agnes E.; M=17 Jan. 1855; G. Huffman, JP. NL.

R.P.; WHITENER, Catharine; M=25 Nov. 1860; PD Moore, Min. NL.

ROCKETT, Calvin W. (25); YOUNT, Sallie J. (16); M=7 Mar. 1878; JC Clapp, Ref. Min. at GDL Yount's; WE Yount, WJD Scherie, JH Moser. NL.

Obed M. (25); MOSER, Jane E. (19); white; M=18 Oct. 1876; JC Clapp, Ref. Min. at GH Moser's; Pierce Moser, William Rockett, Lafayett Yount. NL.

William; HUBERD, Hialdy; M=17 Apr. 1860; Daniel May, Min. NL.

RODERICK, Sephus; BAKER, Adoline; M=20 Dec. 1858; GP Shuford, JP. NL.

ROSEMAN, Alley (50) [Abner Setzer & Rosa Roseman]; CONNOR, Mira (30); black; M=10 Apr. 1879; CW Vanderburg, Min. at Mira Connor's; Jane Carans, Peter Carans, William Brooks. 1-406.

D.F. [Daniel & Anna]; CLINE, Fannie D. [Jonas & Caroline] M=20 Dec. 1871; JH Fesperman, Min. 1-109.

Philo [James Baker & Peggy Roseman]; HUNSUCKER, Harriet [Edmond & Lynnie]; M=6 July 1871; William H. Rockett, JP. 1-110.

Ras. [James Baker & Peggy Baker]; BOST, Harriett [n/g & Chana Bost]; M=24 Feb. 1872; William Brooks, Min. NL.

ROSEMAN, Robert M. (32) [Andrew & Cornelia] of Lincoln Co., NC; FORNEY, Mary (20) [Marcus & Caroline Brown]; white; M=14 May 1879; RE Johnston, Presby. Min. at Mr. Brown's {s.father}; AL Roseman, Katie Roseman, John M. Motz. 1-407.

ROWE, Andrew N. (30); RHODES, Harriet (33); white; M=17 May 1878; JA Foil, Ref. Min. at AJ Foil's; Sue L. Foil, Carrie L. Hagan, A. Hagan. NL.

C.B. [Daniel & Elizabeth]; BOST, Alice E. [Joseph & Polly]; M=25 Nov. 1869; AJ Fox, Min. NL.

Daniel W. (22); SEITZ, Candace (18); white; M=13 Apr. 1876; JH Shuford, Ref. Min. at Moses Yoder's; Moses Yoder, JL Hawn. NL.

James N. (29) of Union Co., NC; GILLELAND, Alice E. (22); white; M=21 Dec. 1876; JA Sherrill, Min. at O. Gilleland's; WE Allen, AW Hager, MG Gilleland. NL.

Junius Q. (21) of Nwtn Twsp; WHITENER, Alace E. (22) of Cline's Twsp; white; M=30 Dec. 1873; JM Smith, Evgl Luth. Min. at D. Yount's; JS Yount, MM Smith, FJ Dellinger. NL.

Lank (21) [Tomas Pearson & Lucinda Rowe]; SIGMON, Mary (18) [Ellick & Edeline] of Hky; black; M=12 Dec. 1879; JH Bruns, JP in Hky; Jane Smyer, Eli M. Smyer, Robert Smyer. 1-408.

M.M. [Daniel & Elizabeth]; BRIDGES, Jane M. [Gilbert & Mehaley]; M=12 Jan. 1870; Daniel May, Min. NL.

Marcus; CLONINGER, Selena; M=23 Feb. 1854; CW Herman, JP. NL.

Marion J. [Daniel & Elizabeth]; HERMAN, Camilla E. [FL & Mahala] M=28 Feb. 1872; EA Warlick, JP. 1-201.

Nelson [Robinson & Mariah]; COULTER, Martha [Willis & Nancy]; M=12 Jan. 1868; EP Coulter, Esq. NL.

Noah; SMITH, Cammila; M=18 Dec. 1851; HB Witherspoon, JP. NL.

Paddy; MCCORKLE, Mandy [Bradford & Emeline]; M=19 Mar. 1868; JW Gabriel, Esq. NL.

Peter J. (23) [Peter L. & Linney L.] of Hky; WHITENER, Mattie A. (18) [Abel & Eliza E.] of Hky; white; M=29 June 1879; JC Clapp, Min. in Nwtn Twsp; Emma Clapp, Carol Clapp, A. Theodore Fry. 1-409.

Pinckney; KEEVER, Senith; M=23 Dec. 1856; JD Caldwell, JP. NL.

Pinkney E. (22) [Noah I. & Cammila]; HERMAN, Ada V. (17) [CW & Elizabeth]; white; M=25 Dec. 1879; JC Clapp, Min. in Nwtn Twsp; JQ Rowe, PG Herman, FG Dellinger. 1-410.

Robert (18) of Hky Tav. Twsp; MOSTELLER, Saphronia (21) of Bandys Twsp; black; M=25 Apr. 1873; Abel Whitener, JP in Hky Tav. Twsp; AP Ward, Joseph L. Deal, Manda Rowe. NL.

RUDISILL, Adolphus Alexander (26); RHONEY, Sarah Ann (29); white; M=8 Apr. 1877; JM Clampit, JP in Bandy's Twsp; JF Rhoney, JW Allson, SA Rudisill. NL.

Daniel R.; SHERRILL, D.L.; M=7 May 1856; Lanely Wood, Min. NL.

E.A.; KILLIAN, C.E.; M=29 Sept. 1862; LM Berry, Min. NL.

Henry P.; YOUNT, Clemma O.; M=15 Mar. 1866; PC Henkel, Min. NL.

Jacob F.; IKERD, Linny C.; M=18 Jan. 1866; J. Lantz, Min. NL.

Jacob F. (35); BLAKELY, Sarah E. (36); white; M=27 Oct. 1876; JC Clapp, Ref. Min. at William Williams'; John Williams, Lou Williams, William Williams. NL.

John P. (25); LINN, Lempie (24); white; M=2 June 1876; Jacob Mosteller, JP in Bandy's Twsp; JF Linn, WP Stalling. NL.

Philip; WORKMAN, Dicy; M=7 Nov. 1857; G. Huffman, JP. NL.

RUDISILL, Philip; MOSTELLER, Elizabeth; M=31 Oct. 1854; PC Henkel, JP. NL.

  Solomon A. (24); SPEAGLE, Alice (21); white; M=25 Apr. 1878; ML Little, Luth. Min. at Carsian Speagle's; Emma Hudson, John A. Rudisill, TJ Leonard. NL.

  Thomas (21); SUMMIT, Nancy Jane (21); white; M=1 Jan. 1875; JW Bandy, JP in Bandy's Twsp; Wade Smith, Jacob Propst, LH Bandy. NL.

RUTLEDGE, John H. (26) of Gaston Co., NC; SHELTON, A.J. (22); white; M=19 Nov. 1878; JA Sherrill, Min. at DW Shelton's; EA Sherrill, DW Shelton, EA Caldwell. NL.

  W.I.; REINHARDT, S.J.; M=5 Jan. 1859; EW Thompson. NL.

  Wade P. (27) of Newton; FRY, Lucy (17) of Newton; white; M=27 May 1873; Daniel May, Meth. Min. in Nwt Twsp; RH Bost, CW Rockett, AJ Seagle. NL.

SAINE, Amos (21) of Lincoln Co., NC; MULL, Ida (17); white; M=10 Nov. 1878; WF Hull, Bapt. Min. at AB Mull's; PM Mull, Calvin Mosteller, WB Mull. NL.

SANDERS, Miles S. [Chesson & Adoline]; COBB, Charlotte [Rufus & Martha]; M=3 May 1869; Archibald Ervin, Min. NL.

SANFORD, Hoses; PAGE, Polly; M=24 Sept. 1865; LB Abernathy, JP. NL.

SCHENK, Monroe (21) [William & Lenie]; WILSON, Synthia (18) [Lewis & Jane]; black; M=29 Nov. 1879; JA Foil, Min. at Newton Twsp; WA Leantz, SC Foil, Robert H. Coulter. 1-411.

SCHEREN, Rev. Simeon; ROSEMAN, Sarah A.; M=6 Feb. 1855; LC Gooseclose, Min. NL.

SCOTS, J.Q.; ROWE, JM; M=9 Jan. 1861; CW Herman, JP. NL.

SCRONCE, Alberta (20); FRY, Leah (37) [Connor & Nancy]; white; M=6 Oct. 1872; JL Huit, JP in Cald. Twsp; Noah Setzer, MH Taylor, Logan Cline. 1-203.

  Thomas [Jacob & Barbara]; MILLER, Caroline [Absalon & Leah]; M=7 Apr. 1872; AJ Fox, Min. 1-204.

SEABOCK, George D. (23); HOUK, Alace (19); white; M=10 Feb. 1876; Abel Barger, JP at Harrison Houck's; AA Spencer, JA Seabock, WP Reinhardt. NL.

  Jacob A. (21) [Jacob A. & Rutha S.] of Hky Tav. Twsp; CLINE, Lou Ellen (17) [n/k & C.R. Cline] of Hky Tav. Twsp; white; M=21 Nov.1872; Moses Teague, P in Hky Tav. Twsp; JA Seabock, GP Seabock, JM Seabock. 1-202.

  James M. (22); HOUK, Emma (18); white; M=25 Mar. 1877; Abel Barger, JP in Hky; ME Houk, CM Seabock, GW Seabock. NL.

  John; CLINE, Mary J.; M=28 Aug. 1862; PC Henkle, Min. NL.

SEAGLE, A.J.; HARRIS, H.H.; M=18 Dec. 1859; J. Davis Wilson, Min. NL.

  Adam; WHITENER, Emeline; M=11 Feb. 1864; PL Rowe, JP. NL.

  Benjamin F. (32) [Daniel & Mary]; HATTWANGER, Josie (25) [Rev. G. & n/k]; white; M=19 May 1880; VR Stickley, Luth. Min. at Western Hotel, Hky; NM Seagle, FB Alexander, HD Abernethy. 2-101.

  Daniel (21); CAHILL, Mary (18); white; M=18 July 1878; JM Smith, Luth. Min. at JM Smith's; FC Sigmon, JPA Herman, RW Robinson. NL.

SEAGLE, Jacob A. (22) [John J. & Barbara] of Lincoln Co., NC;
    CANSLER, Frances R. (20) [Henry & Polly]; white; M=19 Aug.
    1874; ML Little, Min. in Jacob's Fork Twsp; JW Hipp, DL
    Warlick, MK Coon. 1-263.
  John W. (22) [Alfred & Morsisser]; BARGER, Barbara C. (25) [Mose
    & Sallie]; white; M=8 Apr. 1875; Abel Barger, JP in Hky Tav.
    Twsp; JS Cook, John M. Barger, Agnes E. Barger. 1-297.
  Macon; REINHARDT, Harriet L.; M=18 Dec. 1866; RL Davis, Min. NL.
  W.L. [George & Malinda]; RITCHEY, A.E. [Henry & Susanna]; M=20
    Aug.1868; John Watts, Min. NL.
  Wesley [Joseph & Mary]; CLINE, Sarah A. [Aaron & Nancy]; M=16
    Dec. 1871; JW Bandy, JP. NL.
SECREST, Hoke C. (23); STINSON, Maggie (23); white; M=5 Mar. 1877;
    JC Hartsell, Min. in Newton; SM Secrest, FJ Hartsell, Mollie
    M. Hartsell. 1-319.
SEGLE, Andrew [George & Sarah]; RHONEY, Martha Ann [John & Jane];
    M=31 Dec. 1871; JW Bandy, JP. 1-120.
SEITZ, Abel P. (21) [Davis D. & Rebecca]; SIGMON, Fannie E. (16)
    [Jacob & Lina]; white; M=13 Nov.1879; PF Smith, JP in Newton
    Twsp; Sarah Seitz, BM Morrow, FC Smith. 1-412.
  Darius D. (20) of Hky Tav. Twsp; HUFFMAN, Sarah E. (18) of
    Hky Tav. Twsp; white; M=27 Aug. 1873; Abel Whitener, JP of
    Hky Tav. Twsp; Mary Huffman, Catharine Seitz, Jackson
    Huffman. NL.
  F.M. (21) [Levi & Evegeline]; ABEE, C.M. (18) [Ephraim & Law];
    white; M=23 Mar. 1879; JH Bruns, JP in Hky Twsp; DW Rowe,
    JR Whitener, AP Rowe. 1-413.
  J.C.; WARLICK, Rachel C.; M=6 Mar. 1860; Daniel May, Min.
    NL.
  Jones P. (21); WHISENANT, Amanda L. (21); white; M=13 Dec. 1877;
    Jacob Mosteller, PJ in Bandy's Twsp; W. Whisenant, AM Propst.
    NL.
  L.P. [DD & Rebecca]; BAKER, Belza [David & Sarah]; M=20 Feb.
    1868; PC Henkel, Esq. NL.
  Marcus; WILKIE, Caroline; M=6 Nov. 1856; Alexander Aber-
    nathy, Min. NL.
SELF, W.R.; BOST, Mary M.; M=13 May 1858; AJ Fox, Min. NL.
SELVY, J.N. [John & Ann]; HUFFMAN, Nina [Jacob & Caty]; M=26 Mar.
    1868; J. Loretz, Min. NL.
SENS, George Cline; HEFNER, Mary Ann; M=16 June 1863; M. Barger,
    JP. NL.
SETTLEMIRE, David; MILLER, Sarah Ann; M=14 Oct. 1868; EA Warlick,
    JP. NL.
  George; BOST, Anna; M=27 Mar. 1855; William L. Mehaffey, JP.
    NL.
SETTLEMYER, Henry; PONDER, Margaret; M=18 Aug. 1863; Henry Cline,
    JP. NL.
SETTLEMYRE, Allen M. (29); PROPST, Sarah E. (22); white; M=7 Sept.
    1875; GL Hunt, Luth. Min. at GL Hunt's; NW Propst, EE Miller,
    LC Propst. NL.
  George P. (27) of Caldwell Twsp; DEAL, Fannie M. (26)
    of Newton Twsp; white; M=18 Dec. 1873; JM Smith, Luth. Min.
    at Eliza Deal's; MS Deal, ML Setzer, TP Cloninger. NL.
  J.P.; REECE, M.R.; M=21 Nov. 1865; Eli Starr, JP. NL.

SETTLEMYRE, Martin D. (27) [Paul & Clarasey]; SMYRE, Lovina P. (23) [John & Louisa]; white; M=8 May 1879; JM Smith, Luth. Min. in Newton; WM Smyre, SF Huffman, CE Smyre. 1-414.

SETZER, Albentus (22); POWELL, Genelia Sallie (21); black; M=12 May 1874; William Brooks, Min. at Gold Mine; Alex Nail, Mary Nail, Jona Powell. NL.

Albert H. (25); SHUFORD, Dora (18); white; M=12 Dec. 1877; JA Sherrill, Min. at PC Shuford's; J. Turner, LA Shuford, John H. Powell. NL.

Alfred M.; SETZER, Polly; M=25 Nov. 1857; PJ Pitts, JP. NL.

Andrew (22) [Rufus & Mira]; POWELL, Fannie (21) [Davis Holdsclaw & Jane Powell]; black; M=23 Oct. 1879; William M. Brooks, Meth. Min.; Sidna Shaphe, Aryler Shaphe, Burton Shaphe. 1-415.

Calvin; ABERNATHY, Rebecca; M=13 May 1862; LN Wilson, JP. NL.

Carr [Daniel & Susan]; DEAL, M.C. [Henry & Rebecca]; M=22 Dec. 1867; PC Henkel, Min. NL.

Charles A. (26); DEAL, Rhoda (20); white; M=19 Mar. 1876; JM Smith, Luth. Min. at JM Smith's; CT Sipe, AN Sigmon, WB Finger. NL.

Daniel [Daniel & Polly]; WIKE, Martha A. [David & Delila]; M=24 Nov. 1870; PF Smith, JP. 1-35.

David; SETZER, Sarah; M=20 Jan. 1853; WL Mehaffey, JP. NL.

David P.; MULL, Barbara; M=18 Oct. 1855; DE Warlick, Min. NL.

David P.; SHERRILL, Margaret; M=18 Feb. 1852; Hosea Linebarger, JP. NL.

Ellihue (21); CATHEY, Mariah (20); black; M=21 Dec. 1876; WS Shuford, Bapt. Min. at Jack Caldwell's; FC Caldwell, A. Sherrill, Charles Byers. NL.

George C. (24) [Thomas & Elizabeth] of Fairfield Co., SC; ROWE, Sarah Alice (22) [MM & Saling]; white; M=4 Dec. 1879; JC Clapp, Min. in Newton Twsp; LR Clapp, Dan Smyre, MO Sherrill. 1-416.

George W. (23); CARPENTER, Mary Jane (21); white; M=11 Feb. 1874; JC Clapp, Ref. Min. at John Carpenter's; Silas Smyre, John Hapt, Daniel Smyer. NL.

Harrison (22) [Aaron & Polly] of Mt. Crk Twsp; MCCORKLE, Sarah Jenelia (16) [Robert & Aveline] of Mt. Crk Twsp; black; M=17 Aug. 1872; JA Sherrill, Min. in Mt. Crk Twsp; LP Eckard, John W. Gabriel, Fannie E. Gabriel. 1-205.

Henry L. [Jacob & Lillie]; HUIT, Laura; M=1871; Record Missing. NL.

Israel (21); SHERRILL, Caroline (19); black; M=3 Feb. 1876; CW Blalock, Min. at Miles Sherrill's; WW Pope, Andy Setzer, Fayett Shuford. NL.

J.C.; HARRISON, Sally; M=12 Aug. 1857; William L. Mehaffey, JP. NL.

J.H.; LITTLE, M.D.; M=22 Jan. 1861; W. Carson, Min. NL.

J.S.; CLONINGER, Elizabeth C.; M=14 Mar. 1866; J. Lantz, Min. NL.

Jacob; HERMAN, Emmela; M=12 Sept. 1851; William L. Mehaffey, JP. NL.

Jacob; FRAISURE, Nancy M.; M=23 Sept. 1851; HB Witherspoon, JP. NL.

Jacob; FRASURE, Nancy M.; M=4 Oct. 1851; HB Witherspoon, JP. NL.

SETZER, Jacob (73); DEITZ, Patsy Bertha A. (33); white; M=21 Mar. 1878; PK Little, JP in Cline's Twsp; HS Smith, DL Holler, HA Kale. NL.
   James H.; HUNSUCKER, Orpha M.; M=25 Sept. 1851; GJ Wilkie, JP. NL.
   James P.; HAMILTON, Catharine; M=26 July 1866; JA Sherrill, Min. NL.
   James P. (34); HOLBROOKS, Sarah J. (23); white; M=8 Sept. 1878; WC Caldwell, JP in Cald. Twsp; John Withers, George Bell, Pinkney Abernathy. NL.
   John; CONNER, D.M.; M=6 Sept. 1859; LM Berry, Min. NL.
   Joshua (32) of Newton Twsp; DEAL, Sarah (22); black; M=31 Dec. 1873; PF Smith, PJ in Newton; JA Wile, JA Yont, Hosea Deal. NL.
   Marcus; YOUNT, Margaret; M=3 Feb. 1853; Eli E. Deal, JP. NL.
   Marcus C. (22); CARPENTER, Ellen (17); white; M=7 Feb. 1875; Daniel May, Min. at Monroe Sigmon's; Logan Smyre, Daniel Setzer. NL.
   Noah; HUIT, Frances; M=7 Mar. 1866; LN Wilson, JP. NL.
   Noah (22); SIGMON, Ellen (17); white; M=29 Oct. 1874; PF Smith, JP in Newton; MC Setzer, Gerome Bolch, JK Smith. NL.
   Noah (22) of Caldwell Twsp; ABERNATHY, Ann (18) of Caldwell Twsp; white; M=4 Sept. 1873; PF Smith, JP in Newton Twsp; G. Arndt, Eliza Witherspoon, Mame Wilson. NL.
   Patrick [Jacob & Delila]; WITHERSPOON, Margaret [Miles & Sarah]; M=27 Dec. 1871; JL Hewit, JP. 1-112.
   Quincy A. (22) [Reuben & Lovina] of Newton Twsp; SMYRE, Catharine E. (19) [Logan & Emaline]; white; M=13 May 1875; JC Clapp, Min. in Newton Twsp; NH Fry, JM Arndt, JF Smyre. 1-298.
   Thomas A. (21); SMYER, Alace A. (18); white; M=12 Sept. 1878; JC Clapp, Ref. Min. in Newton; Julius Smyer, Daniel Smyer, Elkanah Bolch. NL.
   W.H. [Jacob & Delila]; SMITH, Eveline F. [MM & MC]; M=7 May 1868; D. McD. Yount, Esq. NL.
   William A.; BOST, H.Y.; M=27 Nov. 1860; LN Wilson, JP. NL.
   William B. (24) [Logan & Tabitha]; CALDWELL, Eva (19) [Phillip & Sarah]; white; M=24 Dec. 1879; JC Clapp, Min. in Caldwell Twsp; PH Deal, HH Caldwell, Phillip Caldwell. 1-417.
SHARP, P.M.; KILLIAN, Margaret C.; M=5 Jan. 1864; DE Warlick, Min. NL.
   Solamon G. [Solamon & Hester]; ANGEL, Martha M. [David & Sarah]; M=23 Dec. 1870; ST Wilfong, JP. 1-36.
SHAW, James (37); JAMES, Catharine (20); black; M=7 Oct. 1878; Wm G. James in Hamilton Twsp; Charley Sausm, John Reinhardt, Flaran Hunsucker. NL.
SHELL, John S. (28) of Newton Twsp; MILLER, Sarah Ann P. (18) of Newton Twsp; white; M=28 Aug. 1873; JM Smith, Luth. Min. at JM Smith's; SS Shell, SAC Bost, CR Henkle. NL.
   William (32) of Newton Twsp; CLINE, Callie (23) of Hky Tav. Twsp; white; M=27 Aug. 1873; JM Smith, LUth. Min. at JM Smith's; JS Shell, SAC Bost, AM Settlemyre. NL.
   William G. [RM & Frances]; ABERNATHY, Emma A. [Alburtus F. & Sophia]; M=30 Dec. 1871; Abel Whitener, JP. 1-113.

SHELTON, A.F. (25); CALDWELL, Martha A. (20); white; M=11 Jan. 1877; JA Sherrill, Min. at JA Sherrill's; LA Rudisill, AJ Perkins, ML Sherrill. NL.
  Elihue L. (19) of Lincoln Co., NC; CRANFORD, Nancy Ann (16); white; M=14 Oct. 1874; JW Pruett, Min. at Cranfords; WA Loftin, JF Mundy, AF Shelton. NL.
  Julius P. [John & Lucy]; MONDAY, Francis [Spencer & Susan]; M=25 Feb. 1869; JA Sherrill, Min. NL.
  Thomas [Samuel L. & Palina]; SHERRILL, Ugene [Jepthey & Eliza]; M=10 July 1869; JA Sherrill, Min. NL.
SHEPERD, John; HEFNER, Sarah; M=15 Apr. 1852; JB Little, JP. NL.
SHEPHARD, Polycarp C. (22); DEATZ, Malinda M. (21); white; M=18 Mar. 1877; CT Sigmon, JP in Cline's Twsp; MJ Shephard, LER Sigmon, AM Sigmon. NL.
SHERMAN, Charles H. (39); LOWRANCE, Maggie (28); white; M=23 Oct. 1877; JC Hartsell, Min. at JC Hartsell's; JA Lowrance, JM Blackwelder, John P. Kendall. NL.
SHERRILL, Aaron A. (23) [JH & Juda] of Iredell Co., NC; CALDWELL, Octa (21) [AJ & Sarah]; white; M=16 Dec. 1878; TL Triplett, Meth.Min. at AJ Caldwell's; JW Long, WO Cornelius, Josephus Cornelius. 1-320.
  Alonzo (22) [James A. & Mary] of Newton, NC; DEAL, Amanda (23) [Jonas & Malinda] of Newton, NC; white; M=29 Sept. 1872; PF Smith, JP in Newton Twsp; JS Deal, EL Bowman, John E. Thornton. 1-206.
  Andrew P. [BW & Amanda]; TEAGUE, Mary Ellen [Moses & Margaret]; M=2 Feb. 1871; JH Bruns, JP. 1-114.
  Ben [n/k & Nancy]; PAINE, Emeline [n/k & Chany Wilson]; M=16 Nov. 1868; RA Cobb, JP. NL.
  Burt [Sidney & Lucinda]; SHIPP, Martha [Wesley & Winnie]; M=26 Dec. 1867; JW Gabriel, Esq. NL.
  Calvin W. [Washington & Martha]; LITTEN, Mary Ann R. [Moury & n/k]; M=8 May 1870; JA Sherrill, Min. NL.
  Ceburn (22); WHITENER, Anna (19); white; M=26 Feb. 1879; JA Sherrill, Min. at Elizabteh Whitener's; WF Sherrill, HS Gabriel, AE Sherrill. NL.
  Christopher; CUNENT, Martha; M=11 June 1854; William L. Mehaffey, JP. NL.
  Daniel H. (21) [Reuben & Rodian]; HOOPER, Alice (28) [William & Eliza]; black; M=4 Nov. 1880; William Brooks, Min. in Hamilton Twsp; Pauline Sherrill, Henry Harboryer, William Hooper. 2-102.
  David M. (19) [Robert & Martha]; ALLISON, Rachel (20) [John & Elizabeth]; white; M=13 Feb. 1873; JA Sherrill, Min. in Hamilton Twsp; SC Brown, JH Fisher, Miles Saunders. 1-252.
  E.A. (25); BEATY, Susan V. (17); white; M=29 Jan. 1879; JA Sherrill, Min. at GW Beaty's; John Gabriel, MM Gabriel, MW Sherrill. NL.
  Elihue [William Read & Ludena Sherrill]; GABRIEL, Jane [Andrew & Polly]; M=5 May 1870; JA Sherrill, Min. NL.
  Elisha; SHERRILL, Caroline; M=26 Sept. 1854; William Long, JP. NL.
  Enos; LITTEN, Margaret; M=24 July 1862; SM Berry, Min. NL.
  Francis M. (23); BRADBURN, Susan (33); white; M=5 Jan. 1876; JA Sherrill, Min. at Thomas Bradburn's; SC Brown, TF Bradburn, J. Turner. NL.

SHERRILL, Hiram (21) [Isaac N. & Martha J.]; SHERRILL, Martha J. (16) [Jacob & Harriett]; white; M=8 Oct. 1879; GW Fry, Min. in Denver, NC; WF Sherrill, ?. 1-418.

J.C. [Jacob & Ann]; LITTLE, Manerva [Thomas Cloninger & Sarah]; M=15 Sept. 1869; A. Hayse, Min. NL.

J. Clancy (21); SHERRILL, Ann (21); white; M=8 Apr. 1875; SC Brown, JP in Hamilton Twsp; AE Brown, MJ Brown, ME Day. NL.

J.W. Henderson (20) [John & Mira]; SHERRILL, Jane (19) [Bedford & Barbara]; black; M=30 July 1879; MM Gabriel, JP in Mt. Crk Twsp; John Sherrill, VG Gabriel, William Linn. 1-419.

J. Wesley (22) [Enus & Ruannah]; SHERRILL, Margaret Ann (18) [Marion & Espey]; white; M=27 Feb. 1873; JA Sherrill, Min. in Mt. Crk Twsp; EF Sherrill, SW Sherrill, John Gabriel. 1-253.

Jacob; SHERRILL, Harriet; M=28 Feb. 1855; WC Patterson, Min. NL.

James (26); LITTLE, Mary C. (18); white; M=10 Jan. 1875; LA Lockman, JP in Mt. Crk Twsp; BW Howard, JH ?, HC Barkley. NL.

James A.; MICHAEL, Sarah S.; M=25 Sept. 1866; EA Warlick, JP. NL.

James M. [Washington & Matty]; WILLIAMSON, Hatty [Milton & n/g]; M=1 Jan. 1871; JA Sherrill, Min. 1-115.

Jason A. (24) [Jeptha & Eliza]; SHUFORD, Laura J. (20) [PC & Nancy]; white; M=15 Dec. 1880; PFW Stamey, Min. in Catawba Twsp; CF Powell, FA Sherrill, JP Sherrill. 2-103.

Jasper; LOFTIN, Etta; M=19 Dec. 1865; PJ Pitts, JP. NL.

John [Richard & Mary]; MCCORKLE, Rozanna [n/k & Mary Clark]; M= 7 Apr. 1868; JW Gabriel, JP. NL.

John; YOUNT, S.A.; M=1 May 1866; JA Sherrill, Min. NL.

John (30) of Caldwell {County?/Township?}; TEAGUE, Mattie S. (23); white; M=22 Feb. 1877; JC Hartsell, Min. in Newton; Lucy Foard, Laura Bost, FJ Hartsell. NL.

John N.; HOLDSCLAW, Camela; M=11 Jan. 1860; William Long, JP. NL.

Joseph Henry (34) [Logan N. & Sarah N. Eckard] of Mt. Crk Twsp; BYNUM, Candice (32) [John C. & Candice] of Hamilton Twsp; white; M=11 Dec. 1872; JA Sherrill, Min. in Hamilton Twsp; JW Gabriel, Sarah E. Ekcard, LP Eckard. 1-207.

M.A. [E & R]; BROTHERTON, F.E. [Hugh & T. Brotherton]; M=11 Nov. 1869; JA Sherrill, Min. NL.

M.W.; CORNELIUS, Mattie E.; M=12 Oct. 1865; JA Sherrill, Min. NL.

Miles W.; LEE, Elizabeth; M=12 Sept. 1858; William L. Mehaffey, JP. NL.

Morris [Jack & Dianah]; HOWARD, Rebeccah [Hiram & Violet]; M=29 June 1871; A. Sherrill, JP. 1-116.

Philo (21) [Frank & Camilla] of Alexander Co., NC; POPE, Susan (21) [George & Sallie]; white; M=30 Oct. 1879; PK Little, JP in Cline's Twsp; JB Little, Daniel Shook, David Christopher. 1-420.

R.H.; MUNDAY, Jane; M=2 Mar. 1851; H. Asbury, Min. NL.

Richard [Tobias & Meriah]; WILSON, Jemima [Merissa]; M=18 Dec. 1870; JL Hewit, JP. 1-37.

Robert W. (21) [Wicklif & Elizer]; BROTHERTON, Mary Jane (23) [John & Menervy] of Lincoln Co., NC; white; M=8 Oct. 1879; JA Sherrill, Min. in Mt. Crk Twsp; HD Howard, AB Sherrill, HF? 1-421.

SHERRILL, Sidney; GANTT, Frances; M=30 Jan. 1859; JD Caldwell, JP. NL.
  T. Martin (21); INGRAM, Mira (16); white; M=31 July 1877; SC Brown, JP in Catawba; EC Kate, William L. Rea, JA Ingram. NL.
  Thomas [Nelson & Martha]; TROUTMAN, Linea; M=1871. NL.
  Thomas (24) [Pinkney & Martha]; ROBINSON, Susan Lillie (17) [June & Sarah]; white; M=22 Jan. 1880; JA Sherrill, Min. in Mt. Crk Twsp; PF Bandy, RW Sherrill, TA Sherrill. 1-422.
  Thomas Alex (21); ROBINSON, Laura (17); white; M=21 May 1874; LA Lockman, JP in Mt. Crk Twsp; AE Sherrill, ME Robinson, TF Conner. NL.
  William [Timothy Herman & n/k]; BYARS, Lucinda; M=17 Dec. 1868; F. Caldwell, JP. NL.
  William F. [Isaac N. & Martha J.]; RUDDECK, Mary Jane [William Little & Martha Ann Little]; M=22 Nov. 1871; JA Sherrill, Min. 1-117.
  Woodford; HOWARD, Molly M.; M=17 Aug. 1866; JS Nelson, Min. NL.
SHOOK, Daniel; HUFFMAN, Emeline; M=23 Nov. 1865; DMC Yount, JP. NL.
  Daniel [Daniel & Polly]; SIGMON, Anna [Alanson & Mahala]; M=26 Mar. 1871; William G. James, JP. NL.
  Emanuel [David & Matilda]; HEFNER, Camila [Lewis & Rosanah]; M=6 June 1872; GL Hunt, Min. 1-208.
  Franklin; MOSER, Leah J.; M=19 Apr. 1864; JHA Yount, JP. NL.
  Franklin (21); YOUNT, Azline (19); white; M=8 Feb. 1877; HA Forney, JP in Newton; WD Huffman, Jacob Hefner, Elisha Huffman. NL.
  Fredrick [David & Matilda]; CHRISTOPLE, Manervey [David & Sarah] M=10 Aug. 1871; William H. Rockett, JP. 1-118.
  George R. [Andrew & Nancy]; HEDRICK, Delila [Joseph & Catharine] M=22 Dec. 1870; William H. Rockett, JP. 1-38.
  Henry; MILLER, Barbara; M=21 Feb. 1857; E. Conner, PJ. NL.
  John C. [Fredrick & Barbara]; LOWRANCE, Susan C. [Clinton & Harriet]; M=17 Nov. 1870; JM Smith, Min. 1-39.
  John F.; MOSER, Rhoda; M=15 Sept. 1858; JB Little, JP. NL.
  Lawson; LAEL, Rany; M=28 Nov. 1866; DMD Yount, JP. NL.
  Miles W.; FULBRETH, Manerva; M=8 Feb. 1852; Eli E. Deal, JP. NL.
  Reubin [Jacob & Polly]; HEFNER, Sarah [Miles & Polly]; M=10 Aug. 1871; William H. Rockett, PJ. 1-119.
  Tobus; DEAL, C.E.; M=4 Jan. 1866; GJ Wilkie, Min. NL.
  William; HAGLER, Bettie; M=1 June 1866; JB Little, JP. NL.
  William H. (23); LOWRANCE, Dora (21); white; M=25 Nov. 1874; PL Herman, Min. in Newton; TS Shook, JK Smith, J. Deal. NL.
SHOOPING, Gilbert (19); CLINE, Margaret (17); white; M=8 May 1876; JG Grice, JP in Mt. Crk Twsp; James Starnes, Miller Ann Grice, EM Grice. NL.
SHORES, Eli (35); SHUFORD, Ellen (21); black; M=23 Jan. 1875; JH Bruns, JP in Hky; FA Clinard, John N. Robinson. NL.
  Eli (45) [n/k & Ailsey Shores]; GROSS, Delia (25) [Sandy & Caroline]; black; M=11 Nov. 1880; EJ Harris, Min. at Hky Twsp; Alen Lewis, Harrit Wilson, Franklin Drum. 2-104.
SHRONCE, Ephraim (19) [Syntha Shronce]; LEATHERMAN, Martha SE (19) white; M=29 June 1879; CA Gantt, Meth. Min. in Jacobs Fork Twsp; Eli Johnson, LR Shuford, JH Sigmon. 1-423.

SHUFORD, A.D.L.; SHERRILL, Martha Ann; M=16 May 1866; JA Sherrill, Min. NL.
  Abel A. (31) [Jacob H. & Catherine] of Hky Tav. Twsp; CAMPBELL, Alda V. (22) [Ogbon & Catherine] of Newton Twsp; white; M= 18 Dec. 1873; JC Clapp, Min. in Newton Twsp; John Baker, Capt. Robert Bost, TR Abernathy. 1-254.
  D.H. [Danel & Rosanah]; RAMSOUR, Bell [Alfred & Jane]; M=6 Sept. 1870; AJ Fox, Min. NL.
  D.P. [John M. & Margaret]; SHUFORD, Mary Ann [OC & Rosa]; M=21 Sept.1867; AJ Fox, Min. NL.
  Daniel J. (26); MOSTELLER, Livonia P. (27); white; M=14 Nov. 1876; ML Little, Luth. Min. at J. Mosteller's; DH Shuford, Rufus Mosteller, Daniel C. Shuford. NL.
  Franklin; LARKLIN, Isabel; M=29 Mar. 1856; AJ Whitener, JP. NL.
  Israel (63) of Bandy's Twsp; WEAVER, Levina (53) of Bandy's Twsp; white; M=4 Mar. 1873; JW Bandy, JP in Bandy's Twsp; Frank Shuford, Sal Shuford, AS Hudson. NL.
  Joel F. (21); HOWARD, L. Susan (19); white; M=27 July 1875; John A. Foil, Ref. Min. at Sarah Howard's; JF Howard, WB Shuford, HF Powell. NL.
  John (21) [Solamon & Hanah] of Jacob's Fork Twsp; ROBINSON, Lydia (18) [Thomas & Eliza] of Jacob's Fork Twsp; black; M= 31 July 1872; George McClain, AME Zion Church Min. in Jacob's Fork Twsp. 1-209.
  John L.; ABERNATHY, Salina; M=8 Jan. 1852; George Huffman, JP. NL.
  John M. [Jacob H. & Catherine]; WILSON, Allie A. [MM & Catherine]; M=15 Jan. 1870; JC Clapp, Min. NL.
  Laban R. (22); LINK, Sarah L. (19); white; M=3 Apr. 1877; JL Huit, JP in Caldwell Twsp; William Rabb, Charlie Fry, David Beel. NL.
  Labe [Herve & Sela]; SHUFORD, Charlotte [Lewis Blair & Sarah Shuford]; M=7 Jan. 1872; William Brooks, Min. NL.
  Lafayette [Lewis Cansler & Anna Cansler]; BROOKS, Hanna [William & Hannah]; M=8 Feb. 1868; HA Lowrance, JP. NL.
  Logan H. (24) [Levi A. & Catherine]; PEARSON, Ida N. (21) [Isaac A. & Matilda]; white; M=29 July 1874; PL Herman, Min. in Hamilton Twsp; CH Herman, WE Lowrance, QM Little. 1-264.
  Marion [Jim & Katy]; GOODSON, Caroline; M=18 July 1868; HA Lowrance, JP. NL.
  Maxwell [David & Elizabeth]; RHONEY, Elmainda; M=1871. Record Missing. NL.
  P.C.; TURNER, N.C.; M=15 Sept. 1858; JS Ervin. NL.
  Pink [Robert & Eliza]; ROSEMAN, Sylvia [Augustus & Malinda]; M=3 Oct. 1867; EA Warlick, JP. NL.
  Rufus (47); COWHONE, Elizabeth (26); black; M=4 Apr. 1877; JB Turner, Min. in Hky Twsp; Lee Lutz, Fayett Sigmon, Frank Crowell. NL.
  Thomas F.; MARTIN, H.R.; M=1870. No other information. NL.
  W.P.; RAMSOUR, Emma E.; M=28 Oct. 1866; J. Ingold, Min. NL.
  Wallie S. [George & Mary]; SHERRILL, Jane [Laney & Cinday]; M= 25 Dec. 1867. NL.

SIGMON, A.E.; SHOOK, Polly M.; M=8 Nov. 1857; JB Little, JP. NL.
 A.P. [Jesse & Adoline]; TURNER, Lidia R. [William & Caty]; M=1 Oct. 1868; IH Burns, JP. NL.
 A.S. (34); POLLARD, Martha (17); white; M=24 Dec. 1878; GL Hunt, Luth. Min. at Elizabeth Sigmon's; LA Sigmon, CR Sigmon, GW Settlemyre. NL.
 Aaron Y. (26); WINKLER, Agnes (20); white; M=27 Apr. 1876; Abel Whitener, JP in Hky; Aaron Sigmon, WH Sigmon, HC Sigmon. NL.
 Abel [William & Elizabeth]; LINK, B.P. [David & Polly]; M=9 May 1869; PC Hinkle, Min. NL.
 Adolphus (24); HALLMAN, Anna (23); white; M=26 May 1875; Abel Whitener, JP in Hky Tav. Twsp; DM Whitener, GM Whitener, EA Whitener. NL.
 Adolphus N. (21); DEAL, Fannie A. (18); white; M=11 Nov. 1875; PK Little, Cline's Twsp; JK Smith, CH Sipe, Perry K. Sigmon. NL.
 Alexander H. [Harrison & Sarah]; MONDAY, Jane V. [Spencer & Susan]; M=31 Mar. 1869; JA Sherrill, Min. NL.
 Alfonzo (25); SIGMON, Mary Ellen (20); white; M=1 Dec. 1878; PK Little, JP in Cline's Twsp; MM Smith, WS Setzer, PS Sigmon. NL.
 Benjamin; SIPE, Susan; M=17 Sept. 1859; Wm L. Mehaffey, JP. NL.
 Calvin S.; SMITH, Manerva; M=22 Sept. 1859; PC Hinkle, Min. NL.
 Carrey; NAUGLE, Harriet; M=4 Mar. 1858; Wm L. Mehaffey, JP. NL.
 Churchwell J. (26) [Able & Emeline] of Jacob's Fork Twsp; ABERNATHY, Elizabeth (21) [Moses & Polly] of JF Twsp; white; M=20 Feb. 1873; Robert Helton of Hky Tav. Twsp; HG Seitz, LA Hawn, HM Lentz. 1-255.
 Daniel (25); HARTZOE, Emaline (30); white; M=13 July 1876; Abel Whitener, JP in Hky; OA Sigmon, LH Huggins, Eliza Whitener. NL.
 David; DEITZ, Catharine; M=2 Sept. 1862; JM Yoder, JP. NL.
 David E. [Eli & Mary]; HARTSOWE, Sarah A. [Eli & Sally]; M=14 Dec. 1868; JT Hughes, Min. NL.
 David M. (22); SHRUM, Mary Jane (24) of Lincoln Co., NC; white; M=17 Oct. 1876; JL Huitt, JP in Cald. Twsp; Eliza Keener, F. Shrum, Christena Huitt. NL.
 David S. [Jonas & Jemima]; WITHERSPOON, Catherine [Nelson & Malinda]; M=7 Oct. 1869; JL Huit, JP. NL.
 Dock B.J. (23); FISH, Mattie (18); white; M=13 Apr. 1876; JA Sherrill, Min. at Bryson Fish's; JA Stiles, MA Sigmon, ML Sigmon. NL.
 E.G.; HEFNER, Elema; M=11 Oct. 1860; JHA Yount, JP. NL.
 Elcana; DEAL, Eliza; M=26 Sept. 1852; Eli E. Deal, JP. NL.
 Emanuel (21) [William & Susan]; HUIT, Sarah "Sally" (35) [David & Nancy]; white; M=5 May 1875; PF Smith, JP in Newton Twsp; Perry Deal, Perry A. Bolch, Amy Barringer. 1-299.
 Emanuel [William & ? Lomax]; SETZER, Margaret; M=1871; Record Missing. NL.
 Emanuel; DEAL, Lucinda; M=25 Sept. 1866; D McD Yount, JP. NL.
 Harrison (54); MCKAY, Marrenia (43); white; M=10 Feb. 1874; JA Sherrill, Min. at JA Sherrill's; LA Rudisill, Cal Kerley, ML Sherrill. NL.
 Henry A. (21) [Aranius & Jimina]; BOLCH, Sarah J. (22) [Andrew & Rosa]; white; M=19 Dec. 1880; GL Hunt, Luth. Min. at Newton Twsp; WJ Pharr, JM Poovey, JA Propst. 2-105.

SIGMON, Henry F. (24); PROPST, Mary A. (18); white; M=4 Dec. 1878; AJ Fox, Min. at JW Propst's; A. Anthony, Mary Jarret, Cath E. Sigmon. NL.

Hosea Pinkney (19) [Barnett & Martha Ann]; DOUGLAS, Alice (19) [James & Rosea]; white; M=4 Oct. 1875; JL Hewit, JP of Cald. Twsp; HC Cline, John Keener, James Lineberger. 1-300.

James E. (24); CLINE, Angeline (28); white; M=4 Apr. 1877; Abel Barger, JP in Hky; WH Settlemyre, JW Settlemyre, JP Settlemyre. NL.

James Edney [Eli & Elizabeth]; HARTSOE, Elizabeth [Eli & Sally]; M=19 Sept. 1868; EJ Coulter, JP. NL.

James W.; FISHER, Anna M.; M=26 May 1853; Thomas Ward, JP. NL.

Jesse [Jesse & Adaline]; HAWN, Sarah [John & Elizabeth]; M=9 Mar. 1871; EA Warlick, JP. 1-121.

Jethro; HEVNER, Mary; M=23 Sept. 1852; PC Henkle, Min. NL.

John C.; HARRIS, Nancy C.; M=22 July 1866; Wm L. Mehaffey, JP. NL.

John E. (27); GUTHRIE, Mary (27); white; M=27 Jan. 1875; JL Hewit, JP in Cald. Twsp; Forcus Sipe, Louis Guthrie, Candace Sigmon. NL.

John H. (25) [Noah & Malinda]; WORKMAN, Susan (22) [Henry & Caroline]; white; M=9 Dec. 1875; Robert Helton, Min. in Jacob's Fork Twsp; R. Helton, JW Helton, MA Leonard. 1-301.

John H. (26) of Newton Twsp; RHODES, Julian (21) of Newton Twsp; white; M=23 Dec. 1873; JM Smith, Luth. Min. at Caleb Rhodes'; JF Sitmon, John M. Rhodes, Martin L. Rhodes. NL.

John H. [Lawson & Malinda]; FRY, Julia [Phillip & Clarrisa]; M=29 May 1868; H. Cline, Esq. NL.

John L. (21) [Abel & Elizabeth]; TURNER, Harriett C. (22) [GW & Elmira]; white; M=31 Dec. 1879; JW Mouser, JP in Hky Twsp; AY Sigmon, CC Cody, RF Turner. 1-424.

Jonas T. (23) [Henry L. & Margaret M.] of Cline's Twsp; SMITH, Mary Ellen (21) [David & Catharine] of Hamilton Twsp; white; M=19 Dec. 1872; William H. Rockett, JP in Ham. Twsp; John Brown, Pierce Hoke, Knox Smith. 1-210.

Joshua; SIPE, Elby; M=4 Dec. 1861; JHA Yount, JP. NL.

Julius A. [David & Molly]; REESE, Juliann [Lewis & Amy]; M=31 Dec. 1868; James A. Garvan, JP. NL.

Julius S.; DEAL, Harriet G.; M=8 June 1856; H. Ingold, JP. NL.

Julius T. (26); FORSTER, Hannah (19); white; M=20 Feb. 1879; JC Clapp, Min. at CJ Forster's; MC Setzer, JH Sigmon, JA Douglas. NL.

L.H.; DRUM, E.A.; M=13 Dec. 1857; John Kent, JP. NL.

Lafayett (22) of Hky; JONES, Lydia (23) of Hky; black; M=5 Sept. 1877; JB Turner, Min. in Hky; AN Bowman, Walace Bridges, Birt Bellmore. NL.

Lewis; SETZER, Susan; M=19 Aug. 1851; Wm L. Mehaffey, JP. NL.

M.A.; SIGMON, M.E.; M=30 Jan. 1861; PC Henkel, Min. NL.

M.A.; TURNER, Harriet; M=18 Feb. 1864; E. Yount, JP. NL.

M.A.; RUDISILL, D.L.; M=19 Nov. 1865; JA Sherrill, Min. NL.

M.L. [Lawson & Mahaley]; SMITH, M.A.; M=17 Dec. 1869; PC Hinkle, Min. NL.

Marcus (21); FRY, Mary (20); white; M=8 June 1876; JL Huit, JP in Cald. Twsp; Frank Boyd, John Setzer, George Bost. NL.

SIGMON, Martin [Thomas & Nancy]; LITTLE, Susanah [Nelson Ray & Leanah Little]; M=24 Aug. 1871; Wm H. Rockett, JP. NL.
  Maxwell L. (20); BROWN, Alice S.C. (16); white; M=21 Feb. 1878; PK Little, JP in Cline's Twsp; JS Sigmon, HM Isaac, PC Hoke. NL.
  Miles [Logan & Sarah]; SHOOK, Adaline [Frederick & Barbra]; M=23 Feb. 1871; William G. James, JP. 1-123.
  Miles S. [LH & RE]; SETZER, Louiza [Logan & n/g]; M=3 Sept. 1871; TL Smith, JP. 1-122.
  Monroe (52); FRY, Catharine (21); white; M=9 Nov. 1876; JM Smith, Luth. Min. at Mrs. C. Fry's; PE Fry, ME Fry, JA Witherspoon. NL.
  N.M.; HOKE, Melinda; M=20 Sept. 1860; PC Hinkel, Min. NL.
  Nelson E. (30) [George & Elizabeth] of Cline's Twsp; ROCKETT, Martha J. (19) [William H. & Ann] of Cline's Twsp; white; M=23 Dec. 1873; JC Clapp, Min. in Cline's; Daniel Deal, Jacob Isenhour, WN Hunsucker. 1-256.
  Newson C. (22) [Adolphus & Malinda]; MILLER, Angeline (21) [Franklin & Mary]; white; M=23 Dec. 1880; JM Smith, Luth. Min. in Cline's Twsp; AM Huit, Lewis Huit, AE Sigmon. 2-106.
  Newton M. (37); HOKE, Amanda M. (33); white; M=16 Oct. 1877; JM Smith, Luth. Min. at JM Smith's; PP Hoke, EA Hoke, PC Hoke. NL.
  Noah; FRY, Melinda; M=27 Nov. 1851; Henry Cline, JP. NL.
  Perry [David & Mary]; ABERNATHY, Cate [Miles & Susie Clay]; M=24 Mar. 1870; Daniel May, Min. NL.
  Philo S. [Eli & Anna]; HEDRICK, Harriett [David & Malinda]; M=16 Nov. 1871; CT Sigmon, JP. 1-124.
  Pinkney W. (22) of Jacob's Fork Twsp; HERMAN, Callie (20) of Hky Tav. Twsp; white; M=24 Dec. 1873; JM Smith, Luth. Min. at FL Herman's; Julius Rowe, JS Coulter, John J. Reinhardt. NL.
  Reuben E. [Martin & Sally]; HOFFMAN, Lydia S. [Alfred & Malinda] M=24 Jan. 1869; PC Hinckle, Min. NL.
  Revle; SETZER, Rachel; M=26 Sept. 1858; PJ Pitts, JP. NL.
  Rufus (21) [William & Susan]; HEFNER, Jane (26) [George & Rachel]; white; M=26 Dec. 1880; PK Little, JP in Cline's; PH Hoke, Alfred Hefner, George Pope. 2-107.
  Sidney W. (21); DEAL, Catharine Adoline (20); white; M=26 Mar. 1874; GL Hunt, Luth. Min. at CA Deal's; GW Setzer, EA Sigmon, Elias Longcrier. NL.
  Silvanus (21) [Jerry & Adoline]; HOOVER, Eliza A. (20) [Daniel & Louisa]; white; M=4 Mar. 1875; JH Bruns, JP in Hky Twsp; W. Hoover, C. Hoover, S. Bolch. 1-302.
  Sylvanus (24) [Jessie & Adline]; MILLER, Cammila (21) [Paul & Mira]; white; M=21 Aug. 1879; PC Henkel, Min. at Newton Twsp; AS Ekard, Charles H. Henkel, TJ Wagner. 1-425.
  Thornton (19); LEFEVERS, Laura (20); white; M=16 Mar. 1876; JL Huitt, JP in Cald. Twsp; Sallie Boyd, MH Taylor, George Blankenship. NL.
  V.G. [Eli & Anna L.]; ICENHOUR, Lenor [Philip & Rebecca]; M=20 Sept. 1869; Wm H. Rockett, JP. NL.
  William; PROBST, Adoline; M=21 Dec. 1853; WL Mehaffey, JP. NL.
  William (25); MILLER, Delia (25); white; M=14 Nov. 1878; JH Bruns, JP in Hky; G. Marshall, JB Baker, MF Tomlinson. NL.
  William; HUFFMAN, Delila M.; M=18 Mar. 1855; Timothy Moser, JP. NL.

SIGMON, William B.; HOFFMAN, Mary Ann; M=1870; No other
   information. NL.
   William B.; HARTZOGE, Hala M.; M=17 July 1866; No Minister or
   Justice of the Peace. NL.
   William K. (26); MORROW, Margaret L. (20); white; M=28 Dec.
   1876; JC Clapp, Ref. Min. at WH Morrow's; Burton Morrow,
   Churchill Sigmon, Sidney Whitener. NL.
SILON, J.A. (30) of Virginia; LANTZ, Henryetta C. (24); white;
   M=19 Oct. 1876; JA Foi, Ref. Min. at Mrs. Lantz's; SC Foil,
   EJ Lantz, DLS Summitt. NL.
SIMMONS, Adolphus J. (22); EKARD, Martha J. (18); white; M=28 Feb.
   1879; PK Little, JP at Simon Ekard's; JV Simmons, LM Holler,
   JA Simmons. NL.
   Elijah; HERMAN, Michel; M=12 Mar. 1854; E. Yount, JP. NL.
   Jackson V. (18) [Elijah & Michal]; SIMMONS, Nancy (19) [Daniel
   & Linnie]; white; M=21 Oct. 1880; PC Henkel, Luth. Min. in
   Hky Twsp; WG Holler, PL Miller, James A. Propst. 2-108.
SIMONS, Cicero S. (22); LINTHACUM, Alice (20); white; M=13 July
   1874; JM Smith, Luth. Min. at Noah Townsend's; NL Smith,
   Linna Smith, John Hunsucker. NL.
SIMONTON, Robert [n/g & Polly Houston]; SOUTHERS, Lucinda; M=30
   May 1871; JH Bruns, JP. 1-125.
   Samuel (23); DALTON, Louisa (22); black; M=9 Dec. 1877; JH
   Bruns, JP in Hickory; Mack Coulter, Thomas Holyburton,
   Champion Crowell. NL.
SIMS, Feinck (21) [Britton & Usley]; SHERRILL, Mary (19) [Pinck-
   ney & Martha]; white; M=19 Feb. 1880; JA Sherrill, Min. in
   Mt. Crk Twsp; WE Allen, RW Shelton, WJ Gamble. 2-109.
   John C. [William & Sarah Huffman]; LUTZ, Malinda [Elias &
   Elizabeth]; M=3 Dec. 1868; James A. Garvan, JP. NL.
   John C. (29); POPE, Manervy C. (25); white; M=7 July 1878; R.
   England, JP in Cald. Twsp; WP Cline, JA Whitener, BA White-
   ner. NL.
   William [Green & Millie]; MOORE, Charlotte [Jacob & Hanah]; M=
   4 Feb. 1872; William Brooks, Min. NL.
SIPE, Alfred E. [John & Mary]; BAKER, Sarah J. [George H. & A.
   Barbara]; M=8 Feb. 1872; CT Sigmon, JP. 1-211.
   Cain F. (26); HERMAN, Fannie (20); white; M=19 Apr. 1877; PK
   Little, JP in Cline's Twsp; GW Holler, CH Sipe, Barbara Deal.
   NL.
   Elkanah [Peter & Malinda]; HUFFMAN, Mary Ann [Ambros & Barbara
   Pope]; M=15 Feb. 1872; EA Warlick, JP. 1-212.
   Hartwell (26); HOLLER, Susanah (18); white; M=20 Jan. 1876; PK
   Little, JP in Cline's Twsp; A. Deal, WC Smith, GW Holler. NL.
   James (20) [Peter & Melinda]; MATHAS, Candace (24) [Levi & Me-
   linda; white; M=7 Aug. 1879; HA Forney, JP in Newton Twsp;
   Mary Forney, William Mathis, Levina Mathis. 1-426.
   John; BAKER, Sallie; M=17 Oct. 1866; PC Henkel, Min. NL.
   Titus E. (24); HUFFMAN, Amy M.J. (15); white; M=5 Sept. 1878; DC
   Huffman, Luth.Min. at AM Huffman's; JM Wagner, FJ Huffman, HD
   Wagner. NL.
SLADE, Mayfield (22) of Lincoln Co., NC; SMYRE, Harriett (14);
   black; M=17 Dec. 1873; William Brooks, Min. at Wilson
   Smyre's; Sam Cale, Wilson Smyre, Adol Woodfin. NL.

SLATEN, Julius (21) [Jonathan & Anna] of Lincoln Co., NC; CORNELIUS, Ann (17) [Emerson & Caroline]; black; 25 Oct. 1879; MM Gabriel, JP in Mt. Crk Twsp; Logan Johnston, DW Montgomery. 1-428.

SMITH, Adolphus [John & Barbary]; MILLER, J. [? & Leacil Miller]; M=12 June 1870; AJ Fox, Min. NL.

Alfred [Alexander & Mary]; LOWRANCE, Martha [Peter & Susan]; M=12 Oct. 1870; William Brooks, Min. 1-40.

Andrew (47) [Jerry & Nancy]; HUNSUCKER, Adoline (25) [Andrew Abernathy & Mima]; black; M=6 Jan. 1876; CT Sigmon, JP in Cline's Twsp; Wilburn Baker, Harriet Sigmon, Elkanah Hunsucker. 1-317.

Babel (24) [Sandy Burdick & Margaret Burdick]; RUTHERFORD, Louisa (17) [Isaac Conley & Mary Rutherford]; black; M=10 Nov. 1880; GM Yoder, JP in Newton; LS Yount, GW Michal, GW Cockman. 2-110.

Carson B. (22) [William & Delpha]; HERMAN, Harriett M. (21) [Reuben & Sarah]; white; M=20 Jan. 1880; JA Whitener, JP in JF Twsp; HP Rudisill, SFG Miller, Noah Huffman. 2-111.

David (34); ROWE, Amanda (21); black; M=25 Feb. 1876; JM Smith, Luth. Min. at Camilla Herman's; WH Herman, MS Deal, TP Cloninger. NL.

David H.M. (20); SCRONCE, Sarah A.L. (20); white; M=7 Sept. 1877; Robert Helton, Min. at Robert Helton's; MC Smith, Jane Ballard, Ida C. Helton. NL.

Edmont (53) of Caldwell Co., NC; HOGLIN, Elizabeth (35) of Caldwell Co., NC; white; M=26 May 1873; Daniel May, Meth. Min. in Newton Twsp; Katie May, Susan G. May. NL.

Elisha; KILLIAN, Nancy; M=23 Dec. 1860; GM Yoder, JP. NL.

Elmore B. [Frederic & Adline]; CARPENTER, Sallie [Franklin & Mary Ann]; M=17 Apr. 1872; JM Smith, Min. 1-213.

Franklin (19); LOWRANCE, Polly (18); black; M=3 Dec. 1874; William Brooks, Min. at Peter Lowrance's; Alex Smith, James Smith, Peter Lowrance. NL.

George F. (30); BANDY, Mary E. (22); white; M=27 Jan. 1876; GM Wyant, JP in Bandy's Twsp; AM Johnson, JA Rudisill, WH Smith. NL.

James (21); CLINE, Susan (22); black; M=25 Oct. 1877; QM Smith, JP in Cline's Twsp; George W. Little, Franklin P. Little. NL.

James W. (21) [Jacob & Mary]; REINHARDT, Mary (20) [John & Sally Yoder]; white; M=11 May 1870; Jacob Mosteller, JP in Bandy's Twsp; WP Stallings, Levi ?. 1-427.

John [Joseph & Jane]; STOWE, Sarah [?F & Minta]; M=26 Apr. 1868; D. Hamilton, Esq. NL.

John M.; LAWRANCE, H.S.; M=11 Nov. 1856; PC Hinkle, Min. NL.

M.A. [George Mull & Mary Smith]; WHISENANT, Susan [Adam & Malinda]; M=18 Mar. 1872; JW Bandy, JP. 1-214.

Marcus; WHITENER, Mary Ann C.; M=10 Mar. 1853; GP Shuford, JP. NL.

P.F. [David & Caty]; HUITT, F.C. [Moses M. & Rhoda]; M=4 June 1870; JM Smith, Min. NL.

R.A.; SHERRILL, Sarah J.; M=16 May 1860; J. Finger, Min. NL.

R.C.; CLINE, Eliza; M=12 Oct. 1865; LN Wilson, JP. NL.

Wade H. (23); REINHARDT, Emeline (19); white; M=9 Jan. 1879; MF Hull, JP at MF Hull's; WB McDowell, JA Johnson, RDL Ritchey. NL.

SMITH, William (22) of Hky Tav. Twsp; WORKMAN, Martha J. (23) of
    Hky Tav. Twsp; white; M=27 Oct. 1873; GL Hunt, Luth. Min. at
    GL Hunt's; PM Hunt, LM Hunt, SA Hunt. NL.
  William H.; HARWELL, Margaret; M=31 Dec. 1857; William Long, JP.
    NL.
  William P. [MM & MC]; STINE, Camila C. [John & Sarah]; M=6 May
    1868; D. McD Yount, Esq. NL.
SMYER, A. Byrd [Anthony & Catharine]; JAMES, Martha E. [David &
    Emeline]; M=16 Sept. 1867; GW Wilkie, Min. NL.
  Andrew (31); REINHARDT, Barbra (27); black; M=25 Apr. 1878; CW
    Vanderburg, Min. at Snow Hill [Newton]; Ed Thomas, Albert
    Wood, Caleb Bost. NL.
  Pink [Miles Barringer & Chaney Smyer]; BROOKS, Lizzie [William
    & n/g]; M=4 May 1872; Isaac Wells, Min. NL.
  Robert L. (22) [Wilson & Flora] yellow; REINHARDT, Martha (19)
    [Anderson & Cano] black; M=15 July 1874; Andrews, Sherward,
    Min. in Newton Twsp; Albert Abernathy, Young Wilson, Lafayett
    Wilson. 1-265.
  Silas; HUIT, S. Jane; M=8 Feb. 1866; EE Smyer, Min. NL.
SMYLEY, Thomas M. (32); LUNTZ, Ellen E. (27); white; M=27 May
    1875; John A. Foil, Ref. Min. at Ref. Church; JM Brown, JH
    Shuford, SM Finger. NL.
SMYRE, F.L. [Jacob & MC]; MILLER, S.C. [Ephraim & Amy]; M=30 May
    1870; JM Smith, Min. NL.
  Julius (31); PLONK, Mary J. (22); white; M=12 Feb. 1879; JC
    Clapp, Min. in Newton; PM Rhyne, WE Yount, DL Smyre. NL.
  Logan Q.; ROWE, H.L.; M=30 Dec. 1852; William L. Mehaffey,
    JP. NL.
  M.N.; HUIT, M.M.; M=9 Feb. 1859; PC Henkel, Min. NL.
  Milton (24); WOODFORD, Jane (20); black; M=30 Sept. 1872; EJ
    Harris, Min. at Christian Dacter's; M. Slade, Christian Dac-
    ter, WA Smyer. NL.
  R.A.; SETZER, Mahala; M=22 Dec. 1852; H. Cline, JP. NL.
  Robert [Charles & Tommy Lutes]; PROPST, Meriah [Simon & Hannah];
    black; M=25 Jan. 1871; ST Wilfong, JP. 1-126.
SNIDER, L.F. [Daniel & Caroline]; WITHERS, Adoline [? Keener &
    Catherine]; M=14 Apr. 1870; Miles Goodson, JP. NL.
SOUNTY, Ben [James & Mary Ramsour]; NCNEILL, Cary; M=5 Feb. 1870;
    Wm Brooks, Min. NL.
SOUTHERLAND, Lafayett (32) [Alex & Eliza] of Pender Co., NC;
    BLACK, Fannie J. (22) [KA & Mary A.]; white; M=13 Apr. 1880;
    J. Ingold, Ref. Min. in Hky Twsp; JG Hall, Robert K. Black.
    2-112.
SPAK, Daniel; ROCKET, Amy; M=5 Dec. 1856; AJ Whitener, JP. NL.
SPEAGLE, Aaron; BAKER, Casaan; M=7 Apr. 1856; George Herman, JP.
    NL.
  Daniel [Solamon & Susan]; JOHNSON, Flora [Franklin & Elizabeth];
    M=26 Oct. 1867; GM Yoder, Esq. NL.
  Philip R.; RUDISILL, Rachel; M=16 Sept. 1858; G. Huffman, JP.
    NL.
  Thomas (21); CANIPE, Catharine L. (22); white; M=20 Aug. 1877;
    JH Brendle, Min. at Andrew Fulbright's; A. Fulbright, DH
    Wyant, PW Bangle. NL.
SPENCER, Adison A. (21); HOUK, Laura J. (18); white; M=20 Aug.
    1874; PF Smith, JP at Harrison Houk's; JP Spencer, SE
    Spencer, WP Reinhardt. NL.

SPENCER, David; CAMPBELL, Sophia; M=23 Feb. 1862; JD Caldwell, JP. NL.
   J.P. [Eli & Lucinda]; HERMAN, D.E. [William & Elizabeth]; M=1 Aug. 1867; PC Henkle, Min. NL.
   John W. (54) of Caldwell Co., NC; PUNCH, Elizabeth C. (41); white; M=3 June 1875; PF Smith, JP in Newton; WP Smyre, AP Miller, WL Deal. NL.
   Mas.; MARTIN, S.E.; M=9 May 1861; OL Rowe, JP. NL.
   S.E. [Eli & Lucinda]; TURNER, Emeline [William & Lovina]; M=17 Sept. 1860; EA Warlick, JP. NL.
SPRUNT, Wm H. (24) [Alexander & Jane] of Wilmington, NC; HAMILTON, Bettie M. (22) [Hugh C. & Susan S.] of Hickory; white; M=22 Dec. 1880; CM Payne, Presby. Min. in Hky; JG Hale, HC Dixon, TE Sprunt. 2-113.
SRONCE, Andrew; GOWENS, Mary; M=3 Jan. 1856; GP Shuford, JP. NL.
   Ephraim; BELL, Polly; M=19 Feb. 1862; Joshua Wilson, JP. NL.
   Henry (20) [Caroline Sronce] of Lincoln Co., NC; GOODSON, Milla (20) [Henry & Rachel]; white; M=6 June 1880; WC Caldwell, JP in Cald. Twsp; JG Caldwell, Nancy M. Caldwell, Levi L. Caldwell. 2-114.
   Joseph; PARKER, Nancy; M=9 Mar. 1851; HB Witherspoon, JP. NL.
   William [Conrad & Mary A.]; HEFNER, Mary [Solomon & Lida]; M=14 Apr. 1870; AJ Fox, Min. NL.
   William A. [Jacob & Margaret Cline]; COBB, Masonia S. [Henry & Nancy]; M=16 July 1871; PF Smith, JP. 1-111.
STALLIANS, William P. [Elisha & Mary]; SEAGLE, Martha Ann [Joseph & Mary]; M=4 Apr. 1869; JW Bandy, JP. NL.
STAMEY, Ephreham (20) [n/k & Mary Stamey]; SHERRILL, Elizabeth (15) [Robert & Mary]; black; M=11 July 1872; JA Sherrill, Meth. Min. in Mt. Crk Twsp; BM Sherrill, JC Pain, MC Sherrill. 1-215.
   Ephrem [Manuel & Mary]; READ, Fanny [Robert Read & Mary Sherrill]; black; M=15 July 1871; JA Sherrill, Min. 1-127.
   Whiteford (19) [Alexander & Belzy] of Martinsville, VA; ROBINSON, Fanny (19) [Conor & Sarah] of Lincoln Co., NC; M=15 Jan. 1873; JM Bandy, JP. 1-257.
STARNES, Columbus C. [William & Elizabeth]; WILLIAMS, Sarah [Joseph & Polly]; M=9 Oct. 1870; JL Hewit, JP. 1-41.
   Daniel [Harrison & Mary]; HEFNER, Malinda [Elias & Mary]; M=20 Oct. 1869; William H. Rockett, JP. NL.
   James (39); CLINE, Rebecca (35); white; M=16 Apr. 1876; JL Grice JP in Mt. Crk Twsp; MA Grice, SJ McCombs, Gilbert Shurping. NL.
   Simon W. (24); REITZEL, Laura (21); white; M=30 Apr. 1876; JM Smith, Luth. Min. at A. Reitzel's; JL LIttle, C. Henkle, CM Henkle. NL.
STARR, Alfred (26) of Guilford Co., NC; LANTZ, Emma J. (23) of Newton; white; M=7 Nov. 1878; JC Clapp, Ref. Min. at MN Lantz's; JA Foil, JH Swatzel, EL Clapp. NL.
   Elon M. [Jacob & Margaret]; WAKE, Sarah [Jacob Detter & Catherine Detter]; M=28 Mar. 1872; JM Smith, Min. NL.
   J.A.; RADER, Pheeby G.; M=19 Feb. 1854; William L. Mehaffey, JP. NL.
   Silvanus M.; CLINE, Polly; M=16 Feb. 1851; ER Shuford, JP. NL.

STATEN, Julius (21) [Jonathan & Anna] of Lincoln Co., NC; CORNELIUS, Ann (17) [Emerson & Caroline]; black; M=25 Oct. 1879; MM Gabriel, JP in Mt. Crk Twsp; Logan Johnston, DW Montgomery. 1-428.

STEVENSON, Frank (21); LOWRANCE, Mary (20); black; M=18 Dec. 1877; Wm Brooks, Min. at Peter Lowrance's; Frank Smith, Alfred Smith, McCim Abernathy. NL.

T.L.; RAMER, S.C.; M=3 July 1860; S. Schener, Min. NL.

STEWARD, A.L.; HEFNER, H.R.; M=13 July 1864; GH Moser, JP. NL.

STEWART, Jep; FRY, Margaret; M=20 May 1860; JM Lowrance, JP. NL.

STILES, J.H.; WALDEN, Mary A.S.; M=4 Oct. 1860; JA Sherrill, JP. NL.

J.R. [John & Sallie]; ABERNATHY, Susan [Wilford & Polly]; M=15 July 1870; A. Sherrill, JP. NL.

Jacob A. [William & Matilda]; FISHER, Margaret E. [Benjamin & Elvina]; M=15 Dec. 1867; D. Hamilton, Esq. NL.

William A.; LEE, Emeline; M=14 Nov. 1861; JA Sherrill, JP. NL.

STILLWELL, L.; MILLER, Margaret; M=18 Mar. 1855; Henry Goodson, Min. NL.

STINE, Allen J. (22); ROWE, Lovina C. (19); white; M=7 Jan. 1875; JC Clapp, Ref. Min. at Marcus Rowe's; Marcus Rowe, Daniel Rowe, Lafayette Rowe. NL.

Jacob M. (30); LITTLE, Sarah C. (16); white; M=6 Mar. 1876; JM Smith, Luth. Min. at JB Little's; MG Little, LL Mitchell, Quintus Little. NL.

STIREWALT, Rev. M.J.; SMITH, Camila E.; M=27 Oct. 1858; PC Hinkel, Min. NL.

STOCTON, James (21); SHERRILL, Rosea (21); black; M=16 Mar. 1876; WS Shuford, Bapt. Min. at Reuben Sherrill's; Alf Sherrill, Abram Turner, Morison Sherrill. NL.

STOWE, Joseph M. (24) [Joel A. & Meriah F.] of Lincoln Co., NC; PARKER, Nancy C. (21) [John & Margaret] of Caldwell Co., NC; white; M=21 Nov. 1872; JL Hewit, JP in Cald. Twsp; John Hewit, Marcus Hewit, Julian Parker. 1-216.

STROUP, Peter; COBB, Melinda M.; M=19 Dec. 1851; Lyman Woodford, JP. NL.

STRUTT, George P. (26); MCCASLIN, O. Almena (17); white; M=30 July 1878; SC Brown, JP in Cald. Twsp; Sol Shrum, AC Cloninger, ND Fry. NL.

SUBLET, John W. [John D. & n/g]; PETERSON, Emily A. [John & Hannah]; M=9 Feb. 1871; JH Bruns, JP. 1-128.

SUDDERTH, Standhope; SHUFORD, M.A.; M=3 Nov. 1852; IH Robinson, Min. NL.

SUMIT, John [Jacob & Polly]; LEE, Camila [Lawson & Nelly]; M=17 Dec. 1871; JL Hewit, JP. 1-129.

SUMMERROW, John C. (33) [Jacob & Rachel] of Caldwell Co., NC; SIGMON, Alice A. (21) [Amon & Caroline]; white; M=19 Oct. 1879; JW Mouser, JP in Hky Tavern Twsp; RF Turner, GC Turner, MN Turner. 1-429.

SUMMIT, Levi R.; CLODFELTER, Jane; M=15 Jan. 1860; Henry Cline, JP. NL.

SUMMITS, Isaac L.; ABERNATHY, Perlina; M=1 Feb. 1857; JD Caldwell, JP. NL.

TALLENT, Samuel; JOHNSON, Mary; M=25 Aug. 1856; Amos Helderbrand, Min. NL.
  William (22); MULL, Elmira (26); white; M=19 May 1874; JW Bandy, JP in Bandy's Twsp; NH Hicks, FT Rhodes, MG Goodson. NL.
TATE, Hampton (25); FORNEY, Jane (23); black; M=23 Oct. 1880; Abel Whitener, JP in Hky Twsp; JA Cowan, JN Harbinson, Alice Wilfong. 2-115.
  Junius W. [HA & FE]; ROWE, Mattie [PL & Lynie]; M=16 Jan. 1872; RL Abernethy, Min. 1-217.
TAYLER, John F. (20); DELLINGER, Laura (20); white; M=17 Jan. 1878; GW Ivey, Min. in Denver, NC; LS Bost, WM McCaul, John M. Howard. NL.
TAYLOR, Lewis (30) [Peter & Elizabeth] of Burke Co., NC; ARNEY, Mattie E. (26) [BF & Anna]; white; M=20 Apr. 1880; JH Bruns, JP in Hky; Owen Duggan, Thomas Scales, Michael Brice. 2-116.
  M.H.; ABERNATHY, Eliza; M=21 Aug. 1853; Philip Burns, JP. NL.
  William [William Hunter & Susan Ramseur]; MOSES, Margaret; M=27 Dec. 1867; RA Cobb, Esq. NL.
TEAGUE, Moses (52); HEALON, Rebecca M. (30); white; M=2 Nov. 1875; JH Bruns, JP in Hky; Morgan Griffin, Daniel Whisenant. NL.
  Vandever E. (20); SHERRILL, Amanda (20); white; M=11 Feb. 1877; JH Bruns, JP in Hky; H. Scott, James B. Beard, Rich B. Baker. NL.
THOMAS, Edmon (21); CHAMBERS, Amanda (19); black; M=14 Apr. 1878; CV Vanderburg, Min. at Catawba Station, Catawba, NC; Andrew Smyer, Jane Abernathy, Sid Reinhardt. NL.
THOMASON, George F. (24); CLINE, Laura E. (17); white; M=9 Dec. 1875; JC Clapp, Ref. Min. at Elijah Cline's; Daniel Rowe, Patrick Cline, Jonas Hunsucker. NL.
  Robert H. (24); FRY, Ellen C. (24); white; M=23 Jan. 1879; JC Clapp, Min. at Solomon Fry's; JP Fry, James L. Miller, Samuel E. Killian. NL.
THOMPSON, Abram (19) [Thomas & Rachel] of Lincoln Co., NC; LITTLE, Laura (18) [John & Lucinda]; white; M=8 Aug. 1874; JA Sherrill, Min. in Mt. Crk Twsp; WA Hewitt, FP Sheaton, MA Thompson. 1-266.
  John; POWELL, Mary; M=22 Nov. 1859; JW Gabriel, JP. NL.
  Vance (18) [John & Martha]; HUFFMAN, Mary Ann (19) [Daniel & Rhoda]; white; M=1 Oct. 1879; PK Little, JP in Cline's Twsp; TA Killian, DF Huffman, CC Harvell. 1-430.
THORNBURG, A.M. [George & Polly]; STARR, Margaret [Elam M. & Barbary]; M=14 Oct. 1869; ET Coulter, JP. NL.
THORNTON, John E. (28) of Newton; MEHAFFEY, Harriet, 23; white; M=15 Mar. 1877; JC Clapp, Ref. Min. at Mrs.Mehaffey's; DA Ikerd, EN Herman, S. Herman. NL.
THRONEBURG, Burton (21); FRY, Mary (17); white; M=7 Mar. 1875; GL Hunt, Luth. Min. at Jacob Fry's; WP Fry, Catharine Throneburg, Louisa Throneburg. NL.
  George T. (22); HOKE, Fanny (19); white; M=7 June 1874; JM Smith, Luth.Min. at Silus Poovey's; JL Fry, LJ Lowrance, HA Lowrance. NL.
  John E. (19); CLINE, Mary J. (19); white; M=14 Oct. 1877; GL Hunt, Luth. Min. at George Cline's; JB Bird, Henry J. Reitzell, WE Hallman. NL.

THRONEBURG, L. Lafayett (27); CLINE, Nancy ann (17); white; M=25 Jan. 1874; GL Hunt, Luth. Min. at GL Hunt's; Mary J. Cline, Thomas D. Cline, Mary Throneburg. NL.
TOLBERT, G.H. [MC & Margaret]; SIGMON, Frances [Abel & Lizzie]; M=2 Feb. 1868; D. McD Yount, Esq. NL.
TOWNSEN, Solomon; PROBST, Jemima; M=1 Jan. 1857; GM Yoder, JP. NL.
TOWNSEND, Adam E.; HEFNER, Mahala; M=30 Nov. 1866; E. Yount, JP. NL.
  Levi L. (21); HERMAN, Camilla (25); white; M=22 July 1873; JM Smith, Luth. Min. in Newton Twsp; AL Yount, Alice ?, LH Bynum. NL.
  Monroe (22) [Jacob & Caroline]; HOLLER, Dianah (21) [Israel & Anna]; white; M=11 Mar. 1875; JM Smith, Luth. Min. in Newton Twsp; Noah Townsend, Henry Odem, JP Spencer. 1-303.
  Peter; SIGMON, Charity; M=26 Nov. 1854; E. Yount, JP. NL.
TRAVENSTED, Joseph; LONGCRIER, Rebecca; M=25 Mar. 1855; WL Mehaffey, JP. NL.
  Levi; DEAL, Emoline; M=25 May 1858; William L. Mehaffey, JP. NL.
  Reubin; LOFEN, Polly; M=19 Sept. 1857; JHA Yount, JP. NL.
  W.M.; TRAVENSTED, Elizabeth; M=18 Feb. 1855; W.L. Mehaffey, JP. NL.
  William A.; HAWN, Mariah; M=16 Mar. 1860; PJ Pitts, JP. NL.
TRAVIS, Darius (23); TRAVIS, Rebecca (19); white; M=7 Mar. 1878; PK Little, JP in Cline's Twsp; Mitson Waller, William Travis, Julius Beard. NL.
  Pinkney E. (21); SIGMON, Ellen (19); white; M=22 Jan. 1879; PK Little, JP in Cline's Twsp; AW Sigmon, JF Beard, Lawson Sigmon. NL.
  Washington (22); HUFFMAN, Amy (22); white; M=25 Oct. 1877; QM Smith, JP in Cline's Twsp; George W. Little, Frank P. Little. NL.
TROLLINGER, I.H. [Frederick B. & LE]; SHERRILL, Fanny L. [Enos Sherrill & n/k]; M=10 Feb. 1869; Elijah Allison, Min. at Enos Sherrill's. NL.
  Robert H. (18) [MB & Susan]; SHERRILL, Lillie E. (18) [Surith & Melissie]; white; M=8 Aug. 1880; PFW Stamey, Min. in Mt. Crk Twsp; CL McCaul, SJ Whitener, Worth Mundy. 2-117.
TROUTMAN, William; LINK, Melinda; M=14 Mar. 1860; JD Caldwell, JP. NL.
TUCKER, Demisey; BAILER, Lucinda; M=2 Feb. 1860; G. Huffman, JP. NL.
  Samuel (65); COSBY, FS (44); white; M=25 Mar. 1874; JW Bandy, JP in Bandys Twsp; PM Mull, JN Payne, Jonas Brittain. NL.
TURBILL, Elkanah; CAMPBELL, Plinna; M=14 July 1853; Henry Cline, JP. NL.
TURBYFILL, Francis W. [Anderson & Mary]; PAIN, Elizabeth E. [John & Elizabeth]; M=18 Oct.1871; JA Sherrill, Min. 1-130.
  J.L.; DRUM, Rebecca; M=21 Feb. 1864; William L. Mehaffey, JP. NL.
  J.M.; KILLIAN, Jane R.; M=22 Nov. 1855; H.Asbury, Min. NL.
  Wesley; ELLER, Mary; M=25 Dec. 1864; JM Lowrance, JP. NL.
  William; KALE, Margaret; M=1 June 1856; JM Lowrance, JP. NL.

TURNER, Alexander (21); SMITH., Drucilla (25); white; M=24 Dec. 1876; Jacob Mosteller, JP in Bandy's Twsp; John F. Linn, Luther Mosteller. NL.
  B.S.; SETZER, Layah L.; M=19 Aug. 1851; William L. Mehaffey, JP. NL.
  D.W.; BARGER, Martha; M=14 June 1860; M. Barger, JP. NL.
  George C. [George W. & Elmira A.]; CLONINGER, Lucinda C. [Noah & Perlina]; M=3 Dec. 1870; JL Hewit, JP. 1-42.
  James; HAMILTON, Lavina; M=15 Apr. 1860; Logan Smyre, JP. NL.
  Laban C. (27) [Gabriel & Lucinda] of Newton Twsp; SMYER, Sarah (18) [Walton & Elvira]; white; M=2 Jan. 1873; JM Smith, Min. in Newton Twsp; S. Shell, WA Smith, HS Smith. 1-258.
  Pinkney L. (27) [Gabriel & Lucinda] of Hky Tav. Twsp; MOONEY, Mary Jane (23) [Sidney & Mahala] of Newton Twsp; white; M=19 Sept. 1872; PF Smith, JP in Newton Twsp; JA Yount, PP Hoke, Briton Sims. 1-218.
  William A. (27) [Gabriel & Lucinda]; KILLIAN, Francis (25) [Daniel Hoover & n/g]; white; M=25 Mar. 1880; PFW Stamey, Min. in Newton; LC Turner, C. Hoover, MI Hoover. 2-118.
UNDERWOOD, John; PARKER, Rebecca; M=17 ? 1854; ER Shuford, JP. NL.
VANHORN, Adolphus L. (18); CRUMP, Candace M. (19); white; M=20 Jan. 1876; HA Forney, JP in Newton. NL.
VENHORN, Alexander; PROBST, Louisa A.; M=1 Dec. 1853; George Huffman, JP. NL.
VITA, Augustino (24) [Joseph & Menica] of Charlotte, NC; SHEPARD, Sarah Allen (19) [Joseph & Sarah]; white; M=27 Aug.1880; MJ Rice, Catholic Priest in Hky; John Nulan, James S. Cobb, Patrick McIntyre. 2-119.
WADE, Elisha; BARRINGER, Emeline E.; M=5 Jan. 1855; John Lantz, Min. NL.
  John C.; WARLICK, Eliza; M=10 Aug. 1865; GM Yoder, JP. NL.
  William; SMITH, Catharine; M=3 Apr. 1859; G. Huffman, JP. NL.
WAGNER, Benjamin; HEFNER, Rachel; M=31 Aug. 1851; IR Moser, Min. NL.
  James M. (21); MILLER, Margaret E. (18); white; M=1 Aug. 1878; PC Henkel, Luth. Min. at JM Miller's; JL MIller, WP Huffman, HJ Wagner. NL.
  P.L.; HUFFMAN, Jemima M.; M=24 Dec. 1851; E. Yount, JP. NL.
  T.J.; HERMAN, H.C.; M=29 Sept. 1864; PC Henkel, Min. NL.
  William L.; HERMAN, Nancy M.; M=4 Sept. 1856; PC Henkle, Min. NL.
WAGONER, Charles M. (24) of Iredell Co., NC; CLARK, Margaret A. (18); white; M=2 Mar. 1876; John E. Presly, Presby. Min. at Alex Clark's; Alex Clark, JA White, John T. Goodman. NL.
WALKER, W.I.; SHUFORD, Susan C.; M=18 Nov. 1855; AM Powell, JP. NL.
WALLACE, H.W. [John & Mary Hoffman]; HOFFMAN, S.A. [? & Katy]; M=29 Apr.1868; Israel Hughes. NL.
WARD, H.P.; ROWE, Jennie E.; M=10 Oct. 1866; DS Henkel, Min. NL.
  John S. of Hky Tav. Twsp; WHITENER, Susan A. (19) of Hky Tav. Twsp; white; M=14 May 1873; AG Corpening, JP in Jacob's Fork Twsp; JP Hawn, SE Whitener, JC Corpening. NL.
  Samuel (25); DELLINGER, Mary (15); black; M=21 Jan. 1874; GW Logan, Min. at Mr. Moore's; Mr. Moore, Mrs. Moore, Mr. Moore, Jr. NL.

WARLICK, D. Logan (35) [David & Rachael]; BRADBURN, Matie E. (32) [JW & Malvino]; white; M=19 Dec. 1880; PFW Stamey, Meth. Min. in Newton Twsp; Levi Yoder, Harriet Yoder, Nora A. Sronce. 2-120.

George [Absalam & Sarah]; LINN, Harriett [Daniel & Jemima]; M=7 Nov. 1867; William Abernathy. NL.

John C.; LUTZ, Mary; M=18 Jan. 1866; J. Lantz, Min. NL.

John N.; LANTZ, Nancy N.; M=30 Mar. 1858; O. Crooks, Min. NL.

Lafayet; WAKE, Elizabeth; M=24 Apr. 1859; David E. Warlick, Min. NL.

Stephen (53) of Bandys Twsp; MOSTELLER, Susan (46); black; M=23 Mar. 1873; JW Bandy, JP at Bandys Twsp; Rufus Robinson, Harvey Mosteller. NL.

Steven; ROBINSON, Nancy; M=20 Dec. 1868; Robert Helton, Min. NL.

WARREN, John; ?, Anna; M=17 May 1853; JP Little, JP. NL.

William S. (23); BROWN, Laura A. (19); white; M=29 Oct. 1876; PK Little, JP in Cline's Twsp; JQ Warren, Anna R. Warren, Quint Pope. NL.

WATRON, James W. (29); HERMAN, Mary R. (18); white; M=15 July 1877; CT Sigmon, JP in Cline's Twsp; AM Sigmon, HE Sigmon, BS Sigmon. NL.

WATSON, John E.; SETZER, Catharin; M=5 Oct. 1853; Lyman Woodford, JP. NL.

WATTS, John A.; LOFTIN, Sarah; M=3 May 1853; Thomas Ward, JP. NL.

Monroe (21); BUMGARNER, Mary (19); white; M=26 Apr. 1876; GJ Wilkie, Bapt. Min. at QM Little's; BH Yount, QM Little, JE Wilfong. NL.

Rufus; BUMGARNER, Elizabeth; M=30 Apr. 1856; JD Caldwell, JP. NL.

William Francis (19) [John & Sarah]; BOLCH, Emaline (21) [James & n/g]; white; M=13 Jan. 1876; GW Cansler, JP in Hamilton Twsp; QH Hampton, Thomas S. Long. 1-318.

WAUGH, Silus B. (22) of Iredell Co., NC; BOLCH, Sarah E. (25); white; M=21 May 1874; ME Sigmon, JP in Cline's Twsp; Daniel Deal, Robert Sigmon, Joseph Hunsucker. NL.

WEAVER, Absolom; DEITZ, Caroline; M=27 Oct. 1864; Henry Goodman, Min. NL.

Adam; SPEAGLE, Emoline E.; M=25 Apr. 1858; GP Shuford, JP. NL.

Adolphus (20) [Henry & Nancy] of Jacob's Fork Twsp; MICHAEL, Mary (20) [Berry & Dulcina] of JF Twsp; white; M=26 July 1873; Robert Helton, Min. in JF Twsp; Ida Helton, Harriet Helton, Drucilla Helton. 1-219.

Frederick; SPEAGLE, Barbara; M=17 Mar. 1859; GP Shuford, JP. NL.

James M. (21) [Daniel & Barbara]; MICHAELS, L. Ann (21); white; License Issued 11 May 1880; No officiator; SJ Shore, Robert B.Helton, JR Sonderz {Saunders}. 2-121.

John [Jacob & Fannie]; ABERNATHY, Catherine [John & Caroline]; M=4 Mar. 1869; AJ Whitener, JP. NL.

John; INGLE, Eliza; M=15 Jan. 1857; AJ Whitener, JP. NL.

O.H.; YOUNT, Eliza; M=7 Oct. 1858; E. Yount, JP. NL.

WEBB, Franklin; PROPST, Anna; M=1869; No other information. NL.

James E. (21) [Thomas & Maneta]; BARGER, Sophronio (24) [Thomas & Harriett]; white; M=19 Feb. 1880; JH Bruns, JP in Hky; AY Sigmon, David Pitts, ME Bradford. 2-122

Joseph B.; BRIDGES, Jane C.; M=3 Nov. 1851; JM Lowrance, JP. NL.

WELKER, Rev. G.W.; MASON, Louisa; M=15 Oct. 1851; JH Crawford, Min. NL.

WHISENANT, Daniel (25); LINN, Sarah (23); white; M=31 Aug. 1876; Jacob Mosteller, JP in Bandy's Twsp; James Lynn, Hosea Johnson. NL.

  Daniel (28) [Phillip & Polly]; GANTT, Alice (19) [Joseph & Fanny]; white; M=16 Mar. 1880; Robert Helton, Min. in Jacob's Fork Twsp; RC Sides, Etta Garett, DL Warlick. 2-123.

  John M. (24); WORKMAN, Mary Jane (18); white; M=25 Oct. 1877; JC Hartsell, Min. in Newton; JR Hawn, FJ Hartsell, John M. Barger. NL.

WHISENHUNT, John; DEITZ, Polly Carolina; M=26 Oct. 1850; Bondsman: Andrew Rinck; George Setzer.

  M.E.; HAWN, Caroline; M=6 Aug. 1860; H. Goodman, Min. NL.

  William [Philip & Polly]; PROPST, Harriet [John & Susan[ ]; M=3 Dec. 1868; AJ Whitener, JP. NL.

  William K. (18); LINN, Martha (20); white; M=25 Aug. 1878; WL Hull, Bapt. Min. at Jane Linn's; CB Young, Rufus Huffman, PL Young. NL.

WHISSENHUNT, L.S. [John & Mary]; KILLIAN, Mary M. [Hedrick Killian & n/k]; M=14 Dec. 1868; AJ Whitener, JP at Hedrick Killian's. NL.

WHITAKER, Frances M. (32) [Mason & Elizabeth]; LOWRANCE, Mary C. (32) [Nelson & Harriett]; white; M=11 Apr. 1880; LN Wilson, JP; QM Little, Canny M. Lowrance, LW Robinson. 2-124.

WHITE, George L. (22); WHITE, Rosea M. (16); white; M=11 Nov. 1875; JC Hartsell, Min. at CM White's; WJ Southern, Frank A. Clinard, John N. Bohanan. NL.

  Henry (21) [Eli & Nancy]; MOORE, Ada (20) [Alfred & Catharine]; black; M=1 Aug. 1879; JH Bruns, JP in Hky Twsp; WC Ervin, TL Gibson, Elizabeth Weisiger. 1-431.

  Joseph C.; SIGMON, Candes L.; M=1 Apr. 1862; James H. Rowe, JP. NL.

  Lawson (53) of Alexander Co., NC; FRY, Harriet S. (46); white; M=13 Mar. 1877; JC Clapp, Ref. Min. at JC Clapp's; AC Fox, William Harris, DP Jarrett. NL.

WHITENER, A.J. [George P.& Sallie]; LEONARD, Mary A. [George & Eliza]; M=4 Feb. 1868; GM Yoder, Esq. NL.

  Absolom (28) [Abel & Margaret]; WHISENANT, Dovie (24) [Phillip & Polly]; white; M=21 Oct. 1880; JC Clapp, Min. in Newton Twsp; Emma Clapp, Jennie Rhyne, Mary McCorkle. 2-125.

  Adolphus D. (25); HELTON, Ida (21); white; M=20 Dec. 1877; CW Anderson, Min. at Robert Helton's; JM Leonard, RM Whitener, JT Dellinger. NL.

  Alen (27); HART, Mira E. (23); black; M=10 Feb. 1879; AB Jennings, Min. at Alen Whitener's; Sallie Winters, Lettie Wilfong, Adolphus Costner. NL.

  Allen P. [Nelson Hedrick & Betsy Whitener]; MOSTELLER, Easter [Robert & Susan]; M=13 Feb. 1868; EA Warlick, Esq. NL.

  Andrew (21) [Sandy & Maria]; PROPST, Bell (18) [Ming Wilfong & Lucy Propst]; black; M=6 May 1879; EJ Farris, Min. in Newton Twsp; Alis Baker, Alexander Bost, Can Whitener. 1-432.

  Benjamin A. (22); CLINE, Julia A. (23); white; M=17 Dec. 1874; AJ Fox, Luth. Min. at Roxanah Cline's; AF Lutz, James Cansler, AS Whitener. NL.

WHITENER, C.M. [AM & Linney]; SIGMON, R.E. [Abel & Elizabeth]; M=6 Oct. 1868; William Abernathy. NL.

Daniel H. [William J. & Anna]; SEITZ, Mary Ann [? & Rebecca L.]; M=27 Oct. 1867; PC Henkle, Min. NL.

Ephraim L. (23); SEITZ, Eliza (18); white; M=26 Sept. 1878; JH Bruns, JP in Hky; AP Seitz, JR Whitener, JO Whitener. NL.

George L.; LEONARD, Clary; M=25 Apr. 1852; GP Shuford, JP. NL.

Henry (21) [Simon & Delila]; HART, Polly (21) [William Ikard & Nancy Hart]; black; M=23 Dec. 1880; EJ Harris, Min. in Newton, Snow Hill; Frank Gross, Andrew Morrow, Adline Harris. 2-126.

Hosea H.; REEP, Sarah Ann; M=17 Sept. 1862; Adam Miller, Min. NL.

J.P. [Eli & Sallie]; FRY, Clara [Henry & Elizabeth]; M=9 Aug. 1867; AJ Whitener, Esq. NL.

James S. [George D. & Margaret]; MORROW, Martha Ann [Harry & Elizabeth]; M=26 Dec. 1871; JC Clapp, Min. 1-131.

Jarvis (21); MORROW, Julia (19); white; M=24 July 1873; AG Corpening, JP in Jacob's Fork Twsp; JV Ward, PM Seitz, Sid Whitener. NL.

John W. (21); ODAM, Laura (19); white; M=25 July 1876; PK Little, JP in Cline's Twsp; Henry Odam, LME Huffman, LH Kale. NL.

Joseph (24) [Marcus & Fannie]; WHITENER, Bettie (20) [Logan & Mahala]; white; M=13 Nov. 1879; AG Corpening, JP in Jacob's Fork Twsp; LG Whitener, JA Harbinson, CW McCaslin. 1-433.

L.G.; YOUNT, Clarinda; M=Oct., 1850; ER Shuford, JP. NL.

L.G.; SETZER, Mehala; M=6 Oct. 1853; ER Shuford, JP. NL.

L.R.; SHUFORD, M.J.; M=15 Jan. 1866; J. Lantz, Min. NL.

Levi; YOUNT, Anna; M=19 Mar. 1859; E. Yount, JP. NL.

Levi [Abel & Margaret]; WEAVER, Anna [Ephraim & Polly]; M=5 Feb. 1871; AJ Fox, Min. 1-132.

Levi (23); ROBINSON, Ann (26); black; M=26 Jan. 1879; JC Clapp, Min. at JC Clapp's; Minda Coulter, Missouri Shook. NL.

Levi (24); LAFEVERS, Sarah (19); white; M=6 Mar. 1879; HA Forney, JP at Levi Gooden's; LF Yoder, Levi Whitener, Cora Wilson. NL.

Marcus A. (25) [Andrew & Sina]; WHITENER, Emma (18) [Washington & Gelina]; white; M=2 Dec. 1875; Abel Whitener, JP in Hky Tav. Twsp; JP Whitener, AD Whitener, JA Whitener. 1-304.

Monroe (27); PROPST, Frances (23); white; M=17 Feb. 1878; GL Hunt, Luth. Min. at GL Hunt's; SA Huit, JAM Hunt, GL Hunt. NL.

P.W.; SHUFORD, Catharine; M=29 July 1862; J. Ingold, Min. NL.

Peter A. (22); MILLER, C.M. (21); white; M=26 Sept. 1878; HA Forney, JP in Newton; Cora Wilson, LF Yoder, HA Whitener. NL.

Philip B. [Michael & Elmira]; YODER, Frances [Andrew & Anna]; M=15 Dec. 1870; AJ Fox, Min. 1-43.

Pinkney; BENDLE, Mahala; M=11 Feb. 1854; GP Shuford, JP. NL.

Robert H.S. (21); HILDEBRAND, Elminda (17); white; M=25 Mar. 1875; SC Brown, JP in Hamilton Twsp; AE Brown, MJ Brown, ME Day. NL.

Sidney J. (28) [David & Elizabeth]; CORNELIUS, Addie (22) [Austin & Anna]; white; M=10 Nov. 1880; GW Ivey, Min. in Mt. Crk Twsp; GG Smith, JF Lineberger. 2-127.

WHITFORD, Stamy (19); ROBINSON, Fannie (19); white; M=15 Jan. 1873; JW Bandy in Bandy's Twsp; NL.

WHITING, Horace G. (36) [Janius & Mary K.] of Iredell Co., NC; CALDWELL, Carrie V. (18) [Frank Caldwell & n/g]; white; M= 4 Mar. 1880; TL Triplett, Meth. Min. at Frank Caldwell's; LC Caldwell, Robert W. Shelton, Adolphus Shelton. 2-128.

  Seymour W. (31) [Seymour W. & Hannah M.] of Raleigh, NC; FARROW, Florence H. (24) [Isaac & Carrie] of Hky, NC; white; M=15 Dec. 1880; Thomas G. Thurston, Presby. Min. in Hky; JG Hall, HC Hamilton, JB Ramsour. 2-137.

WIDBY, James R. (23) of Caldwell Co., NC; JAY, Elizabteh A. (21) of Abyville, SC; white; M=18 Nov. 1873; PL Herman, Min. in Newton; JD Little, Fannie Herman, MD Sherrill. NL.

WIKE, Daniel L. (20) [Silas & Malinda]; HUIT, Alice L. (16) [Henry & Nancy]; white; M=12 Aug. 1880; PK Little, JP in Cline's Twsp; WT Wike, RA Little, Charles Little. 2-129.

  Fred Lafayett (21); JAMES, Lissie (19); black; M=21 Feb. 1877; William G. James, JP in Hamilton Twsp; Jenny James, Monroe Connor, LT Cloninger. NL.

  John L. [Jac & Melinda]; WIKE, Margaret [David & Delilah]; M=16 Nov. 1871; JM Smith, Min. 1-133.

  Pinkney (21); ROBINSON, Ellen (18); black; M=20 Aug. 1878; CW Vanderburg, Min. at Snow Hill, Newton, NC; Pink Bost, Laura Dodge, Jean McCorkle. NL.

  William; DETTER, Sarah; M=26 Jan. 1860; William L. Mehaffey, JP. NL.

WILFONG, Charles (22); PROPST, Jane (17); black; M=22 Apr. 1877; Samuel Helton, Min. at Samuel Helton's; JW Leonard, JR Helton, RA Leonard. NL.

  James E. (23); BLACKBURN, Emma (21); white; M=7 Nov. 1874; Julius Shuford, Ref. Min. at Samuel Blackburn's; E. Crowell, M. Ramsour. NL.

  John; ABERNATHY, Sue; M=6 Sept. 1859; John Lantz, Min. NL.

  Martin (35) [Andy & Lucinda]; SMITH, Hanna (19) [Elick & Mary] of Hky; black; M=4 Feb. 1880; JH Bruns, JP in Hky; E. Smyer, Henry Alexander, Jack Philips. 2-130.

  Ned (21) [David Burchet & Patsy] of Jacob's Fork Twsp; WILFONG, Lettie (23) [Sam & Chana]; black; M=23 Mar. 1873; JW Bandy, JP in Bandy's Twsp; JM Link, WH Mosteller, Rufus Hodson. 1-259.

  Newman [Anthony Robinson & Emeline Wilfong]; BROWN, Leah [n/k & Silvy Robinson]; M=1 Sept. 1869; EA Warlick, JP. NL.

  Philip [Ephraim Wilfong & n/k]; WILSON, Laura [Turner McCorkle & Jane Wilson]; M=8 Jan. 1870; EP Coulter, JP. NL.

  Quince [John & Barbara E.]; SHUFORD, Alice A. [Jacob & Catharine]; M=15 Dec. 1870; JC Clapp, Min. 1-44.

  Robert (21) [Nelson & Esther]; ANGEL, Hannah (18) [James & Ivey] black; M=26 Feb. 1880; AG Corpening, JP in Jacob's Fork Twsp; Forney Robinson, Elizabeth Finger, ? Robinson. 2-131.

WILKERSON, Thomas [William & Susan]; EDWARDS, Jane [John Dick & n/k]; M=21 Aug. 1870; JL Hunt, JP. NL.

  William [Math & Elizabeth]; MCCORKLE, Rosa [Thomas & Dolly]; black; M=18 May 1868; GW Gabriel, JP. NL.

WILKIE, Alfred (22) of Burke Co., NC; CLINE, Zora (19); white; M= 16 Nov. 1876; Joseph M. Smith, Bapt. Min. at William Martin's; AJ Smith, NA ?, GW Pendleton. NL.

WILKIE, James A. (GJ & Ann); HAMILTON, Martha Ann [CJ & Delpha]; M=8 Apr. 1868; Elijah Allison, Min. NL.

WILKINSON, Avery M.P. [John & Eliza]; GRICE, Mary Jane [John & Sarah]; M=27 Mar. 1872; JA Sherrill, Min. NL.

    D.O.; MAYE, Rebecca; M=25 Apr. 1852; Alex I. Cansler, Min. NL.

    D.O.; ABERNATHY, Margaret; M=10 Mar. 1861; JD Caldwell, JP. NL.

    John F. [Thomas & Elizabeth]; DRUM, Harriet L. [Porter M. & Catharine]; M=27 Feb. 1868; JA Sherrill, Min. NL.

    Rufus A. [Thomas & Elizabeth]; SHUFORD, Ellen C.; M=1871; Record missing. NL.

    Sidney [John & Eliza]; BOST, Ann [Lawson & Susanah]; M=12 Sept. 1876; EP Coulter, Esq. NL.

    Thomas F. (20); TURBYFILL, Mary (21); white; M=16 Mar. 1876; JL Huit, JP in Caldwell Twsp; George Strout, Charlie Fry, Robert Norwood. NL.

    Wesley; HOWARD, Elizabeth; M=6 Oct. 1858; H. Asbury, Min. NL.

    William H. [Thomas & Elizabeth]; CALDWELL, Mary A.; M=31 Oct. 1871; Record missing. NL.

WILLIAMS, Coleman W. [Franklin & Solina]; HALL, Catharine [Simon & Ann]; M=20 Nov. 1870; JL Hewit, JP. 1-45.

    Edwin L. (21) [Nelson & Annie]; HOOVER, Isadore (18) [Thomas & Sophina]; white; M=5 Aug. 1880; PFW Stamey, Min. in Newton; JR boyd, RH Trolinger, MO Sherrill. 2-132.

    Franklin M. (55); WALLACE, Mary (40); white; M=24 June 1877; JL Huitt, JP in Caldwell Twsp; Marcus Hewit, William Parks, Margaret Abernathy. NL.

    J.M.D. (22) [Osburn & Rebecca]; SIGMON, Eler (18) [Henry & Elizabeth]; white; M=4 Jan. 1880; OW Osburn, JP in Mt. Crk Twsp; JT Beatty, John M. Howard, HW Sherrill. 1-434.

    John; BUMGARNER, Sarah; M=29 July 1863; Philip Burns, JP. NL.

    John P.; BUMGARNER, Latrtha E.; M=14 July 1859; JD Caldwell, JP. NL.

    John W.; RUDISILL, Ann E.; M=22 Aug. 1866; DS Henkel, Min. NL.

    L.M. [Robert & Lucinda A.]; HULL, Harriett [William Jenks & Rutha]; M=5 Sept. 1867; JC Hartsell, Min. NL.

    Laban P. (23) [FM & Salina]; CAMPBELL, Frances J. (18) [n/k & Martha Kirksey]; white; M=28 Mar. 1880; WC Caldwell, JP in Caldwell Twsp; WC Williams, WMA Clark, Levi S. Caldwell. 2-133.

    Osburn; HOWARD, Isabella; M=25 Oct. 1857; JD Caldwell, JP. NL.

    Richert (22); SHERRILL, Harriet L. Ann (16); black; M=3 Oct. 1878; WS Shuford, Bapt. Min. at Alfred Sherrill's; Jim Stocton, Elihue Setzer, Joseph Abernathy. NL.

    Thomas [William & Mary]; TAYLOR, Susan [n/k & Nancy Eaton]; M=28 June 1868; Miles Goodson, Esq. NL.

    William (65) [William & Mary E.]; CODY, Mary (30); white; M=14 Mar. 1880; WC Caldwell, JP in Caldwell Twsp; PW Cody, PD Campbell, JM Reinhardt. 2-134.

WILLIS, John A. (23) of Cleveland Co., NC; JARRETT, Alice (19); white; M=17 Sept. 1876; Robert Helton, Min. at Wesly Chapel; RJ Helton, MA Helton, CT Abernathy. NL.

WILSON, Alfred (26) [Marcus & Mary Ann] of Hamilton Twsp; ROBINSON, Sallie (22) [Elias & Mahala]; of Ham. Twsp; white; M=12 Dec. 1872; JL Hewit, JP in Ham. Twsp; LH Wilson, John Hewit, Eleanoh Bolch. 1-220.

WILSON, Calvin (21); BOST, Nancy (18); black; M=31 Oct. 1878; EJ Harris, Min. at Aaron Bost's; Ceter Mody, Aaron Bost, AE Harris. NL.
  Daniel C.; MILLER, Sarah E.; M=10 May 1866; J. Lantz, Min. NL.
  David (31); WHITENBURG, Elvina (19); black; M=5 Apr. 1877; PK Little, JP in Cline's Twsp; Abner Whitener, Joseph Wilson, Sidney Hunsucker. NL.
  Frank [Frank Moss & Jinnie Moss]; KILLIAN, Mary S. [Peter Shade & Grace]; M=15 Jan. 1869; James A. Garvan, JP. NL.
  George (35); LUTZ, Harriet E. (26); white; M=28 Feb. 1878; JC Clapp, Ref. Min. at Laban Lutz's; Henry Hass, RW Robinson, AM Settlemyer. NL.
  George W. (21); MILLER, Jane C. (19); white; M=19 Apr.1874; JH Burns, JP in Hky; Max E. Brown, Isaac Hartzell, Mollie E. Burns. NL.
  Henderson (19) of Caldwell Twsp; BOST, Laura (16) of Hamilton Twsp; white; M=23 Oct. 1873; JL Hewit, JP at JL Hewit's; Laura Bost, John Lepard, Augustus Kale. NL.
  Hoyle [Edmont Jennings & Lilla]; LEWIS, Jane [Bill Robinson & Cassie Wilfong]; M=19 May 1872; AG Corpening, JP. NL.
  J.I.; PROPST, Sarah E.; M=27 Sept. 1865; LN Wilson, JP. NL.
  Jacob (22); HART, Jane (21); black; M=15 Nov. 1874; GW Logan, Min. in Hky Tav. Twsp; David Herman, George Feamster. NL.
  Jeremiah (21) [Harry & Manerva]; WADKINS, Mary (22) [Frank & n/g]; black; M=18 Aug. 1872; William Brooks,Min. in Hamilton Twsp; Mira Conner, Hariet Roseman, Judy Smyre. 1-221.
  Jerry (21) of Newton Twsp; WITHERSPOON, Margaret (18) of Cline's Twsp; black; M=25 Dec. 1873; Edward Harris, Min. Jesse Smyre, Louis Yount, Rich Witherspoon. NL.
  John (19) [Samuel & Nelly]; BOSTIAN, Vina (25) [Abram & Betsy]; black; M=9 Dec. 1879; William Brooks, Min. in Hamilton Twsp; M. Conor, A. Ritchmond, M. Muttz. 1-435.
  John (34); SETZER, Ann (22); black; M=17 Oct.1878; HA Forney, JP in Newton; JE Forney, ME Lowrance, GW Setzer. NL.
  John H. (27) [JL & RS]; JONES, Nancy M.C. (17) [James & Caroline]; white; M=3 Sept. 1879; WC Caldwell, JP in Caldwell Twsp; SA Robinson, JE Hass, CC Propst. 1-436.
  John Lee (20) [Miles G. & Emeline]; SUMMIT, Lucinda (18); black; M=Dec. 1875; S. Carter at Snow Hill, Newton; A. Abernethy, Pinkney Hull, Luke Phillips. 1-305.
  Pompai(24); COULTER, Ann (20); black; M=24 Mar. 1878; R. England, JP in Caldwell Twsp; M. Coulter, Robert Ikerd, Peter England. NL.
  Reuben (20) [Ed Ramsour & Fanny Wilson]; HOKE, Caroline (18) [Anderson & Margie]; black; M=8 June 1879; EJ Harris, Min. in Newton Twsp; JW Cane, J. Hary Sims, Thomas Golden. 1-437.
  Robert (21) of Hamilton Twsp [yellow]; THOMAS, Cenus (22) of Ham. Twsp [black]; M=11 May 1873; William Brooks, Min. in Ham. Twsp; Julius Setzer, Pinkney Smyre, Pinkney Thomas. NL.
  William; KILLIAN, Lucy; M=21 Apr. 1861; W. Carson, Min. NL.
  William P.; BESHERER, Arelia; M=9 July 1860; PC Henkel, Min. NL.
WINEBARGER, Anderson (23) of Cline's Twsp; SPENCER, Julia E. (18) of Cline's Twsp; white; M=14 Dec. 1873; NE Sigmon, JP in Cline's Twsp; Daniel Deal, JA Epps, PE Isenhour. NL.

WINEBARGER, Daniel; HETERICK, Helana; M=2 Dec. 1855; H. Ingold, JP. NL.

  Noah; LANIER, Martha Ann; M=7 Sept. 1851; Elijah Huffman, JP. NL.

  William J. (22) [Noah & Rosanah]; WHITE, Candace L. (34) [Eli & Anna]; white; M=23 Dec. 1875; CT Sigmon, JP in Cline's Twsp; PS Sigmon, NM Sigmon, David Ekard. 1-306.

WINGATE, Franklin; ABERNATHY, Hannah; M=3 Nov. 1862; Lyman Woodford, JP. NL.

  Thomas; STINE, Nancy; M=3 Aug. 1859; JD Caldwell, JP. NL.

WINKLER, James W. [Mike & Jane]; CLONINGER, Malinda C. [Noah & Paline]; M=19 Mar. 1870; PF Smith, JP. NL.

WINKLEY, Jerry (27); WILFONG, Emma (24); black; M=12 Mar. 1876; Robert Helton, Min. at Robert Helton's; Ida C. Helton, Harriett Helton, JA Wells. NL.

WINTERS, Marion (22); WHITENER, Sallie (22); black; M=3 Sept. 1876; Abel Whitener, JP in Hky; Lillie Rowe, Phillip Rowe. NL.

  William R. (22) [James & Elizabeth] of Burke Co., NC; DEAL, Frances M. (22) [Frank & Melila]; white; M=17 Dec. 1875; GL Hunt, Luth. Min. in Newton Twsp; N.Huit, TL Huit, EE Longcrier. 1-307.

WISE, Daniel [John & Mary]; ROBINSON, Sallie [David & Anna]; M=31 Dec. 1867; J. Loritz, Min. NL.

  David (26) of Lincoln Co., NC; WHITENER, Catharine (23); white; M=14 Sept. 1876; Alfred J. Fox, Luth. Min. at Hosea Whitener's; WP Rudisill, JP Strutt, JA Whitener. NL.

WISEMAN, William H.; CONNOR, Lucian E.; M=8 Aug. 1865; WH Rockett, JP. NL.

WITHERS, Alfred (19) [Laban & Adoline] of Caldwell Twsp; DETTER, Susanah (18) [Frederick & Lovine] of Cald. Twsp; white; M=21 Nov. 1872; JL Hewitt, JP in Cald. Twsp; Aron Keener, George Blankenship, Cansady Cline. 1-222.

  John (20) [Laben & Adline]; FRY, Dealy Luaner (18) [n/k & Nancy Fry]; white; M=21 Dec. 1880; WC Caldwell, JP in Caldwell Twsp; Czar Gabriel, JB Caldwell, ST Caldwell. 2-135.

  William [Laban & Adoline]; ABERNATHY, Emeline [Jerry & Mary]; M=13 July 1870; JL Huit, JP. NL.

WITHERSPOON, David C.; GANTT, Emily; M=12 July 1857; JD Caldwell, JP. NL.

  James A. [Calvin & AC; FRY, Martha [NH & Catherine]; M=2 Jan. 1870; JM Smith, Min. NL.

  John H. (20) [Cahoun & Emily]; PROPST, Maggie (21) [Lawson & Linda]; white; M=27 Nov. 1879; LH Wilson, JP in Caldwell Twsp; MI Wilson, Mary Propst, Lee Witherspoon. 1-438.

  Thomas A. (23); MILLER, Arkansas (20); white; M=28 Dec. 1876; JC Hartsell, Min. at Joel Miller's; JW Mouser, JW Campbell, JM Witherspoon. NL.

  William C. [NH & Catherine]; FRY, Harriett P. [Calvin & AC]; M=7 Feb. 1870; JM Smith, Min. NL.

WOOD, Aaron [Heckter & Sylvia]; MULL, Bettie [Auther & Elvira]; M=24 Aug. 1871; JC Clapp, Min. 1-134.

  William (27) [Daniel & Hanah]; HELMS, Sarah (21) [Hiram & Elizabeth]; white; M=17 Nov. 1879; Jacob Mosteller, JP in Jacob's Fork Twsp; GW Clay, TS Michaels. 1-439.

WOOD, William W. [Daniel & Hannah]; PARKER, Martha Ann [John & Magdalene]; M=3 Oct. 1871; JL Hewit, JP. 1-135.
WOODFORD, Adolphus (n/g & Harriet Woodford]; SMYER, Mary Jane [Wilson & Elizabeth]; M=6 Jan. 1870; EA Warlick, JP. NL.
WOODRING, Joseph; MOSER, Rebecca; M=24 May 1857; PC Hinkle, Min. NL.
  Joseph (56); CONNS, Sarah Ann (25); white; M=1 Mar. 1877; JM Smith, Luth. Min. at Henry Coon's; MM Coons, Rebecca Hefner, PC Coons. NL.
WOODWARD, C.H.; ABERNATHY, S.E.; M=15 Nov. 1859; John Lantz, Min. NL.
WORKMAN, Danel; REINHARDT, Mary; M=19 May 1859; GW Yoder, JP. NL.
  John A. [Henry & Caroline]; LEATHERMAN, Mary Catharine [Jonas & Elizabeth]; M=3 Nov. 1870; Robert Helton, Min. 1-46.
  Solomon; REINHARDT, S.C.; M=20 Aug. 1865; GM Yoder, JP. NL.
WYANT, Daniel T. (21); LEFEVER, Sarah A. (21); white; M=23 Jan. 1879; ML Little, Min. at John Rocket's; CA Wyant, AM Wyant, JF Leonard. NL.
  Pinkney A. (25); BRITTON, Eliza J. (19); white; M=23 Mar. 1876; DM Wyant, JP in Bandy's Twsp; CA Wyant, AA Rudisill, JF Hudson. NL.
WYCHE, James E. (27) of Cabarrus Co., NC; BOBBITT, Rosa L. (19) of Cabarrus Co., NC; white; M=26 July 1878; FM Jones, Min. in Hky; Pattie A. Bobbitt, Minnie H. Marshall, Thomas P. Hinson. NL.
WYCKOFF, Jacob; ABERNATHY, Epsey; M=1 Sept. 1851; JM Lowrance, JP. NL.
  John W.; ELLER, Sarah E.; M=21 Jan. 1866; PJ Pitts, JP. NL.
YODER, A.A. [Jacob & Catherine]; MILLER, Adoline C. [Danel & Lovenia]; M=9 Dec. 1869; PC Hinckle, Min. NL.
  Alfred M. [JA & Elizabeth]; BRIDGES, S.M.C. [JS & MC]; M=9 Dec. 1869; John B. Marsh, Min. NL.
  Andrew; HAWN, Catharine; M=18 June 1857; PL Rowe, JP. NL.
  Calvin [Eli & Elizabeth]; REINHARDT, Sarah [John Fulbright & Lizzie]; M=13 Oct. 1867; EP Coulter, Esq. NL.
  Cyrus; LEONARD, Elizabeth; M=22 Feb. 1855; John Lantz, Min. NL.
  Daniel; WHITENER, Sacy E.; M=23 July 1854; Henry Goodman. NL.
  Daniel A. (41); MCCASLIN, Jane E. (35); white; M=26 Feb. 1876; AJ Fox, Luth. Min. at Mathew McCaslin's; JJ Cansler, A. Fulbright, A. Yoder. NL.
  Francis A. (23) of Jacob's Fork Twsp; COULTER, Katie C. (19) of Newton Twsp; white; M=20 Jan. 1873; JC Clapp, Ref. Min.; MM Wilson, Frank Ikerd, Perry Bost. NL.
  George M. (51); YODER, Eliza E. (36); white; M=26 Apr. 1877; AJ Fox, Luth. Min. at Moses Yoder's; Jane C. Yoder, Mattie A. Yoder, Moses Yoder. NL.
  J.M.; RICE, S.A.; M=13 Sept. 1860; William L. Mehaffey, JP. NL.
  Jacob M. [Andrew & Anna]; HOBBS, Mahala (Conrad Fry & n/g); M=29 Dec. 1870; EA Warlick, JP. 1-47.
  Jason E. (24) [Daniel & Sarah]; YODER, Jane C. (22) [Moses & Sarah]; white; M=18 Aug. 1880; JM Smith, Luth. Min. in Jacob's Fork Twsp; PL Smith, JP Yoder, LS Yoder. 2-138.
  Levi F. [John & Tollie]; GROSS, Harriet A. [Adam & Retha]; M=2 Sept. 1868; GM Yoder, JP. NL.

YODER, Michael A.L. (22); ABERNATHY, Martha I. (18); white; M=20 Feb. 1879; JC Clapp, Min. at JC Clapp's; J. Clapp, EL Clapp, WA Lants. NL.
  Moses; WARD, Sarah E.; M=14 Oct. 1855; Henry Goodman, Min. NL.
  Peter R. (22) [Cyrus & Elizabeth]; SEITZ, Sarah E. (18) [DD & Rebecca]; white; M=4 Nov.1880; PC Henkel, Luth. Min. in Newton Twsp; PF Smith, PC Hawn, ME Ekard. 2-139.
  Reubin; REAP, Mary C.; M=12 Apr. 1857; AJ Fox, Min. NL.
  Reubin; REEP, D.E.; M=5 Apr. 1863; John Lantz, Min. NL.
  William (22) of Lincoln Co., NC; MOSTELLER, Sarah Ann (27) of Bandy's Twsp; white; M=10 Dec. 1873; ML Little, Luth. Min. at Jacob Mosteller's; P. Baker, WH Mosteller, FL Mosteller. NL.
YOUNG, Andrew [Charley Cline & Hannah Cline]; SMITH, Julia [n/k & Nancy Smith]; M=11 Nov. 1869; William G. James, JP. NL.
  John; JOHNSON, Nancy R.; M=11 Jan. 1860; George Huffman, JP. NL.
  Marcus [George & n/k]; FOX, L.C. [PC Hinckle & Rebecca]; M=1868; PC Hinckle, Min. NL.
  Peter [David & Caty C.]; BOST, Luiza [Moses & Patty]; M=30 Dec. 1869; PF Smith, JP. NL.
  Peter (23); ABERNATHY, Retta (26); black; M=13 Mar. 1873; Isaac Wells, Min. in Mt. Crk Twsp; Ann Sherrill, John Hooper, Lucinda Sherrill. NL.
YOUNT, Ambrose; LOWRANCE, Jenetia; M=15 Feb. 1866; GJ Wilkie, Min. NL.
  Andrew; KALE, Sarah; M=17 Oct. 1861; JM Lowrance, JP. NL.
  D.M.L.; ROSEMAN, E.D.; M=14 Sept. 1865; PC Henkel, Min. NL.
  D.P.; REECE, Sally M.; M=28 Sept. 1865; E. Yount, JP. NL.
  D.P. [David & Malinda]; PROPST, Nancy R. [J. & Delila]; M=17 Oct. 1867; PC Henkel, Min. NL.
  David [Peter Moser & Viola Yount]; TRAVELSTRET, Mahala [Peter & Hannah]; M=12 Sept. 1867; Thomas Fry, Min. NL.
  Emanuel A.; HAWN, Amanda M.; M=26 Oct. 1851; PC Hinkle, Min. NL.
  George M. (23) [JHA & Sophia]; MURRY, Nannie C. (19) [Lambert & Elizabeth]; white; M=25 Apr. 1875; JC Hewit, JP in Newton Twsp; Jess Bost, Jess Yount, ? Murry. 1-308.
  George W.; LITTEN, Nancy R.; M=4 Aug. 1863; JB Little, JP. NL.
  Henry; MILLER, Mary M.; M=21 Aug. 1851; PC Henkel, Min. NL.
  James N. [Joseph & Catharine]; YOUNT, Harriet [WA & Lovina]; M=4 Feb. 1868; D McD. Yount, Esq. NL.
  John L. (22) [Elcanah & Dianah] of Cline's Twsp; CLONINGER, Mary (20) [Michael & Rosanah] of Cline's Twsp; white; M=5 Dec. 1872; JM Smith, Min. in Cline's Twsp; JP Yount, MW Cloninger, AE Whitener. 1-223.
  John Walter (22); HUNSUCKER, Alace (15); white; M=16 Feb. 1875; GL Hunt, Luth. Min. at Sarah Hunsucker's; Vance Yount, Wash cloninger, Wash Yount. NL.
  Jones (19); YOUNT, Leanah (18); white; M=15 Feb. 1877; JM Smith, Luth. Min. at D. Yount's; MM Smith, JL Yount, JP Yount. NL.
  Joseph P. (21); BOLCH, Sarah (15); white; M=31 Dec. 1874; JM Smith, Luth. Min. at AE Bolch's; WJ Yount, MW Cloninger, Noah Setzer. NL.
  Joshua A. [John & Elizabeth]; SUMMITT, Lena [Alexander & Sally]; M=2 Sept. 1869; PC Hinckle, Min. NL.
  L.H.; WHITENER, Margaret R.; M=2 Nov. 1854; John Lantz, Min. NL.

YOUNT, Laban E. (22); MILLER, Mary (22); white; M=15 Feb. 1877; PK Little, JP in Cline's Twsp; AJ Holler, JHC Hewit, Wilson Isenhour. NL.
   Levi (50); NEWTON, Cintha (44); white; M=26 Feb. 1874; JC Hartsell, Min. at Settlemyre's; AA Yoder, HS Settlemyre, JWM Abernathy. NL.
   Lewis (50); SHERRILL, Mary (27); black; M=24 Dec. 1878; WG James, JP in Catawba; McAdams, Leroy Linney, W. Menberry. NL.
   Miles; HEFNER, Catharine; M=6 July 1856; JB Little, JP. NL.
   Moses (25); WHITENER, Susan J. (24); black; M=1 July 1875; NE Sigmon, JP in Cline's Twsp; Pink Smith, Hannah Herman, Delphy Hedrick. NL.
   Pinkney L. (23) [Elcana & DE]; CLONINGER, Annotie (16) [Michael & Rosanna]; white; M=18 May 1879; JM Smith, Luth. Min. at Michael Cloninger's; JL Yount, MW Cloninger, NA Brady. 1-440.
   Samuel; MACK, Laura; M=22 Mar. 1857; E. Conner, JP. NL.
   Sidney [Peter Moser & Violet Yount]; LITTLE, Martha [n/k & Kissie Little]; M=31 Oct. 1869; JC Clapp, Min. NL.
   Stephen A. (31) of Caldwell Twsp; POOVEY, Harriet J. (21); white; M=25 Jan. 1877; Abel Barger, JP in Hky; CE Graham, JG Marshall, James E. Wilfong. NL.
   Timothy J. [Ephraim & Catherine]; HOFFMAN, Emeline [Nelson & Rhoda]; M=7 Apr. 1870; JM Smith, Min. NL.
   Walton C. (27) of Hky Tav. Twsp; YOUNT, Filecta (22) of Hky Tav. Twsp; white; M=16 Apr. 1873; JM Smith, Luth. Min. in Hky Tav. Twsp; SE Yount, AE Townsend, ME Deitz. NL.
   William (21); SMITH, Laura L. (16); white; M=13 May 1875; JM Smith, Luth. Min. at MM Smith's; QM Smith, BE Smith, HS Smith. NL.

- END OF BOOK -

BRIDE'S CROSS-INDEX

?, Anna - Warren, John
?, Manah - Propst, J.H.
Abee, C.M. - Seitz, F.M.
Abee, Jane E. - Martin, William P.
Abee, Martha L. - Fry, J.D.
Abee, Sarah - Hildebran, Jacob A.
Abernathy, Abigail - Edwards, Howard
Abernathy, Alice - Hefner, Adolphus
Abernathy, Ann - Setzer, Noah
Abernathy, Barbara - Bumgarner, Alfred
Abernathy, Belza L. - Bowman, Luther
Abernathy, Caroline - Cline, Francis M.
Abernathy, Caroline - Harvell, Frances
Abernathy, Cate - Sigmon, Perry
Abernathy, Catherine - Weaver, John
Abernathy, Eliza - Taylor, M.H.
Abernathy, Elizabeth - Fry, James H.
Abernathy, Elizabeth - Sigmon, Churchwell J.
Abernathy, Emeline - Withers, William
Abernathy, Emma A. - Shell, William G.
Abernathy, Fannie - Ramsour, Edward
Abernathy, Epsey - Wyckoff, Jacob
Abernathy, Hannah - Wingate, Franklin
Abernathy, Jane E. - Herman, Charles H.
Abernathy, Jenna - Abernathy, R.D.
Abernathy, L. - Covington, B.
Abernathy, M.A. - Beatty, Calvin
Abernathy, Margaret - Wilkinson, D.O.
Abernathy, Martha - Helderbrand, Daniel
Abernathy, Martha A. - Caldwell, J.D.
Abernathy, Martha I. - Yoder, Michael A.L.
Abernathy, Mattie A. - Richard, Charley
Abernathy, Miery - Caldwell, Henderson
Abernathy, N.J. - Propst, J.S.
Abernathy, N.T. - Anthony, R.L.
Abernathy, Nancy E. - Abernathy, John P.
Abernathy, Nancy P. - Hawkins, Miles H.
Abernathy, Perlina - Summits, Isaac L.
Abernathy, Rebecca - Setzer, Calvin
Abernathy, Retta - Young, Peter
Abernathy, Rhoda - Beal, Ephraim
Abernathy, S.E. - Woodward, C.H.
Abernathy, Salina - Shuford, John L.
Abernathy, Sarah A. - Abernathy, Osburn F.
Abernathy, Sarah A. - Helton, William
Abernathy, Sarah Ann - Grice, James M.
Abernathy, Sarah Jane - Hewitt, M.W.
Abernathy, Sophia - Cobb, Rufus
Abernathy, Sue - Wilfong, John
Abernathy, Susan - Cornelius, John
Abernathy, Susan - Stiles, J.R.
Abernethy, Rebecca D. - Crouse, Robert
Abernethy, Willie - Boyd, Thomas
Akins, Anna C. - Berry, Osburn
Albright, Mary - Jones, Isaac G.
Albright, Sallie E. - Jarrett, John R.
Alexander, Caroline - Chambers, Henry A.
Allen, Mary M. - Linebarger, John W.
Allen, Sarah S. - Edwards, Miles
Alley, Laura - Bost, Matthew E.
Allin, Margaret - Little, James B.
Allison, Jinnie - Litten, J.A.
Allison, Rachel - Sherrill, David M.
Allran, Mary - Glasgo, Zach
Angel, Alice - Robinson, Lewis
Angel, Bena - Anthony, Churchill
Angel, Caroline - Hildebrand, James
Angel, Hannah - Wilfong, Robert
Angel, Martha M. - Sharp, Solamon G.
Anthony, Ann - Dellinger, William P.
Anthony, Catharine - Propst, Franklin
Anthony, Isabel - Cansler, Jesse
Anthony, Manday - Finger, Hugh
Arney, Mattie E. - Taylor, Lewis
Arnt, T.S. - Robb, J.F.
Arwood, Anna - Arndt, John Henry
Arwood, Mary - Killian, J. Franklin
Ashebraner, Catherine - Hudson, Franklin
Ashley, Genelia - Marlow, W.H.
Austin, Mary - Clayton, John
Austin, Mattie - Bumgarner, Franklin
Bailer, Lucinda - Tucker, Demisey
Baker, Adoline - Roderick, Sephus
Baker, Belza - Seitz, L.P.

Baker, Candace Angeler - Killian, Sylvanus
Baker, Casaan - Speagle, Aaron
Baker, Ellen - Hefner, Levi
Baker, Eva - Killian, William L.
Baker, Florence - Hefner, David F.
Baker, Jane - Bost, Andrew
Baker, Jane - Mosteller, Lawson
Baker, Julia - Milligan, Gilbert P.
Baker, R.L. - Bowman, Jacob
Baker, Sallie - Sipe, John
Baker, Sarah - Abernathy, Calvin L.
Baker, Sarah J. - Sipe, Alfred E.
Baker, Victoria - Brown, Avery
Ball, Mary - Eads, Joel
Bandy, Chantz M. - McGinnis, John J.
Bandy, Dovey - Goodman, Columbus
Bandy, Jane E. - Jones, Samuel Gregory
Bandy, Mary E. - Smith, George F.
Bandy, Mary Ellenor - Edwards, James L.
Banks, Sarah - Mathis, Daniel Forney
Barger, Barbara C. - Speagle, John W.
Barger, Dinah - Cline, Maxwell
Barger, Eveline - King, Jacob
Barger, Fannie - Erwin, Maxwell E.
Barger, Flora M. - Harris, H.L.
Barger, Margaret C. - Fry, Marcus
Barger, Martha - Turner, D.W.
Barger, Rebecca - Newton, David
Barger, Rhoda - Herman, Frederick
Barger, Sophronio - Webb, James E.
Barkley, Mary - Robinson, Pinckney
Barkley, Sarah E. - McCall, James A.
Barringer, Emeline E. - Wade, Elisha
Barringer, Lina - Cline, M.N.
Barringer, Mary Jane - Deal, Robert H.
Beal, Anna E. - Bandy, Robert H.
Beal, Mary - Bandy, Daniel A.
Beal, Mary - Alexander, Daniel A.
Beard, Caroline - Pitts, Daniel
Beard, Eva - Beard, Asbury B.
Beatty, Elizabeth - Linebarger, Worth
Beatty, Florence E. - Gabriel, Joseph W.
Beatty, M.J. - Abernathy, Mitten
Beatty, Martha Ann - Loftin, John A.

Beatty, Nancy - Little, William
Beaty, Susan - Gabriel, David P.
Beatty, Vira - McCorkle, David
Beaty, Elizabeth - Barkley, John A.
Beaty, Susan V. - Sherrill, E.A.
Bell, Polly - Sronce, Ephraim
Bendle, Mahala - Whitener, Pinkney
Benfield, Catherine - Pope, Augustus
Benfield, Mahaly - Huffman, Sillis
Benfield, Sarah - Miller, William Marcus
Benfield, Sarah - Porter, John R.
Bennick, F.H. - Brady, F.A.
Bennick, Jane - McCorkle, Henry M.
Besherer, Arelia - Wilson, William P.
Bever, Lucy - Cain, John W.
Bishener, Louisa - Hollar, George W.
Black, Fannie J. - Southerland, Lafayett
Blackburn, Emma - Wilfong, James E.
Blackburn, Georgia Ann - Fry, Joseph A.
Blackburn, Mary - Robinson, Aarin
Blackburn, Rhoda - Ramsour, Milton H.
Blakely, Sarah E. - Rudisill, Jacob F.
Bobbitt, Rosa L. - Wyche, James E.
Bogle, Julia - McRorie, Jacob
Bolch, Amy - Flowers, John
Bolch, C.M. - Hefner, H.
Bolch, C.M. - Hefner, S.
Bolch, Carmila - Poovey, John Zeno
Bolch, Caroline - Pope, Henry
Bolch, Elizabeth - Cline, William A.
Bolch, Emaline - Watts, William Francis
Bolch, Emaline E. - Mires, Thomas P.
Bolch, Gemima - Raby, John
Bolch, Laura E. - Hoover, Daniel
Bolch, Lovina - Bost, Sidney M.
Bolch, Manerva - Heterick, John H.
Bolch, Martha - Miller, George
Bolch, Mary M. - Bruner, Reuben W.
Bolch, Nancy E. - Hallman, Laban
Bolch, Patsey - Harbinson, A.S.
Bolch, Polly J. - Bolch, Marcus H.
Bolch, Salina E. - Punch, Joseph L.
Bolch, Sarah - May, Samuel Y.
Bolch, Sarah - Yount, Joseph P.

Bolch, Sarah E. - Waugh, Silus B.
Bolch, Sarah J. - Sigmon, Henry A.
Bolch, Sophiah - Cline, Noah
Bolch, Sophronia - McDurgher, John
Bolch, Susan - Propst, William
Bolch, Susan E. - Fry, Alfred H.
Bolch, Susanah - Gibson, J.M.
Bolinger, Martha - Herman, Peter D.
Bollinger, Isabella - Huffman, Alfred B.
Bollinger, Polly J. - Rinck, George F.
Boovey, Nira Malinda - Kaylor, Joseph E.
Boovy, M.J. - Eckard, Simon
Bost, Alice E. - Rowe, C.B.
Bost, Allace - Baker, Milas
Bost, Ann - Wilkinson, Sidney
Bost, Ann A. - Miller, Absalom
Bost, Anna - Settlemire, George
Bost, Elizabeth - Harris, Augustus
Bost, Ella - Faucette, Edward W.
Bost, Ella Gertrude - Alison, Thomas A.
Bost, Ellen - James, McDuffey
Bost, Emma Jane - Fry, William P.
Bost, H.Y. - Setzer, William A.
Bost, Harriet E. - Know, Robert A.
Bost, Harriet - Roseman, Ras.
Bost, Ider S. - Alexander, Yount
Bost, Julia A. - Keener, David
Bost, Julia C. - Cline, William P.
Bost, Laura - Fox, William
Bost, Laura - Wilson, Henderson
Bost, Laura N. - Cline, M.L.
Bost, Luiza - Young, Peter
Bost, Mary - McRee, Peter
Bost, Mary M. - Self, W.R.
Bost, Nancy - Wilson, Calvin
Bost, Sarah - Forney, J.J.
Bost, Sarah A. - Hallman, William E.
Bost, Sarah A. - Robb, James P.
Bost, Selia - Kale, Marcus Augustus
Bost, Sophrona - Lael, Calvin
Bostain, A.E. - Little, Thomas
Bostian, Frances G. - Danner, Henry S.
Bostian, Vina - Wilson, John
Boston, R.M. - Conner, Henry W.

Bowman, Candace E. - McGee, Jonas M.
Bowman, Frances S. - Miller, Abel P.
Bowman, Harriet E. - Drum, Miles
Bowman, Harriet S. - Fry, Moses
Bowman, Mary - Coons, Jacob
Bowman, Rhoda E. - Bolch, H.J.
Bowman, Sarah C. - Hoke, Thomas M.
Bowman, Susan - Brinkley, Daniel
Bowman, Zenith A. - Murphy, Joseph S.
Boyd, Francis - Perry, Henry H.
Boyd, Mary - Bynum, Pink
Bradburn, Mary - Gilleland, E. Casper
Bradburn, Matie E. - Warlick, D. Logan
Bradburn, Susan - Sherrill, Francis M.
Braddy, Laura - Henkle, Charles H.
Bradshaw, Alice R. - Propst, Daniel A.
Bradshaw, Harriet S. - Caldswell, Rufus A.
Brady, M.A. - Abernathy, Milton A.
Brendle, Frances - Carpenter, William Pinkney
Bridges, Elizabeth - Abernathy, James M.
Bridges, Ellon - Howard, James
Bridges, Henrietta - James, William
Bridges, Jane C. - Webb, Joseph B.
Bridges, Jane M. - Rowe, M.M.
Bridges, M.M. - Laller, H.L.
Bridges, Nancy M. - Fisher, William H.
Bridges, S.M.C. - Yoder, Alfred M.
Brinkley, Jane - Hallman, Noah W.
Brittain, Susan - Hubbard, Franklin
Britton, Annie E. - Abee, Jefferson
Britton, Eliza J. - Wyant, Pinkney A.
Brooks, Hanna - Shuford, Lafayette
Brooks, Lizzie - Smyer, Pink
Brooks, Mary - Moore, Henry
Brotherton, F.E. - Sherrill, M.A.
Brotherton, Mary Jane - Sherrill, Robert W.
Brown, Alice S.C. - Sigmon, Maxwell L.
Brown, Catharine - Jones, Evelind H.
Brown, Laura A. - Warren, William S.
Brown, Leah - Wilfong, Newman
Brown, Manerva - Clark, D.S.
Brown, Mary Ann - Miller, Franklin
Brown, Mary Etta - Rhyne, Burton C.
Brown, Mary J. - Holdsclaw, Alexander

Brown, Mat[ilda] - Miller, Larkin
Brown, Patsey - Hoke, Henry L.
Brown, Rebecca - Miller, Lancan
Bumgarner, A.B. - Parker, Charley
Bumgarner, Camila M. - Abernathy, Pinkney
Bumgarner, Catherine - Bumgarner, Pinkney
Bumgarner, Covy - Abernathy, Miles
Bumgarner, Elizabeth - Watts, Rufus
Bumgarner, Frances A. - Martin, Harry L.
Bumgarner, Huldah - Cash, S.B.
Bumgarner, Jane - Cloninger, Perry C.
Bumgarner, Jemima - Byers, Henry
Bumgarner, Latrtha E. - Williams, John P.
Bumgarner, Mary - Watts, Monroe
Bumgarner, Mary C. - Bumgarner, J.M.
Bumgarner, Nancy - Abernathy, L.
Bumgarner, Rhoda C. - Miller, B.J.
Bumgarner, S.E. - Painter, O.P.
Bumgarner, Sarah - Williams, John
Bumgarner, Susan - Bumgarner, Sidney A.
Burch, Ellen - Megee, Hiram
Burke, Martha - Painter, J.L.
Burns, Caroline - Lafevers, Daniel
Burton, E.E. - Harwell, R.A.
Burton, Lizzie - Rankin, Will
Byars, Lucinda - Sherrill, William
Bynum, Candice - Sherrill, Joseph Henry
Bysing, A.A. - Robinson, D.S.
Cahill, Mary - Seagle, Daniel
Caldwell, Ada O.V. - Clark, James Mel
Caldwell, Carrie V. - Whiting, Horace G.
Caldwell, Debbie - Clark, John W.
Caldwell, Elizabeth - Jones, John Turner
Caldwell, Eva - Setzer, William B.
Caldwell, Fannie E. - Drum, Pinkney D.
Caldwell, Lizey S. - Cranford, W. Manley
Caldwell, Margaret M. - Laney, Noah E.
Caldwell, Margaret R. - Drum, William H.
Caldwell, Martha - Hoover, Jacob
Caldwell, Martha A. - Shelton, A.F.
Caldwell, Mary A. - Clark, William M.A.
Caldwell, Mary Ann - Wilkinson, William H.
Caldwell, Mella H. - Hoover, Monroe
Caldwell, Nancy - Drum, Rufus L.

Caldwell, Octa - Sherrill, Aaron A.
Caldwell, Rhoda M. - Drum, John P.
Caldwell, Sarah - Reep, Susan (sic)
Caldwell, Susan - Kirksey, William
Campbell, Alda V. - Shuford, Abel A.
Campbell, Frances J. - Williams, Laban P.
Campbell, Janie - Abernathy, Theodore R.
Campbell, Plinna - Turbill, Elkanah
Campbell, Rhoda - Carter, John C.
Campbell, Rosanah - Campbell, John W.
Campbell, Sophia - Spencer, David
Canipe, Catharine L. - Speagle, Thomas
Cansler, Frances R. - Seagle, Jacob A.
Canup, Emaline - Huffman, Adolphus
Carkerham, J.F. - Curtis, A.F.
Carpenter, Barbara - Dellinger, Robert
Carpenter, Ellen - Setzer, Marcus C.
Carpenter, Francis L. - Brown, Ruffin
Carpenter, Hannah - Hollyburton, Thomas
Carpenter, Martha A. - Deitz, H.C.
Carpenter, Mary Jane - Setzer, George W.
Carpenter, Sallie - Smith, Elmore B.
Carpenter, Sarah Ann - Hoke, George A.
Carter, Clementine - Hicks, Levi
Carter, M.C. - Ingle, Levi
Carter, Martha E. - Armstrong, Daniel M.
Carter, Sarah - Bumgarner, David
Cathey, Mariah - Setzer, Ellihue
Chambers, Amanda - Thomas, Edmon
Chambers, Catherine L. - Robards, Burtin
Chambers, Elizabeth - Abernathy, James H.
Chapman, Elizabeth - Cline, A.
Childers, Emma C. - Rink, Daniel
Christopher, Catherine - Holler, Jonas
Christophle, Manervey - Shook, Fredrick
Chumn, M.E. - Arney, J.C.
Clark, Margaret A. - Wagoner, Charles M.
Clark, Mary - McCorkle, Carry
Clark, Mary L. - McKinzie, Jonathan
Clark, Rebecca - Drum, James M.
Cline, Adoline L. - Bolch, Phillip H.
Cline, Amanda E. - Poovey, Henry L.
Cline, Angeline - Sigmon, James E.
Cline, B.S. - Deal, A.

Cline, Callie - Shell, William
Cline, Camila - Burris, John
Cline, Candace - Mooney, William Pinkney
Cline, Candace M. - Hunsucker, William Nelson
Cline, Caroline - Huit, Henderson
Cline, Caroline - Patrick, Calvin
Cline, Catharine - Killian, Henry
Cline, Clarinita - Hass, Daniel
Cline, Eliza - Barringer, Noah
Cline, Eliza - Hudson, Andrew
Cline, Eliza - Smith, R.C.
Cline, Emeline - Bumgarner, Eli
Cline, Fannie D. - Roseman, D.F.
Cline, Frances - Hunsucker, Burton
Cline, Harriet - Raby, William
Cline, Harriet J. - Hartzoge - Abel C.
Cline, Julia A. - Whitener, Benjamin A.
Cline, Juliann C. - Miller, John
Cline, Kesiah - Hefner, Marcus
Cline, Laura E. - Thomason, George F.
Cline, Lou Ellen - Seabock, Jacob A.
Cline, Mahala - Huffman, Jeremiah
Cline, Mahala - Huit, Carry
Cline, Margaret - Flowers, Calvin
Cline, Margaret - Shooping, Gilbert
Cline, Margaret E. - Hudson, William S.
Cline, Margaret R. - Poovey, Amianal
Cline, Martha S. - Miller, Rufus
Cline, Mary C. - Helton, Abel A.
Cline, Mary J. - Seabock, John
Cline, Mary J. - Throneburg, John E.
Cline, Mary Jane - Cline, John P.
Cline, Mattie - Huit, W. Adolphus
Cline, Nancy - Bolch, Manuel
Cline, Nancy Ann - Throneburg, L. Lafayett
Cline, Patsey - Newbin, Thomas
Cline, Polly - Abernathy, William
Cline, Polly - Starr, Silvanus M.
Cline, R.E. - Drum, John P.
Cline, Rebecca - Starnes, James
Cline, Rhoda - Abernathy, Adam A.
Cline, Rhoda E. - Helton, Clingman
Cline, Sarah - Eldridge, Jasper
Cline, Sarah A. - Seagle, Wesley
Cline, Susan - Reese, George
Cline, Susan - Smith, James
Cline, Trefena - Huffman, Martin
Cline, Zora - Wilkie, Alfred
Clipard, Elizabeth - Bradshaw, Thomas J.
Clipard, L.C. - Fry, Jacob
Clippard, Lovina R. - Reel, Hamilton
Clippard, Nancy J. - Clippard, Rufus W.
Clodfelter, Catharine - Coley, G.D.
Clodfelter, Francis S. - Hedgepeth, John
Clodfelter, Jane - Summit, Levi R.
Clodfelter, Sarah P. - Bumgarner, Sidney
Cloninger, Annotie - Yount, Pinkney L.
Cloninger, Carmilla - Herman, M.C.
Cloninger, Elizabeth C. - Setzer, J.S.
Cloninger, Lucinda C. - Turner, George C.
Cloninger, Malinda C. - Winkler, James W.
Cloninger, Manerva - Little, Jacob L.
Cloninger, Martha E. - Brady, Noah E.
Cloninger, Mary - Yount, John L.
Cloninger, Meriah - Bridges, Wallie
Cloninger, Sarah C. - Hunsucker, Jonas
Cloninger, Selena - Rowe, Marcus
Cobb, Charlotte - Sanders, Miles S.
Cobb, Emma - Croson, H.H.
Cobb, Lovina F. - Clark, P.M.
Cobb, Masonia S. - Sronce, William A.
Cobb, Melinda M. - Stroup, Peter
Cobb, Minta - Reinhardt, Frank
Cochran, Celila - Livinston, John
Cochran, Louisa S. - Coffey, Henry N.
Cochrane, Martha V. - Cashion, Leonard
Cody, Mary - Williams, William
Collett, Harriett - Alexander, Julius
Colter, Manga - Robinson, Martin
Conley, Candace - Gross, Allen
Conley, Lon - Gibbs, James
Conner, D.M. - Setzer, John
Conner, Harriet - Howard, Pinckney B.
Connor, Lucian E. - Wiseman, William H.
Connor, Mira - Roseman, Alley
Conrad, Adoline - Cline, Darus
Conrad, Mary - Nance, Franklin
Cook, M.E. - Fisher, N.H.

Coons, Camila - Lail, Gerard
Coons, Elizabeth - Houston, J.M.
Coons, Mary Ann - Lael, Sylvanus
Coons, Sarah Ann - Woodring, Joseph
Cornelius, Addie - Whitener, Sidney J.
Cornelius, Alace - Monday, Miles
Cornelius, Ann - Slaten, Julius
Cornelius, Ann - Staten, Julius
Cornelius, Fannie - Calicutt, James
Cornelius, Jane - Conner, William
Cornelius, Mattie E. - Sherrill, M.W.
Correll, Margaret M. - Abernathy, Miles C.
Cosby, F.S. - Tucker, Samuel
Coulter, A.A. - Bost, W.R.D.
Coulter, Ann - Wilson, Pompai
Coulter, Fanny - Ramsour, George
Coulter, Katie C. - Yoder, Francis A.
Coulter, Laura - McCorkle, Henry
Coulter, Louisa - Huffman, Noah
Coulter, Martha - Rowe, Nelson
Coulter, Martha J. - Ikerd, Franklin C.
Coulter, Mary Ann - Berry, J.M.
Coulter, Sallie - Gibbs, Charles
Coulter, Sallie - Robinson, Noah
Covington, Charity C. - Grice, John W.
Cowhone, Elizabeth - Shuford, Rufus
Cranford, Laura R. - Loftin, William Alex
Cranford, Mary M. - Allen, William E.
Cranford, Nancy Ann - Shelton, Elihue L.
Crowell, Mildred - Ellis, William H.
Crump, Candace M. - Vanhorn, Adolphus L.
Crutchfield, Elizabeth E. - Bailey, John
Cunent, Martha - Sherrill, Christopher
Daetos, J.C. - Bost, E.J.
Dagenhardt, Missouri - Nance, William H.
Dagenhart, Barbara T.E. - Huffman, James M.
Dagerheart, Cacean - Deitz, Solamon
Dalton, Louisa - Simonton, Samuel
Davidson, Emeline - Hunter, Alex
Davis, Malinda - Edwards, Henderson
Davis, Mary Sue - Forney, Albert
Davis, Violett - Robinson, William
Dawthitte, Ella A. - Cline, James E.
Day, Elizabeth - Price, William C.

Day, Margaret - Brown, S.C.
Day, Rachel A. - Brown, R. Hosea
Deal, Ada - Bowman, William P.
Deal, Adoline - Cline, D.W.
Deal, Adoline - Johnson, C. Perry
Deal, Amanda - Sherrill, Alonzo
Deal, C.E. - Shook, Tobus
Deal, Catharine Adoline - Sigmon, Sidney W.
Deal, Eliza - Sigmon, Elcana
Deal, Eliza E. - Deal, John S.
Deal, Ellen P. - Epps, John A.
Deal, Emoline - Travensted, Levi
Deal, Fannie A. - Sigmon, Adolphus N.
Deal, Fannie M. - Settlemyre, George P.
Deal, Frances M. - Winters, William R.
Deal, Harriet G. - Sigmon, Julius S.
Deal, Harriett L. - Moose, Daniel W.
Deal, Jane E. - Fox, Joseph
Deal, Julian - Hoke, F.A.
Deal, L.A. - Lee, Osburn
Deal, Laura A. - Baker, Martin L.
Deal, Linnie - Hefner, Lewis
Deal, Lucinda - Sigmon, Emanuel
Deal, Lymie E. - McGee, John L.
Deal, Lynia - Megee, John L.
Deal, M.C. - Setzer, Carr
Deal, Mary Jane - Lutz, James
Deal, Mary Jane - Frazier, William Bruce
Deal, Nancy - Clodfelter, Elias
Deal, Nisy - Bowman, J.L.
Deal, Rhoda - Setzer, Charles A.
Deal, Rosanah M. - Miller, Wesley
Deal, Sarah - Setzer, Joshua
Deal, Sarah A. - Isenhour, Daniel
Deal, Susan J. - Mosteller, Franklin P.
Deal, Susanah - Hollar, Jacob
Deatz, Malinda M. - Shephard, Polycarp C.
Deitz, Caroline - Fry, A.D.
Deitz, Caroline - Weaver, Absolom
Deitz, Catharine - Sigmon, David
Deitz, Celia - Garland, F.R.
Deitz, Celia - Parland, F.R.
Deitz, Eliza - Hider, William
Deitz, Martha - Hawn, James Knox Polk

Deitz, Patsy Bertha A. - Setzer, Jacob
Deitz, Polly Carolina - Whisenhunt, John
Deitz, Polly S. - Haiman, Hiram
Dellinger, Anna - Eckard, George
Dellinger, Barbara C. - Bolch, Cany
Dellinger, Catherine E. - Bolch, Benjamin
Dellinger, Eliza - Davis, William D.
Dellinger, Laura - Tayler, John F.
Dellinger, Margaret - Morgan, Lafayette
Dellinger, Mary - Ward, Samuel
Dellinger, Sarah - Fry, Calvin
Detter, Carolina - Blankenship, Elisha
Detter, Catharine Y. - Keever, Aaron
Detter, L.C. - Hileman, A.F.
Detter, Mary M. - Logan, William
Detter, Sarah - Wike, William
Detter, Susanah - Withers, Alfred
Dietz, Barbara E. - Bolch, William M.
Dietz, Ellen - Lail, George W.
Dockert, Nancy - Herman, Benjamin
Doctor, M.E. - Moose, Daniel
Douglas, Alice - Sigmon, Hosea Pinkney
Douglass, Jane - Mingus, George
Downs, Margaret - Mull, John
Drum, A.M. - Hefner, B.C.
Drum, Camila - Eckard, Wesley D.
Drum, Catharine - Loftin, William
Drum, Cynthia - Miller, Reuben
Drum, Dorothy - Huffman, Elisha
Drum, E.A. - Sigmon, L.H.
Drum, E. Jane - Miller, Albert A.
Drum, Ellen - Reep, Gilbert N.
Drum, Gillie - Fry, Enos Grover
Drum, Harriet L. - Wilkinson, John F.
Drum, Leah - Lackey, J.H.
Drum, Londie - Huffman, William P.
Drum, Martha J. - Cook, James M.
Drum, Mary - Benfield, Noah
Drum, Mary - Price, Israel C.
Drum, Mulvina - Bandy, Theodore L.
Drum, N. Callie - Flowers, John H.
Drum, Rebecah - Fulbright, William S.
Drum, Rebecca - Killian, Alfred L.
Drum, Rebecca - Turbyfill, J.L.

Drum, Rebecca M. - Lofton, Adolphus G.
Drum, Roxanah - Cline, John
Drum, Sarah Ann - Hagar, Clemmline
Duck, Martha - Gross, Allen
Eades, Catharine - Burris, George W.
Eckard, A. - Huffman, Setthial
Eckard, Eliza - Fisher, N.J.
Eckard, T.S. - Cline, L.J.
Eckerd, Susanna C. - Icenhour, John
Eckert, Emeline E. - Lanier, Burton N.
Edwards, Jane - Wilkerson, Thomas
Edwards, Martha Ann - Edwards, John
Edwards, Mary - Raby, W.A.
Edwards, Sallie Ann - Keever, Alexander
Ekard, Ellen B. - Holler, Lawson M.
Ekard, Isabell - Costner, Franklin
Ekard, Martha E. - Hetrick, Alfred H.
Ekard, Martha J. - Simmons, Adolphus J.
Ekard, Susan - Hefner, L.S.
Ekard, Veronica B. - Reitzel, Henry J.
Ekerd, Candace C. - Coons, Marcus M.
Eldridge, Camila - Bumgarner, Julius
Eller, Jane M. - Brown, William E.
Eller, Mary - Turbyfill, Wesley
Eller, Sarah E. - Wyckoff, John W.
Elliott, Mary - James, James
Elliott, Mary C. - Cody, John
Ellis, Susan - Newton, Eboneezer
England, Catherine - Finger, Lalon
England, Julia - Ekerd, Bob
England, Lydia Ann - Gibbs, Thomas
Ervin, Ann - Pitts, David
Ervin, Clara - Reinhardt, Graham
Farrow, Florence H. - Whiting, Seymour W.
Finger, Malinda - Keener, J. Frank
Finger, Martha E. - Hicks, J.J.
Finger, Mary Jane - Fry, J.E.
Finger, S.J. - Hicks, J.J.
Finger, Synthia R. - Michael, A.
Fish, Eliza - Blalock, Andrew A.
Fish, Emily - Kale, Palsen
Fish, Lina - Ennis, John
Fish, Mattie - Sigmon, Dock B.J.
Fish, Nannie - Cline, James

Fish, Rebecca - Cline, Calvin
Fisher, Anna M. - Sigmon, James W.
Fisher, Caroline - Bolch, W.P.
Fisher, Emeline - Long, William T.
Fisher, Faney E. - Long, John W.
Fisher, Margaret E. - Stiles, Jacob A.
Fisher, Roxanna - Childers, Daniel W.
Fisher, Thelethia - Hass, J.A.
Fleming, Elizabeth J. - Long, John W.
Fleming, Martha - Harwell, J. Horace
Flowers, Elmina - Bolch, N.A.
Flowers, H.R. - Cline, Rufus
Forney, Jane - Tate, Hampton
Forney, Mary - Roseman, Robert M.
Forney, Sarah C. - Brown, Anderson A.
Forster, Hannah - Sigmon, Julius T.
Fox, Amy - Moser, J.C.
Fox, Barbara C. - Dellinger, John C.
Fox, E.M. - Moore, J.P.
Fox, L.C. - Young, Marcus
Fox, Mag - Drum, Joshua
Fox, Mary Ann - Mathis, Elcanah
Fox, Sarah - Benfield, Secrtus (Socrates)
Fox, Susan - Mingus, And[y]
Fradt, Susan - Klutz, Levi
Fraisure, Nancy M.- Setzer, Jacob
Frasure, Laura - Kale, Albert E.
Frasure, Nancy M. - Lanier, Jacob Setzer
Frasure, Nancy M. - Setzer, Jacob
Frazier, Laura - Brown, John J.S.
Frazier, Martha A. - Neill, George C.M.
Frazier, Mildred N. - Carpenter, William W.
Fry, Allice V. - Fry, Frederick L.
Fry, Angeline - Kale, Polsen
Fry, Barbara M. - Leonard, James M.
Fry, Caroline - Deal, Henry
Fry, Caroline - Lefevers, William E.
Fry, Catharine - Sigmon, Monroe
Fry, Catherine - Beal, Aaron
Fry, Clara - Whitener, J.P.
Fry, Dealy Luaner - Withers, John
Fry, E.T. - Douglas, E.L.
Fry, Eliza M. - Carpenter, John
Fry, Ellen C. - Thomason, Robert H.
Fry, Emily E. - Poovey, Silas
Fry, Emma - Mosteller, Forney M.
Fry, Frances - Killian, Samuel E.
Fry, Frances C. - Miller, Emanuel W.
Fry, Frances L. - Miller, James F.
Fry, Harriet S. - White, Lawson
Fry, Harriett - Hoyle, John
Fry, Harriett - Keener, Michael
Fry, Harriett P. - Witherspoon, William C.
Fry, Jane C. - Houston, Sidney A.
Fry, Jinnie - Deal, Amsie
Fry, Joanna - Allen, B.C.
Fry, Julia - Sigmon, John H.
Fry, Laura - Bailey, William
Fry, Laura - Fulbright, Lawrence A.
Fry, Laura J. - Abernathy, David G.
Fry, Leah - Scronce, Alberta
Fry, Linny E. - Hoke, John D.
Fry, Lucy - Rutledge, Wade P.
Fry, Lucy E. - Finger, Daniel A.
Fry, Mahala - Hobbs, John
Fry, Margaret - Campbell, A.L.
Fry, Margaret - Stewart, Jep
Fry, Martha - Witherspoon, James A.
Fry, Martha E. - Ekerd, Eli D.
Fry, Mary - Hass, David H.
Fry, Mary - Throneburg, Burton
Fry, Mary - Sigmon, Marcus
Fry, Mary J. - Finger, William J.
Fry, Melinda - Sigmon, Noah
Fry, Minnie J. - Gaither, Junius P.
Fry, Nancy S. - Fry, Perry
Fry, Sally C. - Hovis, Melkiah
Fry, Sarah C. - Miller, James L.
Fry, V.B. - Eckard, Daniel
Fulbreth, Manerva - Shook, Miles W.
Fulbright, Mahala - Reese, Martin L.
Fulbright, Sarah C. - Bollinger, James F.
Fulbright, Susan C. - Jarrett, H.R.
Fulbrite, Sarah - Reinhardt, John
Gabriel, Ada M. - Robinson, William
Gabriel, Callie - Linebarger, Augustus
Gabriel, Fannie - Howard, Edmond
Gabriel, Fanny - Robinson, Francis O.

Gabriel, Jane - Sherrill, Elihue
Gabriel, Laura M. - Barkley, John M.
Gabriel, Mary - Jones, Able
Gaither, Candace - McClellan, Monroe
Gaither, Emeline - Bost, Adolphus
Gaither, Euphemia R. - Ellis, John
Gaither, Laura M. - Foard, Robert O.
Gamble, Sarah - Reinhardt, Ephraim B.
Gant, Sina J. - Cline, J.
Gant, Sue F. - Herman, Joseph F.
Gantt, Alice - Whisenant, Daniel
Gantt, Emily - Witherspoon, David C.
Gantt, Frances - Sherrill, Sidney
Gapet, Melinda A. - Raby, William R.
Gibbs, Annie - Dickson, John A.
Gibbs, C. Sophia - Lanier, Cornelius G
Gibbs, Cassiann - Robinson, William
Gibbs, Elizabeth - Fry, Pink
Gibbs, Emma - Carpenter, Wallace
Gibbs, Jane - Loretts, Fayette
Gibbs, Sarah Jane - Boyd, William
Gill, Bettie L. - Bost, Robert H.
Gilleland, Alice E. - Rowe, James N.
Gilleland, Catharine - Bolch, Isaac
Gilleland, Elizabeth - Litten, Elcany
Gilleland, Emoline - Clark, David
Gilleland, Jenelia - Moss, [George]
Gilliland, Jane - Nickson, Munroe
Goble, Martha A. - Dagenhardt, Rufus
Goode, Frances - McCorkle, Levi
Goodman, Victoria - Baker, Calvin
Goodson, Caroline - Shuford, Marion
Goodson, Malinda - Abernathy, Jacob
Goodson, Milla - Sronce, Henry
Gowens, Mary - Sronce, Andrew
Graham, Mariah - Fry, Sam
Green, Amanda M. - Herman, James
Green, Jane - Deal, N.S.
Green, Martha - Propst, Harvy
Green, Mary Jane - Killian, Henry C.
Green, Sarah S. - McGee, Noah H.
Grice, Mary Jane - Wilkinson, Avery M.P.
Grimes, Eve - Keller, Henry
Gross, Delia - Shores, Eli
Gross, Harriet A. - Yoder, Levi F.
Gross, Nancy J. - Dickson, Fredrick
Gross, Sarah - Haynes, G.M.
Guthrie, Mary - Sigmon, John E.
Hafer, Elizabeth - Christopher, Ephraim
Hager, Julian E. - Harwell, A.W.
Hagler, Bettie - Shook, William
Hale, Miriam - Daley, George W.
Hall, Catharine - Williams, Coleman W.
Hallman, Anna - Sigmon, Adolphus
Hallman, Camila - Killian, Gabriel
Hallman, Jermina C. - Miller, James M.
Hallman, Julie E. - Miller, James Monroe
Hamesly, Catharine - Murphey, Frank D.
Hamilton, Bettie M. - Sprunt, Wm H.
Hamlton, Catharine - Setzer, James P..
Hamilton, Julina - Patterson, Calvin
Hamilton, Lavina - Turner, James
Hamilton, Martha Ann - Wilkie, James A.
Hamilton, Sarah J. - Holdbrooks, E.B.
Harbeson, Caroline - Gilleland, Daniel
Harman, Elanora - Holler, Marcus
Harman, Jane - Propst, George W.
Harman, Malinda - Hollar, Daniel L.
Harmon, Lina - Alexander, Henry
Harris, H.H. - Seagle, A.J.
Harris, Nancy - McCorkle, Richard A.
Harris, Nancy C. - Sigmon, John C.
Harris, Yarmetty - Abernathy, John P.
Harrison, Mahala - Cline, Joseph T.
Harrison, Sally - Setzer, J.C.
Hart, Jane - Wilson, Jacob
Hart, Margery - Raby, James C.
Hart, Mira E. - Whitener, Alen
Hart, Polly - Whitener, Henry
Hartsoe, Dovey G. - Hicks, James M.
Hartsoe, Elizabeth - Sigmon, James Edney
Hartsowe, Sarah A. - Sigmon, David E.
Hartzoe, Barbara - Raby, H.A.
Hartzoe, Emaline - Shuford, Daniel
Hartzoe, L.L. - Huffman, Marcus
Hartzoge, Hala M. - Sigmon, William B.
Harval, C.C. - Fisher, F.M.
Harwell, Adoline - Hudspeth, George

Harwell, Ann E. - McCall, F.G.
Harwell, Margaret - Smith, William H.
Harwell, Nancy - Harbinson, Israel
Harwell, Sarah - Propst, Elcanah
Harwell, Susan P. - Harwell, John
Hass, Barbara - Cook, L.O.
Hass, Meriah - Cline, Coleman M.
Hattwanger, Josie - Seagle, Benjamin F.
Hawn, Amanda M. - Yount, Emanuel A.
Hawn, Barbara Jane - Hawn, Wesley M.
Hawn, Caroline - Whisenhunt, M.E.
Hawn, Catharine - Yoder, Andrew
Hawn, Elnore - Hawn, Lawson J.
Hawn, Flora - Abee, Ephraim
Hawn, Flora E. - Jarrett, James F.
Hawn, Jane - Jarrett, O.M.
Hawn, Julia - Killian, John
Hawn, Martha Ann E. - Barger, Marcus
Hawn, Mary - Flanegan, Luther
Hawn, Meriah - Travensted, William A.
Hawn, S.E. - Peterson, J.A.
Hawn, Sarah - Sigmon, Jesse
Haynes, Mary Etta - Hinton, Robert W.
Healon, Rebecca M. - Teague, Moses
Hedrick, Delila - Shook, George R.
Hedrick, Harriett - Sigmon, Philo S.
Hedrick, Lucinda - Bolch, Elcahan
Hedrick, Sarah C. - Hudson, D.M.
Heffner, Anna - Fulbright, Joseph
Heffnre, Harriet - Hollar, Eli S.
Heffner, Harriett - Little, Stanley
Hefner, Abigail - Miller, P.L.
Hefner, Camila - Fox, Adolphus
Hefner, Camila - Shook, Emanuel
Hefner, Candace - Isaac, John F.
Hefner, Candice - Graham, Benton S.
Hefner, Caroline - Hefner, Ambrose
Hefner, Catharine - Yount, Miles
Hefner, Donie E. - Deitz, Emanuel M.
Hefner, Elema - Sigmon, E.G.
Hefner, Eliza J. - Reinhardt, George H.
Hefner, Ellen - Brady, Jonas G.
Hefner, Emaline - Hefner, Hosea
Hefner, Emma F. - Reinhardt, James L.

Hefner, H.R. - Steward, A.L.
Hefner, Harriett - Keller, Pinkney L.
Hefner, Isabel - Ekard, Wesley
Hefner, Jane - Sigmon, Rufus
Hefner, Kesiah - Hass, Henry
Hefner, Linnie - Benfield, Silvanus
Hefner, Lucinda - Isenhour, Joseph R.C.
Hefner, Lucy - Drum, Hosea
Hefner, Mahala - Christopher, William
Hefner, Mahala - Townsend, Adam E.
Hefner, Malinda - Starnes, Daniel
Hefner, Mary - Sronce, William
Hefner, Mary Ann - Cline, George
Hefner, Mary Ann - Sens, George Cline
Hefner, Mary Jane - Huffman, William J.
Hefner, Rachel - Wagner, Benjamin
Hefner, Roxanna - Gantt, F.M.
Hefner, Ruanah - Hefner, George
Hefner, Salinda E. - Eads, Ransome
Hefner, Sally - Pope, Alfred
Hefner, Sarah - Hefner, Peter
Hefner, Sarah - Shook, Reubin
Hefner, Sarah - Sheperd, John
Hefner, Sarah Ann E. - Kanup, Enos
Hefner, Sida - Pope, David
Hefner, Sonova A. - Propst, Daniel E.
Hefner, Susanah - Hefner, Pinkney
Hefner, Susanah C. - Bowman, Gilbert P.
Helderbrand, J.S. - Carpenter, Solomon
Helderbrand, Nancy C. - Mull, Marion A.
Helms, Sarah - Hood, William
Helms, Sarah - Wood, William
Helton, Caroline - Bowman, N.L.
Helton, Ida - Whitener, Adolphus D.
Henderson, Emma - Clemons, Alexander
Henkle, S.C. - Fox, Rev. D.E.
Herman, A.L. - Hunsucker, L.A.
Herman, Ada V. - Rowe, Pinkney E.
Herman, Allace C. - Bost, Philip E.
Herman, Amanda J. - Bolch, Lemuel
Herman, Callie - Sigmon, Pinkney W.
Herman, Camilla - Townsend, Levi L.
Herman, Camilla E. - Rowe, Marion J.
Herman, Candace A. - Little, Marcus L.

Herman, Clarinda - Hunsucker, Jonas
Herman, D.E. - Spencer, J.P.
Herman, Emeline - Herman, H.A.
Herman, Emmela - Setzer, Jacob
Herman, F. Virginia - Mingus, John F.
Herman, Fannie - Sipe, Cain F.
Herman, Gracie - Baker, Franklin
Herman, H.C. - Wagner, T.J.
Herman, Harriet L. - Deal, Alfred W.
Herman, Harriett M. - Smith, Carson B.
Herman, Irene - Herman, Philo G.
Herman, Leah - Lennre, J.L.
Herman, Linnie E. - Fox, David P.
Herman, Louisa - Bolch, Henry P.
Herman, Martha A. - Bost, T.J.
Herman, Martha C. - Eckard, Rufus
Herman, Mary A. - Herman, Ephraim
Herman, Mary R. - Watron, James W.
Herman, Michel - Simmons, Elijah
Herman, Nancy M. - Wagner, William L.
Herman, Ruby L. - Flowers, Adam
Herman, Sally - Hefner, Herman
Herman, Sally L. - Hoke, Martin S.
Herman, Saponia A. - Coulter, John S.
Heterick, Anna - Null, Ambrose
Heterick, Eliza C. - Isenhower, David
Heterick, Emma - Fox, Marcus
Heterick, Helana - Winebarger, Daniel
Heterick, Polly - Hampton, J.F.
Hetrick, Martha Ann - Canup, Abel
Hevner, Mary - Sigmon, Jethro
Hewit, Emma - Hawn, Polycarp C.
Hewitt, Amanda - Lutz, Alonzo F.
Hicks, Elizabeth - Johnson, Bartlet
Hicks, Julian - Bost, J.C.
Hicks, L.C. - Martin, William
Hicks, Nancy - Beard, Watsel
Hicks, Susanah - Robinson, Isaac
Hildebrand, Elminda - Whitener, Robert H.S.
Hildebrand, Saphronia - Robinson, Benjamin
Hill, Anna Rebecah - Crockleton, Hamilton
Hill, Florence - Kidder, George W.
Hill, Lucy - Robinson, George
Hill, Rachel - Helderman, A.J.

Hinkle, Eliza - Abernathy, Ephraim
Hobbs, Avoline - James, James G.
Hobbs, Mahala - Yoder, Jacob M.
Hoffman, Emeline - Yount, Timothy J.
Hoffman, Jemima C. - Miller, Lemuel C.
Hoffman, Lydia S. - Sigmon, Reuben E.
Hoffman, Mary Ann - Sigmon, William B.
Hoffman, S.A. - Wallace, H.W.
Hoglin, Elizabeth - Smith, Edmont
Hoke, Amanda M. - Sigmon, Newton M.
Hoke, Caroline - Wilson, Reuben
Hoke, Eliza M. - Hefner, C.R.
Hoke, Emoline - Baker, John P.
Hoke, Fanny - Throneburg, George G.
Hoke, Frances - McRee, James
Hoke, Mary - Jenkins, William
Hoke, Melinda - Sigmon, N.M.
Hoffman, Sarah Ann - Eckert, Morgan
Holbrooks, Sarah J. - Setzer, James P.
Holder, Lura J. - Bollinger, Elbirt M.
Holdsclaw, Camela - Sherrill, John N.
Holdsclaw, Roxann - Moore, Andrew
Hollar, C.C. - Fulbright, Iben
Hollar, Elizabeth, Pitts, Abel
Hollar, M.A. - Ramsey, S.J.
Holler, Amanda - Huffman, Solomon E.
Holler, Belle - Black, Samuel H.
Holler, Belzosa - Huffman, Burle
Holler, Candice - Bumgarner, W.P.
Holler, Caroline - Huggins, Lawson A.
Holler, Dianah - Townsend, Monroe
Holler, Dora J. - Holler, John E.
Holler, Martha - Howard, James L.
Holler, Melinda - Pitts, James M.
Holler, Polly Maria - Lail, Noah
Holler, Prucilla - Pitts, Conrad
Holler, Sarah - Deal, Adam
Holler, [Sarah] - Reitzel, [Jerome Cass]
Holler, Susanah - Sipe, Hartwell
Holler, Susanah E. - Odom, Henry
Honeycutt, Mary - Childreis, Miles W.
Honeycutt, Mary - Childers, Miles W.
Honeycutt, Rebecah A. - Brotherton, Hiram
Hooper, Alice - Sherrill, Daniel H.

Hooper, Elisa - McNeley, Julius
Hooper, Elizer - McNely, Julius
Hoover, Anna C. - Angel, Lawrence W.
Hoover, Barbara E. - Hoover, C.A.
Hoover, Eliza A. - Sigmon, Silvanus
Hoover, Elizabeth - Bollinger, W.B.
Hoover, Emaline - Hull, William Pinkney
Hoover, Frances - Killian, W. F.
Hoover, Isadore - Williams, Edwin L.
Hoover, M.J. - Herman, George D.
Hoover, Sarah - Cline, Laben Wilson
Hoover, Sarah A. - Hildebrand, P.M.
Hoover, Sarah A. - Hitterbrand, P.M.
Hop, Malinda - Griffin, Isaac
Hopp, Catharine - Cline, Coleman M.
Hopp, Meriah - Cline, Coleman M.
Houk, Alace - Seabock, George D.
Houk, Emma - Seabock, James M.
Houk, Laura J. - Spencer, Adison A.
Houstin, Margaret - Heterick, John
Houston, Lettie - Knox, Ephraim
Houston, Mary A. - Girvan, Charles L.
Howard, Dovey - Goodson, Ezell Jenkins
Howard, Elizabeth - Wilkinson, Wesley
Howard, Fanny A. - Powell, H.F.
Howard, Isabella - Williams, Osburn
Howard, Juliann - Brotherton, James F. Alex
Howard, L. Susan - Shuford, Joel F.
Howard, Lucinda - Riley, Andrew
Howard, M.A. - Moose, D.F.
Howard, M.C. - Robinson, F.O.
Howard, Mahala - Childers, Gilbert L.
Howard, Molly M. - Sherrill, Woodford
Howard, Nancy E. - Fisher, William J.
Howard, Patsey - Ingle, Jacob
Howard, Rebeccah - Sherrill, Morris
Howard, Susanna - Childers, Thomas C.
Howser, Sarah - Hoyle, N.M.
Hoyle, C.L.C. - Philips, C.L.
Hubbard, P.M. - Johnson, David
Huberd, Hialdy - Rockett, William
Hudson, Elizabeth V. - Bowman, John A.
Hudson, Mary F. - Ford, Frederic L.

Huffman, Amanda L. - Baker, Barton
Huffman, Amy - Travis, Washington
Huffman, Amy M.J. - Sipe, Titus E.
Huffman, Anna - Isaacs, Levi
Huffman, Camila - Ekard, Marcus E.
Huffman, Catharine - Mathes, Daniel
Huffman, Catharine L. - Fox, James
Huffman, Catharine M. - Killian, Noah
Huffman, Catherine - Ingle, John
Huffman, Ceda - Christopher, Adolphus
Huffman, Delia S. - Deitz, Julius
Huffman, Delila - Hedrick, Daniel
Huffman, Delila M. - Sigmon, William
Huffman, Eliza - Pope, Franklin
Huffman, Ema E. - Huffman, Doctor R.
Huffman, Emeline - Shook, Daniel
Huffman, Emoline E. - Eckard, Daniel B.
Huffman, Erpha - Leffon, Noah
Huffman, Francis - Benfield, Perry
Huffman, Harriett - Fox, George
Huffman, Jemima M. - Wagner, P.L.
Huffman, Julian - Killian, William
Huffman, Lavina - Fulbright, Joseph
Huffman, Mahala M. - Lail, Levi
Huffman, Malinda - Christopher, Henry
Huffman, Mary Ann - Childers, Henry H.
Huffman, Mary Ann - Sipe, Elkanah
Huffman, Mary Ann - Thompson, Vance
Huffman, Mary L. - Pope, Marcus
Huffman, Nina - Selvy, J.N.
Huffman, Polly A. - Hefner, Devalt
Huffman, Polly R. - Ekard, W.D.E.
Huffman, Salina - Hedrick, William S.
Huffman, Sarah - Lutz, David
Huffman, Sarah E. - Seitz, Darius D.
Huffman, Senelda E. - Hefner, Calvin
Huit, Alice L. - Wike, Daniel L.
Huit, Ann - Cuman, Jacob
Huit, Barbara - Lutz, Franklin
Huit, Eliza - Abernathy, F.M.
Huit, Ellen M. - Carpenter, L.A.
Huit, Emoline - Bandy, William
Huit, Frances - Setzer, Noah

Huit, Jane - Kael, Samuel
Huit, Lucy Jane - Deal, Perry
Huit, M.M. - Smyre, M.N.
Huit, Mahala L. - Barringer, Noah
Huit, Mary - Jones, James
Huit, Michael - Bolch, Perry
Huit, S. Jane - Smyer, Silas
Huit, Sarah - Gray, John
Huit, Sarah "Sally" - Sigmon, Emanuel
Huit, Susan C. - Fox, John
Huitt, Delphia - Beal, William P.
Huitt, F.C. - Smith, P.F.
Hull, Ella - Keller, W.A.
Hull, Harriett - Williams, L.M.
Hull, M.N. Alice - Hoke, Franklin J.
Hullit, Sarah - Mason, John T.
Hunsucker, ? - Little, Peter
Hunsucker, Adoline - Smith, Andrew
Hunsucker, Alace - Yount, John Walter
Hunsucker, Amanda - Cansler, Moses G.
Hunsucker, Caroline - Hunsucker, Levi
Hunsucker, Catharine - Miller, David
Hunsucker, Harriet - Isenhour, Jacob
Hunsucker, Harriet - Roseman, Philo
Hunsucker, Laura - Reinhardt, Leban
Hunsucker, Mary - Baker, William
Hunsucker, Mary - Fry, Rufus
Hunsucker, Orpha M. - Setzer, James H.
Hunsucker, Susan - Lee, Rufus
Hunsucker, Violet - Hooper, Isaah
Hunt, Fannie E. - Huffman, Jefferson M.
Hunt, Laura - Setzer, Henry L.
Hunt, Nancy C.R. - Huffman, Davidson C.
Icenhour, Belzy S. - Hoke, P.C.
Icenhour, Emma - Henkel, Solan
Icenhour, Froney - Hull, William P.
Icenhour, Lenor - Sigmon, V.G.
Ikard, Louisa E. - Bost, Amzie
Ikerd, Linny C. - Rudisill, Jacob F.
Ikerd, Polly - Finger, Franklin
Ingle, Eliza - Weaver, John
Ingold, Alice E. - Murrill, John F.
Ingold, Laura I. - Pitts, John Henry
Ingold, M.B. - Fry, Hansen S.

Ingram, Mira - Sherrill, T. Martin
Isaacs, Lovina - Brown, Calvin
Isaacs, Munervy - Holler, Alfred L.
Isanhour, Harriet - Isanhour, Wilson M.
Isenhour, Cnadace - Little, Solon C. (1st)
Isenhour, Candace - Little, Solon C. (2nd)
Isenhour, Harriett - Dellinger, Jonas
Isenhour, Harriett - Isenhour, Martin M.
Isenhour, Mary - Pope, Carry
Isenhour, Rachel - Houston, William N.
Isenhour, Sallie H. - Houston. Daniel N.
Isenhour, Sidney Jane - Michal, Albert
James, Catharine - Shaw, James
James, Lissie - Wike, Fred Lafayett
James, Maggie - Gunn, John
James, Malinda - Hunsucker, Milus
James, Martha E. - Smyer, A. Byrd
James, Mary - Huit, Thomas
James, Nancy - Hunsucker, Silas A.
James, Norah - Lockman, Jones D.
James, Sally - Herman, N.M.
Janet, Catharine - Propst, John W.
Janet, H.A. - McCaslin, J.C.
Janet, P.L. - Carpenter, Jonas
Jarrett, Alice - Willis, John A.
Jarrett, Clara E. - Keever, Daniel C.
Jarrett, E.J. - Hawn, C.L.
Jarrett, Isabell - Jarrett, Alfred
Jarrett, Mary M.A. - Hefner, Andrew
Jarrett, Sarah - Childers, L.P.
Jarrett, Susan Jane E. - Killian, Pinkney A.
Jay, Elizabeth A. - Widby, James R.
Jenkins, Mary E. - Baker, Henry
Jennings, Mattie K. - Greenwade, Washington
Johnson, Catharine - Rhoney, Franklin
Johnson, Elizabeth - Lynn, James
Johnson, Elizabeth - Hetrick, Anderson
Johnson, Ellen - Bowman, Nelson
Johnson, Flora - Speagle, Daniel
Johnson, Harriet - Glasgo, Thomas
Johnson, Mary - Tallent, Samuel
Johnson, Mary A. - Boyd, Franklin
Johnson, Mattie - Hildebrand, Christopher
Johnson, Nancy - Bollinger, Henry L.

Johnson, Nancy R. - Young, John
Johnson, Sarah E. - Bollinger, Levi A.
Jones, Allice - Harman, James
Jones, Caroline - Linebarger, Frederick L.
Jones, China - Campbell, Samuel D.
Jones, Emaline - McGee, Thomas N.
Jones, Fannie L. - Gabriel, Harison S.
Jones, Gertrude E. - Clinard, Francis A.
Jones, Jane - Oswalt, John
Jones, Julia A. - Jones, John W.
Jones, Laura Annette - Hewitt, William A.
Jones, Louisa - Goodman, Martin
Jones, Lovinia - Bumgarner, Perry
Jones, Lydia - Sigmon, Lafayette
Jones, Mary J. - Fisher, Pinkney C.
Jones, Nancy M.C. - Wilson, John H.
Justice, Mary Ann - Barger, Babel
Kale, Angeline - Massey, William L.
Kale, Elizabeth - Litten, Thomas
Kale, Elmira - Brown, Elbert Lorenzo
Kale, Fannie - Ingram, John L.
Kale, Julia - Abernethy, Mack R.
Kale, Lucinda - Bruner, Josephas
Kale, Margaret - Turbyfill, William
Kale, Ruth - Howard, William Pinkney
Kale, Sarah - Yount, Andrew
Kanup, Malinda - Bolch, Elcanah
Kaylor, Gemima - Pope, Daniel
Kaylor, Harriet - Austin, Larkbury
Kaylor, Rhoda - Hefner, John
Kaylor, Susan D. - Huffman, Freeman J.
Keener, Adaline - Parker, Samuel
Kenner, Francis - Parker, Lemuel P.
Keener, J.C. - Propst, N.E.
Keener, Sarah - Finger, D.F.
Keener, Susan - Hovis, Rufus
Kees, Sarah - Murphy, Syirus M.
Keever, Martha - Jarrett, W.S.
Keever, Senith - Rowe, Pinckney
Keller, Emma L. - Baker, Barney
Keller, Mira - Keller, Peter
Kelly, F. Ellen, Hill, Isaac L.
Kent, Phebe - Herman, Abel
Kesiah, Sarah Ann - Campbell, D.A.

Kestler, Alice - Jarrett, David M.
Kestler, ELiza J. - Linn, Philo R.
Killian, Adeline - Deal, Jacob
Killian, Allis - Carpenter, Elijah
Killian, C.E. - Rudisill, E.A.
Killian, Clarinda A. - Honeycutt, McDaniel
Killian, Dora - Gibbs, Benjamin
Killian, Elizabeth - Raby, George W.
Killian, Francis - Turner, William A.
Killian, Jane R. - Turbyfill, J.M.
Killian, Julia E. - Hefner, Josiah A.
Killian, Laura L. - Keever, Franklin
Killian, Lucy - Wilson, William
Killian, Margaret C. - Sharp, P.M.
Killian, Martha Ann - Helton, William
Killian, Mary M. - Whissenhunt, L.S.
Killian, Mary S. - Wilson, Frank
Killian, Nancy - Smith, Elisha
Killian, Permira - Hawn, Jonas
Killian, Rebecca - Barger, Hosea
Killian, Sophina - Hallman, Ephraim
Kirksey, Eliza - Ingle, Michael
Kirksey, Margaret - Bumgarner, A.P.
Lackey, Susan A. - Mace, William
Lael, Catharine - Holler, Lawson
Lael, Catharine - Pope, Milus
Lael, Eliza - Herman, J.C.
Lael, Mary - Miller, John
Lael, Mary - Bowman, Calvin
Lael, Rany - Shook, Lawson
Lagle, Elizabeth - Lanier, Canny
Lagle, Elizabeth - Lanaer, Carry
Lail, Catherine E. - Bolch, Caleb M.
Lail, Juliann - Miller, Jacob Conrad
Lail, Matilda - Pope, Alfred
Lail, Susan - Abernathy, James W.
Lanier, Agnes Susan - Gilbert, George Ellis
Lanier, Martha Ann - Winebarger, Noah
Lanier, Sallie T. - Griffin, Nicholas M.
Lantz, Emma J. - Starr, Alfred
Lantz, Henryetta C. - Silon, J.A.
Lantz, Nancy N. - Warlick, John N.
Larklin, Isabel - Shuford, Franklin
Larr, Elizabeth - Killian, Andrew

Lawrance, H.S. - Smith, John M.
Lawrence, Mag E. - Lawrence, William H.
Leatherman, Isabella - Hoover, Leo
Leatherman, Martha S. E. - Shronce, Ephraim
Leatherman, Mary Catharine-Workman, John A.
Lee, Camila - Sumit, John
Lee, Elizabeth - Gant, John
Lee, Ellizabeth - Sherrill, Miles W.
Lee, Emeline - Stiles, William A.
Lee, Martha - Martin, A.F.
Lee, Mary - Potter, A.J.
Lee, Sarah - Parker, John J.
Lefevers, Laura - Sigmon, Thornton
Lefevers, Sarah - Whitener, Levi
Lefevers, Sarah A. - Wyant, Daniel T.
Lemmon, Sarah Ann - Bowman, John
Lenhart, Leah A. - Chatman, H.A.
Leonard, Clary - Whitener, George L.
Leonard, Elizabeth - Yoder, Cyrus
Leonard, Harriet A. - Link, John M.
Leonard, Mary - Lore, E.
Leonard, Mary A. - Whitener, A.J.
Leonard, Sarah E. - Isly, James H.
Leonard, Susan - Petre, M.
Lewis, Jane - Wilson, Hoyle
Lewis, Rachael - Hoyle, Sandy
Lewis, Sarah - Lowery, Randolph
Limonton, Jane - Abernathy, William H.
Linch, Sarah - McKinzie, David A.
Lindsey, Anna E. - Ogburn, Charles J.
Linebarger, Mary - Jones, William
Linebarger, Mary M. - Hill, Isaac L.
Linebarger, Sarah A. - Drum, William C.
Linebarger, Susan - Jones, Nelson
Linebarger, Susan E. - Killian, Luther
Linebarger, Dovy - Robinson, Martin M.
Lineberger, Susan - Cline, Reubin F.
Link, B.P. - Sigmon, Abel
Link, Catharine - Burke, Johnson
Link, Catharine S. - Raby, John W.
Link, Charity E. - Cline, John r.
Link, Elizabeth - Cline, Sylvanus
Link, Emma - Abernathy, Jerry J.
Link, Eve C. - Huntley, Virgil
Link, Margaret - Campbell, John D.
Link, Melinda - Troutman, William
Link, Olive L. - Clippard, Andrew
Link, Pamphiliam - Huit, Miles
Link, Sarah E. - Cline, John R.
Link, Sarah L. - Shuford, Laban R.
Link, Susan - Gross, Daniel
Linn, Harriett - Warlick, George
Linn, Lempie - Rudisill, John P.
Linn, Martha - Whisenhunt, William K.
Linn, Missouri C. - Fulbright, Jacob
Linn, Patsey - Knipe, John M.
Linn, Sarah - Whisenant, Daniel
Linthacum, Alice - Simons, Cicero S.
Litten, Candes - Brown, Andrew E.
Litten, Lizzie - McKay, A.J.
Litten, Lizzie - McCay, A.J.
Litten, Margaret - Robinson, N.L.
Litten, Margaret, Sherrill, Enos
Litten, Mary Ann R. - Sherrill, Calvin W.
Litten, Nancy Emaline-Caldwell, William David
Litten, Nancy R. - Yount, George W.
Litten, Sarah - Allison, B.L.
Litten, Sarah S. - Edwards, B. Perry
Little, Alice - Little, Franklin P.
Little, Alverda - Holler, A.J.
Little, Elisebeth - Fisher, William G.
Little, Elizabeth F.E. - Howard, Allen M.
Little, Ellen - Huffman, John
Little, Henrietta A.J. - Moose, Ceredlons? M.
Little, Jinnie - McDade, Joseph
Little, Laura - Thompson, Abram
Little, Louisa M. - Downs, Benjamin F.
Little, M.D. - Setzer, J.H.
Little, Manerva - Sherrill, J.C.
Little, Martha - Yount, Sidney
Little, Martha G. - Ingram, William D.
Little, Mary - Crouse, L.R.
Little, Mary - Jarrett, Jonas
Little, Mary C. - Sherrill, James
Little, Rebecca - Hannah, John
Little, Sarah C. - Stine, Jacob M.
Little, Susan - Linebarger, Henry D.M.
Little, Susanah - Sigmon, Martin

Littlejohn, Emily - Goldsmith, William W.
Litton, Anna - Robinson, Hiram
Litton, M.E.- Brotherton, J.H.
Lockman, Mattie - James, Auther
Lofen, Polly - Travensted, Reubin
Loftin, Barbara - Miller, Andrew
Loftin, Etta - Sherrill, Jasper
Loftin, Harriet - McKinnis, G.A.
Loftin, Mary - Drum, Francis M.
Loftin, Sarah - Watts, John A.
Long, Ceda - Edwards, Elbert
Long, Jane E. - Cansler, G.W.
Long, Martha A. - Little, Thomas A.
Long, Ruth V. - Neill, William S.
Longcrier, Lydia - Herman, Moses
Longcrier, Rebecca - Travensted, Joseph
Longcryer, Delila - Deal, Franklin
Lourence, Mag E. - Lourance, William H.
Love, Allie - Reinhardt, Alexander
Love, Sally V. - McCaslin, H.Y.
Lowe, Mary - Robinson, Willis
Lowrance, Cammilla - Lael, A.D.
Lowrance, Catherine - Kale, Pinckney C.
Lowrance, Dora - Shook, William H.
Lowrance, Fannie - Abernathy, McClain
Lowrance, Ida - McGee, William S.
Lowrance, Jenetia - Yount, Ambrose
Lowrance, M.A. - Fraysure, H.Y.
Lowrance, M.C. - Johnson, Eli
Lowrance, Maggie - Sherman, Charles H.
Lowrance, Martha - Smith, Alfred
Lowrance, Mary - Stevenson, Frank
Lowrance, Mary C. - Whitaker, Frances M.
Lowrance, Melinda - Dellinger, J.H.
Lowrance, Polly - Smith, Franklin
Lowrance, Sarah M. - Gilleland, H.A.
Lowrance, Susan C. - Shook, John C.
Luntz, Ellen E. - Smyley, Thomas M.
Lutz, A.E. - Reep, W.F.
Lutz, Ellen - Huit, Noah
Lutz, Harriet E. - Wilson, George
Lutz, Jane - Lentz, Jacob
Lutz, Malinda - Sims, John C.
Lutz, Martha - Mehaffey, Joseph

Lutz, Mary - Warlick, John C.
Lutz, Sarah Ann - Carpenter, David
Mace, Seana E. - Arnt, Henry
Mace, Seana E. - Ornt, Henry
Mack, Laura - Yount, Samuel
Maise, Sally - Huffman, Miles
March, Cynthia Ann - Mull, John
Marshall, Mary - Lee, Robert
Marshall, Nelly - Baker, William
Marshall, Sarah - Lee, Robert G.
Martin, Ada - McCombs, Robert
Martin, Anna M. - Lowrance, C.E.
Martin, Catharine - Huffman, Rufus C.
Martin, H.R. - Shuford Thomas F.
Martin, Lucy Ann - Lee, J. Hart
Martin, Mary J. - Grice, Francis M.
Martin, Mary J. - Grier, Francis M.
Martin, S.E. - Spencer, Mas.
Martin, Sophronia - Fry, Eph. N.
Martin, Susan - Davis, William
Mason, Louisa - Welker, Rev. G. W.
Mathas, Candace - Sipe, James
Mathews, Elizabeth - Christopher, Lawson
Mathews, Rhoda M. - Bailey, John
Matthews, D.C. - Matthews, Julius
Mauney, Vira - Keener, George
May, C. Ada - Davis, J.W.
Maye, Rebecca - Wilkinson, D.O.
Mays, Frances - Bostian, Omar C.
McCall, Rachael - Massey, Logan
McCaslin, Jane E. - Yoder, Daniel A.
McCaslin, Margaret Ella-Cloninger, Archibald
McCaslin, O. Almena - Strutt, George P.
McCombs, Ellen - Martin, A.F.
McCombs, Ida - Martin, J.W.
McCorkle, Dolly - Knox, Hiram
McCorkle, Eliza - Hull, Silas
McCorkle, Elizer - Linch, George
McCorkle, Jane - Burton, Robert
McCorkle, Mandy - Rowe, Paddy
McCorkle, Nancy - Riggins, Archey
McCorkle, Rosa - Wilkerson, William
McCorkle, Rozanna - Sherrill, John
McCorkle, Sraah Jenelia - Setzer, Harrison

McCoy, Julia A. - Corkill, William M.
McDowell, Mollie - Crowell, Frank
McGee, Adoline - Deal, George
McGee, Eliza - Drum, Filden W.
McGinnis, Lydia - Deaton, Rufus
McKay, Marrenia - Sigmon, Harrison
McKinsey, Susan Rebecca Jane - Loftin, James Edmon
McKinzie, Juliett - Cook, James
McNeill, Cary - Sounty, Ben
Mehaffey, Harriet - Thornton, John E.
Michael, Mary - Weaver, Adolphus
Michael, Sarah r. - Bolch, S.A.
Michael, Sarah S. - Sherrill, James A.
Michaels, L. Ann - Weaver, James M.
Michal, Eliza Ann - Reinhardt, Pinkney M.
Michals, Mary M. - Reinhardt, Isaac
Michel, Mary Julia E. - Drum, Pinkney A.
Micher, Elizabeth - Kelly, Samuel
Miller, Ada M. - Davidson, Leonados
Miller, Adoline C. - Yoder, A.A.
Miller, Amanda - Cook, Ellis L.
Miller, Angeline - Sigmon, Newson C.
Miller, Anna Rosabell - Huffman, Julius
Miller, Arkansas - Witherspoon, Thomas A.
Miller, Barbara - Shook, Henry
Miller, C.M. - Whitener, Peter A.
Miller, Cammila - Sigmon, Sylvanus
Miller, Candace - Cline, Jason J.
Miller, Candice B. - Bolch, Joshua
Miller, Caroline - Miller, Joseph
Miller, Caroline - Scronce, Thomas
Miller, Catharine - Barger, Allin
Miller, Catharine - Mouser, Eli
Miller, Catharine - Maye, William
Miller, Ceda - Cline, Alfred
Miller, Delia - Sigmon, William
Miller, Elenora - Isenhour, Marcus
Miller, Emoline - Rink, Andrew
Miller, F.S. - Bumgarner, Robert L.
Miller, Fannie E. - Killian, M.A.
Miller, Frances E. - Hunt, Peter M.
Miller, Genela - Bolch, Gerard
Miller, H.C. - Leonard, Eli
Miller, Harriett - Leatherman, Newton A.
Miller, Harriet M. - Huffman, Davidson C.
Miller, J. - Smith, Adolphus
Miller, Jane C. - Wilson, George W.
Miller, Louisa S. - Herman, Elijah
Miller, Louisa V. - Carpenter, Adolphus J.
Miller, Lovina L. - Huffman, Levi S.
Miller, M.L. - Nangle, Levi J.
Miller, Margaret - Stillwell, L.
Miller, Margaret E. - Herman, Adolphus
Miller, Margaret E. - Wagner, James M.
Miller, Martha Ann G. - Punch, Adolphus
Miller, Martha C. - Holler, A.D.
Miller, Mary - Yount, Laban E.
Miller, Mary Ann - Holler, Elisha
Miller, Mary M. - Fry, David S.
Miller, Mary M. - Yount, Henry
Miller, Mary M. - Hunsucker, John F.
Miller, R.M. - Hefner, J.W.
Miller, Rachel - Kahill, Daniel
Miller, Rocksana - Brown, James M.
Miller, Rosanah - Cline, Elkana
Miller, Ruphena - Cline, L.H.G.
Miller, S.C. - Smyre, F.L.
Miller, Sally M. - Rinck, Paul
Miller, Sarah - Hunsucker, Elkanah
Miller, Sarah - Powell, John Enza
Miller, Sarah Ann - Settlemire, David
Miller, Sarah Ann P. - Shell, John S.
Miller, Sarah E. - Wilson, Daniel C.
Miller, Susana E. - Mouser, John W.
Miller, Volara L. - Heffner, Poley
Milligan, Jane C. - Harwell, James L.
Milligan, Lizzie - Gabriel, A.A.
Milligan, Martha R. - Abernathy, M.A.
Milligan, Sarah - Eckard, Logan Pinkney
Mingus, Margaret - Pope, Logan
Mitchael, Elizabeth - Little, Quintus
Mobley, Nellie - Reinhardt, Calvin
Mody, Lucinda - McCall, John C.
Monday, Arther - Loftin, Eldridge L.
Monday, Esther - Bost, Alexander
Monday, Francis - Shelton, Julius P.
Monday, Jane V. - Sigmon, Alexander H.
Moody, Mary H. - Lowrance, B.A.

Mooney, Mary Jane - Turner, Pinkney L.
Moore, Ada - White, Henry
Moore, Charlotte - Sims, William
Moore, Dollie - Robinson, Lawson A.
Moore, Jinney S. - Hawn, John L.
Moore, Lydia - Hart, Isaac
Moore, Mary - Paine, John W.
Moose, Barbara - Keener, David
Moose, Margaret A. - Keener, Marcus
Moose, Margaret Ann - Keener, Alexander L.
Moose, Mary - Richey, George Pinkney
Moose, Susan A. - Kale, Absalam
Moretz, Susan - Houk, Coleman
Morrow, Emma - Beard, Henry C.
Morrow, Julia - Whitener, Jarvis
Morrow, Margaret L. - Sigmon, William K.
Morrow, Martha Ann - Whitener, James S.
Moser, Annie - Hedrick, James L.
Moser, Candis - Carpenter, Daniel
Moser, Eliza - Bowman, Joshua
Moser, Jane E. - Rockett, Obed M.
Moser, Laura - Pope, Quincey E.
Moser, Leah J. - Shook, Franklin
Moser, Maria - Killian, Laban
Moser, Rebecca - Woodring, Joseph
Moser, Rhoda - Shook, John F.
Moses, Margaret - Taylor, William
Mosteller, Easter - Whitener, Allen P.
Mosteller, Elizabeth - Rudisill, Philip
Mosteller, Hildy - Finger, Calvin
Mosteller, Livonia P. - Shuford, Daniel J.
Mosteller, Mary Ann - Ervin, George
Mosteller, Mina - Floyd, Marion
Mosteller, Saphronia - Rowe, Robert
Mosteller, Sarah Ann - Yoder, William
Mosteller, Sarah E. - Burns, Hosea
Mosteller, Susan - Warlick, Stephen
Mouser, Harriet B. - Hedrick, Franklin M.
Mouser, Rosanah C. - Hawn, Joseph
Mouser, Susan M. - Lefevers, Daniel M.
Mull, Adline - Hunt, Hiram
Mull, Barbara - Setzer, David P.
Mull, Barbara Alice - Mull, Wallace B.
Mull, Bettie - Wood, Aaron

Mull, Eliza - Lanier, Joseph
Mull, Elmira - Tallent, William
Mull, Emoline - Mull, Peter
Mull, Ida - Saine, Amos
Mull, Malinda A. - Hoyle, Israel G.
Mull, Sophronia - Johnson, Pink
Munday, Disie - Bost, John
Munday, Fannie - Gabriel, Connor
Munday, Jane - Sherrill, R.H.
Munday, Julia A. - Proctor, S.H.
Munday, Mary J. - Barkley, Henry C.
Munday, Rebeker - Munday, D.
Mundy, Nancy C. - Brady, J.A.
Murphy, Martha J.-Bollinger, Sidney L
Murphy, Mary - Fulbright, Logan S.
Murphy, Susan - Moore, Samuel
Murry, Nannie C. - Yount, George M
Nail, Isabella - Brooks, Jason
Nail, Molly - Mose, Peter
Nance, Frances R-Dagenhart, Martin L
Nance, Julia - Dagenhardt, Henry V.
Nangles, Frances C. - Barger, John M
Naugle, Harriet - Sigmon, Carrey
Naugle, Nancy - Holder, Jesse David
Neil, Arrenia - Costner, Henry F.
Neill, Lucy - Robeson, George
Newton, Cintha - Yount, Levi
Nipper, Elizabeth-Plonk, Jacob L.
Norwood, Mary - Miller, Absalom
Norwood, Mary E. - Lippard, John
Norwood, Sarah - Fulbright, Peter A.
Norwood, Susanah - Lee, James S.
Norwood, Theodocia - Canipe, J.F.
Null, Louisa - Hetrick, Levi
Null, Marthy A. - Kale, Sidney
Odam, Laura - Whitener, John W.
Odam, Sarah J. - Carpenter, Luther C.
Odem, C.E. - Kale, L.H.
Odom, Anna A. - Fox, Noah
Packet, Mary - Crowell, Champion
Page, Polly - Sanford, Hoses
Pain, Elizabeth E.-Turbyfill, Francis W
Paine, Emeline - Sherrill, Ben
Paine, Rosanah - Jones, Thomas J.

Painter, Harriet - Bumgarner, Pinckney
Painter, Mary J.E. - Calaway, J.T.
Painter, Perlina - Armstrong, Joseph
Painter, Sarah F. - Hall, Humphry
Parker, Alice - Price, Waitsell A.
Parker, Jane - Harwell, Elbert
Parker, Martha Ann - Wood, William W.
Parker, Nancy - Sronce, Joseph
Parker, Nancy C. - Stowe, Joseph M.
Parker, Rebecca - Underwood, John
Parks, Amanda - Gabriel, William P.
Partis, Lucinda N. - Rhine, John
Pattent, Sarah - Kaylor, David E.
Patterson, C.A.M. - Caldwell, James B.
Patton, Mary R. - Hefner, Levi
Peacock, Virginia W. - Killian, Frank
Perason, Barbara E. - Caldwell, Avery P.
Pearson, Ida N. - Shuford, Logan H.
Peterson, Emily A. - Sublet, John W.
Petra, Mary N. - Carpenter, John W.
Phelps, Nancy - Deal, Soloman
Pitts, Hattie - Beard, Asbury
Pitts, Laura E. - Coulter, John H.
Pitts, Malinda C. - Beard, Julius
Pitts, Sarah - Arney, John
Plonk, Mary J. - Smyre, Julius
Pollard, Martha - Sigmon, A.S.
Ponder, Margaret - Settlemyer, Henry
Pool, Anna Matilda - Correll, Hugh McCaslin
Pool, Elvery C. - Fish, Brisan
Pool, Nancy H. - Caldwell, William C.
Poovey, A.M.C. - Barger, Noah
Poovey, E.R. - Poovey, D.S.
Poovey, Elizabeth - Honeycutt, Solomon
Poovey, Elizabeth - Hunicut, Solomon
Poovey, Harriet J. - Yount, Stephen A.
Poovey, Nancy - Huit, Marcus
Poovey, Sallie M. - Fulbright, Jonas M.
Pope, Alice - Holler, Jefferson
Pope, Anna M. - Conner, C.F.
Pope, Barbara - Huffman, Ambrose
Pope, Belza - Pope, Jeff
Pope, Candace - Mathis, Jonas
Pope, Delilia - Huffman, Able B.

Pope, Ella - Heffner, William M.
Pope, Gemima - Rector, John
Pope, Manervy C. - Sims, John C.
Pope, Nancy - Ivens, J.W.
Pope, Nancy - Evens, J.W.
Pope, Orphy M. - Mayse, Jack
Pope, Ruah - Benfield, Silvanus
Pope, S.E. - Gantt, E.
Pope, Susan - Sherrill, Philo
Powell, Eva L. - Little, Quintus M.
Powell, Fannie - Setzer, Andrew
Powell, Genelia Sallie - Setzer, Albentus
Powell, Mary - Neill, Alexander
Powell, Mary - Thompson, John
Price, Emaline - Miller, John
Probst, B.A. - Campbell, Ennas L.
Probst, Jemima - Townsen, Solomon
Probst, Louisa A. - Venhor, Alexander
Probst, Patsy - Burns, J.F.
Propst, Adoline - Arney, Pinkney M.
Propst, Adoline - Sigmon, William
Propst, Anna - Webb, Franklin
Propst, B.A. - Campbell, Ennas L.
Propst, B.G. - Propst, J.C.
Propst, Bell - Whitener, Andrew
Propst, Caroline R. - Bolch, Ephraim
Propst, Catharine - Bumgarner, John S.
Propst, Catherine - Mitcham, John Wesley
Propst, Clara - Keever, Amos
Propst, Frances - Whitener, Monroe
Propst, Harriet - Whisenhunt, William
Propst, Jane - Wilfong, Charles
Propst, Julia - Huitt, M.M.
Propst, Lucinda - Hoyle, Manuel E.
Propst, Maggie - Witherspoon, John H.
Propst, Margaret E. - Leonard, D.E.
Propst, Mary A. - Link, David E.
Propst, Mary A. - Sigmon, Henry F.
Propst, Mary E. - Mouser, William H.
Propst, Mary J. - Fry, Perry E.
Propst, Meriah - Smyre, Robert
Propst, Nancy - Yount, D.P.
Propst, Patsy - Burns, J.F.
Propst, Phebe C. - Rink, Christian F.

Propst, R.E. - Bowman, Q.E.
Propst, Sarah E. - Settlemyre, Allen M.
Propst, Sarah E. - Wilson, J.I.
Propst, Susan J. - Deitz, Washington M.
Punch, Elizabeth C. - Spencer, John W.
Punch, Laura - Flowers, Nicholas
Punch, Martha - Jones, Osbum
Punch, Sarah - Gilleland, H.A.
Punch, Selina - Rees, Calvin
Rabb, Harriett - Murry, William
Rabb, Margaret - Cloninger, Monroe
Rabb, Sarah - Huit, J.L.
Raby, Caroline - Miller, Samuel E.
Rader, Lima - Cline, E.E.
Rader, Martha J. - Fry, William P.
Rader, Pheeby G. - Starr, J.A.
Rain, Cora Ann - Hoke, Joseph
Ramer, S.C. - Stevenson, T.L.
Ramsaur, Barbara Ann - Hooper, Isaac
Ramsey, Mary E. - Burns, Phillip
Ramsour, Bell - Shuford, D.H.
Ramsour, Benna - Cansler, G.P.
Ramsour, Emma E. - Shuford, W.P.
Ramsour, Fannie B. - Corpening, John E.
Ramsour, Harriet - Coulter, Merida
Ramsour, Henrietta - Link, Mitus
Ramsour, Jane J. - Baker, Barton
Ramsour, Mary - Hoke, Joseph
Ramsour, Mollie - Ramsour, P.W.
Ray, Julia A. - Hughes, Israel P.
Read, Fanny - Stamey, Ephrem
Reap, Mary C. - Yoder, Reubin
Rector, Camila - Bailey, John
Rector, Candace - Little, Jason C.
Reece, Linny - Garver, John H.
Reece, M.R. - Settlemyre, J.P.
Reece, Sally M. - Yount, D.P.
Reed, Lovena - Howard, Andrew
Reep, D.E. - Yoder, Reubin
Reep, Sarah Ann - Whitener, Hosea H.
Reepe, Margaret - Jarrett, John J.
Rees, Lavina M. - Rees, Aarin R.
Rees, Rosanah - Bolch, Jacob
Reese, Jane - Flowers, Joseph V.

Reese, Juliann - Sigmon, Julius A.
Reese, Sarah - Eades, Joel
Reinhardt, Alice - Ramsour, D.W.
Reinhardt, Ann - Robinson, Jim
Reinhardt, Barbra - Smyer, Andrew
Reinhardt, Eliza - Abernathy, William Albert
Reinhardt, Ellen - Bost, Henry
Reinhardt, Emeline - Smith, Wade H.
Reinhardt, Frances - Britton, Adolphus Monroe
Reinhardt, Harriet L. - Seagle, Macon
Reinhardt, Ida - Bost, Pinkney
Reinhardt, Jance C. - Ramsour, Thomas
Reinhardt, Julia - Graham, Stephen
Reinhardt, Lizzie - Boyd, Britton
Reinhardt, Margaret - Robinson, William
Reinhardt, Martha - Smyer, Robert L.
Reinhardt, Mary - Smith, James W.
Reinhardt, Mary - Workman, Danel
Reinhardt, Mary E. - Boyd, Marcus
Reinhardt, Rhoda - Bost, Alfred
Reinhardt, S.C. - Workman, Solomon
Reinhardt, S.J. - Ritledge, W.I.
Reinhardt, Sarah - Cline, James
Reinhardt, Sarah - Yoder, Calvin
Reister, Mattie E. - Bost, Ed R.
Reitzel, Hance C. - Fry, David W.
Reitzel, Lucinda C. - Deitz, C.L.
Reitzel, Laura - Starnes, Simon W.
Reitzel, Lydia S.E. - Rink, Christian R.
Reitzel, S.L. - Gant, A.L.
Reitzel, S.L. - Garret, A.L.
Rendleman, C.J. - Butler, Rev. Thomas
Reynolds, Theresa Ann - Harwell, John
Rhodes, C.E. - Linebarger, J.Y.
Rhodes, Julian - Sigmon, John H.
Rhoney, Catharine - Clampet, James
Rhoney, Elmainda - Shuford, Maxwell
Rhoney, Harriett - Goodnight, Joseph
Rhoney, Martha - Martin, Zebedee B.
Rhoney, Martha Ann - Segle, Andrew
Rhoney, Sarah Ann - Rudisill, Adolphus A.
Rhoney, Sarah Susan - Bass, S.H.
Rice, S.A. - Yoder, J.M.
Richey, Sarah - Michum, Lawon

Rinch, Mary C. - Hawn, Abner
Rinehardt, Martha - Fry, Robert M.
Ring, Ellen - Evans, Richard
Rink, Eliza - Cline, Abe J.
Rink, Frances E. - Herman, George W.
Rink, Jane - Herman, Ephard
Ritchey, A.E. - Seagle, W.L.
Ritchey, Marthey - Mitchell, Hosea
Robards, Annie K. - Roberts, Henry H.
Robinson, Ann - Lutz, Jacob
Robinson, Ann - Whitener, Levi
Robinson, Ann M. - Mills, H.M.
Robinson, Anna E. - Little, J.A.
Robinson, Caroline - Johnson, R.W.
Robinson, Catharine - Abernathy, Robert
Robinson, Ellen - Wike, Pinkney
Robinson, Fannie - Angel, Robert
Robinson, Fannie - Whitford, Stamy
Robinson, Fanny - Stamey, Whiteford
Robinson, Harriet - Finger, John
Robinson, Jane - Friday, John A.
Robinson, Jane - Howard, William
Robinson, Laura - Sherrill, Thomas Alex
Robinson, Lydia - Shuford, John
Robinson, M.A. - Jones, M.J.
Robinson, Margaret - Feimster, George W.
Robinson, Martha Eveline - Robinson, Jackson A.
Robinson, Mary Ann - Peeler, David H.
Robinson, Nancy - Warlick, Steven
Robinson, Phillis - Jones, Jim
Robinson, Polly - Mull, Andrew
Robinson, Rachel - Howard, John M.
Robinson, S.C. - Forney, M.L.
Robinson, Sallie - Wilson, Alfred
Robinson, Sallie - Wise, Daniel
Robinson, Sarah Ann - England, N.B.
Robinson, Sarah Ann - Rabb, George W.
Robinson, Susan - Howard, Joseph A.
Robinson, Susan Lillie - Sherrill, Thomas
Rocket, Agnes E. - Rocket, E.M.
Rocket, Amy - Spak, Daniel
Rocket, Jane M. - Abernathy, S.O.
Rocket, Sarah - Hoyle, Wesley
Rockett, Agnes E. - Johnson, John
Rockett, Martha J. - Sigmon, Nelson E.
Roseman, E.D. - Yount, D.M.L.
Roseman, Harriet - Rowe, Andrew N.
Roseman, Martha - Holdsclaw, Rufus
Roseman, Mita - Flowers, Alexander
Roseman, Sarah A. - Scheren, Rev. Simeon
Roseman, Sylvia - Shuford, Pink
Row, Catharine A. - Null, John
Rowe, Amanda - Smith, David
Rowe, Ellen - Dellinger, Franklin J.
Rowe, H.L. - Smyre, Logan Q.
Rowe, J.M. - Scots, J.Q.
Rowe, Jennie E. - Ward, H.P.
Rowe, Lizzie - Cline, J. Patrick
Rowe, Lovina C. - Stine, Allen J.
Rowe, Lucy - Keller, Mitchell
Rowe, M.A. - Pain, Coleman
Rowe, Mattie - Tate, Junius W.
Rowe, Rosabella - Cline, William
Rowe, Sarah Alice - Setzer, George C.
Ruddeck, Mary Jane - Sherrill, William F.
Rudisill, Ann - Robinson, Robert
Rudisill, Ann E. - Williams, John W.
Rudisill, D.L. - Sigmon, M.A.
Rudisill, Eliza Ann - Reinhardt, Monrow
Rudisill, Ellena - Mason, Andrew
Rudisill, Rachel - Speagle, Philip R.
Rush, Patsey - Haynes, John
Rutherford, Louisa - Smith, Babel
Sanders, Willie A. - Fisher, Joel H.
Sayne, Roxanna J. - Hicks, Nicholas F.
Schofield, Alice - Abernathy, Henry
Scott, Rilla - McCorkle, Bradford
Scronce, Sarah A.L. - Smith, David H.M.
Seabock, Mary T. - Hatley, Rufus P.
Seagle, Martha Ann - Stallians, William P.
Seagle, Mary Ann - Link, Henry J.
Seapoth, H.E. - Barger, Abel
Seitz, Candace - Rowe, Daniel W.
Seitz, Cath - Hollar, Paul
Seitz, Catharine - Huffman, Dainel M.
Seitz, Eliza - Whitener, Ephraim L.
Seitz, Jane E. - Flowers, Burgess G.
Seitz, Leah - Hollar, M.C.

Seitz, Mary Ann - Whitener, Daniel H.
Seitz, Pheribee C. - Abernathy, William L.
Reitz, Rosea - Baker, Calvin
Seitz, Sarah E. - Yoder, Peter R.
Settlemyer, Alace - Bolch, Christian F.
Settlemyer, Angeline - Cline, Jonathan
Settlemyer, Ellen C. - Cline, Eli P.R.
Settlemyer, Mary M. - Cloninger, Thomas P.
Settlemyre, Alice - Holder, Elias
Settlemyre, Rhody - Cline, Cicero
Setzer, Ann - Wilson, John
Setzer, Ann C. - Jones, J.F.
Setzer, Catharin - Watson, John E.
Setzer, Catharine - Barger, M.W.
Setzer, Fannie - Bailey, John
Setzer, Jane - Poovey, Eli F.
Setzer, Jennie-Houston, Robert Bruce B.
Setzer, Kate - Rabb, W.H.
Setzer, L. Alice - Cline, Alfred K.
Setzer, Layah L. - Turner, B.S.
Setzer, Louiza - Sigmon, Miles S.
Setzer, Mahala - Herman, Elkanah
Setzer, Mahala - Smyre, R.A.
Setzer, Margaret - Sigmon, Emanuel
Setzer, Martha - Holler, George W.S.
Setzer, Mary - Isenhour, David
Setzer, Mary Ann - Lutz, J.S.
Setzer, Mehala - Whitener, L.G.
Setzer, Menerva - Perkins, Henry
Setzer, Phebe - Deal, Goan
Setzer, Polly - Setzer, Alfred M.
Setzer, Rachel - Sigmon, Revle
Setzer, Saphronia - Keener, David A.
Setzer, Sarah - Setzer, David
Setzer, Sina - Norwood, R.C.
Setzer, Susan - Deal, Camy
Setzer, Susan - Sigmon, Lewis
Shell, E.A. - Carpenter, Joshua
Shell, Elizabeth M. - Rink, Eli F.
Shell, Fannie - Herman, Hosea M.
Shell, Sarah C. - Miller, Daniel A.
Shell, Malinda - Hefner, Daniel
Shelton, A.J. - Rutledge, John H.
Shelton, Laura J. - Powell, Robert S.
Shelton, Martha Ann - Caldwell, J.E.A.
Shelton, Mary E. - King, Adolphus H.
Shelton, S.J. - Proctor, R.G.
Shepard, Ellen - Bolch, Polycarp
Shepard, Mary L. - Lafon, Timothy
Shepard, Sarah Allen - Vita, Augustino
Shepard, Susan - Mathis, John
Sheppard, Jane - Price, Gilbert E.
Sherrill, Amanda - Teague, Vandever E.
Sherrill, Ann - Sherrill, J. Clancy
Sherrill, Ann E. - Cornelius, James B.
Sherrill, Ann E. - Gabriel, Jacob
Sherrill, Caroline - Setzer, Israel
Sherrill, Caroline - Sherrill, Elisha
Sherrill, Catharine - Fisher, William Sidney
Sherrill, Cenia - Rea, William L.
Sherrill, D.L. - Rudisill, Daniel R.
Sherrill, Dorcas S. - Cochran, John L.
Sherrill, E.E. - Cornelius, William O.
Sherrill, Elizabeth - Chesser, Ephraim A.
Sherrill, Elizabeth - Propst, William
Sherrill, Elizabeth - Gantt, J.L.
Sherrill, Elizabeth - Stamey, Ephreham
Sherrill, Elizabeth - Long, Pearson
Sherrill, Ellar M. - Caldwell, Elijah
Sherrill, Fanny L. - Trollinger, I.H.
Sherrill, Harriet - Sherrill, Jacob
Sherrill, Harriet L. Ann - Williams, Richert
Sherrill, Jane - Sherrill, J.W. Henderson
Sherrill, Jane - Shuford, Wallie S.
Sherrill, Jane C. - Robinson, John S.
Sherrill, Jane J. - Bynum, John P.
Sherrill, Julia A. - Lyttle, Joseph N.
Sherrill, Julia A. - Cannon, F.A.
Sherrill, Julie E. - Harwell, Henderson
Sherrill, L.V. - Ritchey, P.C.
Sherrill, Laura - Cline, J.R.
Sherrill, Laura - Cline, Robert B.
Sherrill, Lillie E. - Trollinger, Robert H.
Sherrill, Louise - Cornelius, William
Sherrill, Lovina - Harwell, M.J.
Sherrill, Mahala - Fry, J.P.
Sherrill, Margaret - Setzer, David P.
Sherrill, Margaret Ann - Sherrill, J. Wesley

Sherrill, Margaret E. - Harwell, James T.
Sherrill, Martha - Erney, Franklin
Sherrill, Martha - Hill, Cyrus
Sherrill, Martha - Robinson, William R.
Sherrill, Martha Ann - Shuford, A.D.L.
Sherrill, Martha J. - Sherrill, Hiram
Sherrill, Mary - Yount, Lewis
Sherrill, Mary - Sims, Feinck
Sherrill, Mary - Cornelius, Benjamin F.
Sherrill, Mary J. - Conner, Charles
Sherrill, Mary J. - Gabriel, Miles
Sherrill, Mary L. - Edwards, J.S.
Sherrill, Matty - Brown, Francis M.
Sherrill, N.E. - Gabriel, M.M.
Sherrill, Nancy - Little, Alexander M.
Sherrill, Octavia E. - Mayhew, Henry L.
Sherrill, R.E. - Chenault, W.W.
Sherrill, Rosea - Stocton, James
Sherrill, Ruth - Ford, William A.
Sherrill, Rutha - Proctor, Samuel
Sherrill, S.J. - Jones, Mitten
Sherrill, Sarah - Hagar, Thomas
Sherrill, Sarah - Robinson, James
Sherrill, Sarah J. - Smith, R.A.
Sherrill, Susan - Jones, G.W.
Sherrill, Susan - Linebarger, Robert
Sherrill, Susan L. - Pain, Isaac R.E.
Sherrill, Ugene - Shelton, Thomas
Shipp, Margaret - Abernathy, Cain
Shipp, Martha - Sherrill, Burt
Shipp, Sarah - McCorkle, Charles
Shitte, Jane E. - Keistler, Joseph
Shook, Adaline - Sigmon, Miles
Shook, Catharone - Heffner, Jacob W.
Shook, E.L. - Maize, G.W.
Shook, Elizabeth - Propst, Eli
Shook, Elizabeth - Rector, Brett
Shook, Jemima - Huffman, David
Shook, Leah - Rector, Burton
Shook, Lydia - Camp, Philo
Shook, Lydia - Canup, Philo
Shook, Malinda - Huffman, Allin
Shook, Mary - Robinson, Augustus
Shook, Mattie - Pope, Henry

Shook, Meriah - Christopher, Adolphus
Shook, Orpha E. - Dellinger, William
Shook, Polly M. - Sigmon, A.E.
Shook, Sarah - Drum, David
Shook, Sarah - Pope, George
Shook, Susan - Reitzel, C.G. [Christian Guido]
Shores, Amelia - Coulter, Isaac
Shrum, Mary Jane - Sigmon, David M.
Shuford, Alace - Abernathy, Adolphus S.
Shuford, Alice A. - Wilfong, Quince
Shuford, Annie - Carpenter, Wade A.
Shuford, Catharine - Neill, Henry
Shuford, Catharine - Whitener, P.W.
Shuford, Charlotte - Shuford, Labe
Shuford, Dora - Setzer, Albert H.
Shuford, Ellen - Shores, Eli
Shuford, Ellen C. - Wilkinson, Rufus A.
Shuford, Etta - Houston, Hugh
Shuford, Isabel - Helton, Robert J.
Shuford, Laura - Beal, Daniel
Shuford, Laura - Ramsour, Eli
Shuford, Laura J. - Sherrill, Jason A.
Shuford, Lettie - Dewy, James T.
Shuford, M.A. - Sudderth, Standhope
Shuford, M.C. - Lutz, J.F.
Shuford, M.C. - Lentz, J.F.
Shuford, M.J. - Whitener, L.R.
Shuford, Mary Ann - Shuford, D.P.
Shuford, Roda C. - Helton, John W.
Shuford, Susan - Monday, Marcus
Shuford, Susan C. - Walker, W.I.
Sigmon, Agnis - Bolch, Jorden
Sigmon, Alace - Jones, Andrew L.
Sigmon, Alice A. - Summerrow, John C.
Sigmon, Angelene - Cline, Logan
Sigmon, Ann - Reitzel, Anderson
Sigmon, Anna - Cloninger, Miles W.
Sigmon, Anna - Shook Daniel
Sigmon, Bell - Hefner, Daniel
Sigmon, Belzie - Bradshaw, J.B.
Sigmon, C.E. - Miller, J.F.
Sigmon, Candes L. - White, Joseph C.
Sigmon, Catharine - Arndt, George
Sigmon, Catharine - Bolch, Abel

Sigmon, Catharine - Blaylock, Joseph H.
Sigmon, Catharine G. - Dellinger, G.M.
Sigmon, Charity - Townsend, Peter
Sigmon, E.S. - Pope, F.L.
Sigmon, Eler - Williams, J.M.D.
Sigmon, Ellen - Reinhardt, J.J.
Sigmon, Ellen - Setzer, Noah
Sigmon, Ellen - Travis, Pinkney E.
Sigmon, Ellen K. - Heavener, John J.
Sigmon, Espy M. - Drum, Phillip L.
Sigmon, Fannie E. - Seitz, Abel P.
Sigmon, Ferdona S. - Ekard, Poly C.
Sigmon, Frances - Tolbet, G.H.
Sigmon, Frances M. - Murry, Robert V.
Sigmon, Harriet - Cline, Rufus
Sigmon, Jinnie - Deal, Jefferson C.
Sigmon, Julie Ann - Poovey, James M.
Sigmon, Larisa E. - Fry, J.A.
Sigmon, Louisa - Jenkins, William
Sigmon, Lovina B. - Alexander, J.Q.
Sigmon, Lucinda - Clemmer, E.P.
Sigmon, Lucinda S. - Hawn, John A.
Sigmon, M.E. - Sigmon, M.A.
Sigmon, M.S.A. - Bostin, T.W.
Sigmon, Mahala - Clemor, Jonas
Sigmon, Malinda - Gilbert, J.H.
Sigmon, Malinda - Poovey, Miles M.
Sigmon, Margaret M. - Bolch, Henry C.
Sigmon, Martha - Edwards, Spencer
Sigmon, Mary - Rowe, Lank
Sigmon, Mary A. - Allen, John
Sigmon, Mary Ellen - Sigmon, Alfonzo
Sigmon, Mary J. - Hass, John A.
Sigmon, Olivia C. - Miller, Jacob H.
Sigmon, Polly - Bumgarner, Andrew
Sigmon, Polly Ann - Burns, John
Sigmon, R.E. - Whitener, C.M.
Sigmon, Rachael - Deal, Henry
Sigmon, Sallie C. - Huit, Abel M.
Sigmon, Sarah - Hedrick, Quintis A.
Sigmon, Sarah Ann - Ekard, Elkanah
Sigmon, Sarah E. - Cook, E.G.
Sigmon, Sarah H. - Lail, Levi F.
Sigmon, Sarah P. - Bolch, Elias P.

Sigmon, Susan - Cook, Jacob
Sigmon, Susan - Hoke, Monroe
Sigmon, Susanah - Jones, Pinckney
Sigmon, Susie - Connor, Marion
Sigmon, Tabitha H. - Reitzel, Leroy M.
Sigmon, Texas - Blankenship, George
Simmons, A.M. - Bumgarner, Thomas
Simmons, Alice - Bowman, Daniel L.
Simmons, Fanny - Bolch, A.J.
Simmons, Margaret - Drum, Albert J.
Simmons, Nancy - Simmons, Jackson V.
Simmons, Rhoda S. - Eckard, Emanuel
Sims, H.A. - Reynolds, John F.
Sipe, Candace - Christopher, Larkin
Sipe, Elby - Sigmon, Joshua
Sipe, Mary - Mathis, Peter
Sipe, Saphronia - Killian, Caleb P.
Sipe, Susan - Sigmon, Benjamin
Smallwood, Sallie - Bost, John L.
Smith, Alice - Bollinger, M.M.
Smith, Alice - Miller, William A.
Smith, Camila C. - Smith, William P.
Smith, Camila E. - Stirewalt, Rev. M.J.
Smith, Cammila - Rowe, Noah
Smith, Catharine - Wade, William
Smith, Catharine E. - Little, Peter K.
Smith, Catherine - Deal, Lemuel
Smith, Drucilla - Turner, Alexander
Smith, Emaline - Nance, John
Smith, Eveline F. - Setzer, W.H.
Smith, Francis A. - Hunsucker, J.P.
Smith, Hanna - Wilfong, Martin
Smith, Harriett - Helton, Robert
Smith, Harriet A. - Bolch, Junius
Smith, Jane - Hoyle, B.W.
Smith, Julia - Young, Andrew
Smith, Laura A. - Baker, Fielden N.
Smith, Laura L. - Yount, William
Smith, M.A. - Sigmon, M.L.
Smith, Manerva - Sigmon, Calvin S.
Smith, Martha A. - Love, Valentine
Smith, Mary Ellen - Sigmon, Jonas T.
Smith, Ovina - Deal, Reubin
Smith, Rhoda S. - McCorkle, D.N.

Smith, Susan - Linn, Jacob
Smith, Susan - Hoke, David
Smyer, Alace A. - Setzer, Thomas A.
Smyer, Barbara M. - Huffman, Elijah
Smyer, Ellen M. - Miller, Abel P.
Smyer, Genela - Frazier, Cyrus J.
Smyer, Jane - Ikerd, Willis
Smyer, Mary Jane - Keener, Alfred L.
Smyer, Mary Jane - Woodford, Adolphus
Smyer, Mary M. - Arndt, John M.
Smyer, S. Ellen - Bost, O. Perry
Smyer, Sarah - Turner, Laban C.
Smyre, Amanda - Lutz, Lee Andrew
Smyre, C.A. - Hilterbran, P.M.
Smyre, Catharine E. - Setzer, Quincy A.
Smyre, Delia - Bost, William Perry
Smyre, Frances - Fry, Noah
Smyre, Harriett - Slade, Mayfield
Smyre, Julian - Propst, D.L.
Smyre, Lovina P. - Settlemyre, Martin D.
Smyre, Sarah - Little, Columbus
Southers, Lucinda - Simonton, Robert
Speagle, Alice - Rudisill, Solomon A.
Speagle, Barbara - Weaver, Frederick
Speagle, Clary - Johnson, John M.
Speagle, Emoline E. - Weaver, Adam
Speagle, Fanny - Huffman, John P.
Speagle, Harriet J. - Hood, G.W.
Spencer, Amy - Price, Smith
Spencer, Elizabeth - Hefner, Michael
Spencer, Emeline - Kirksey, J.W.
Spencer, Julia E. - Winebarger, Anderson
Spencer, Sallie - Propst, John H.
Spinks, Laura A. - Isenhour, George W.
Sronce, Janie O. - Cox, Henry C.
Sronce, Mary Ann - Carpenter, Jonas
Sronce, Molly M. - Howard, W.H.
Stamey, Bettie - Harman, Stephen
Stamey, Ellen - Dellinger, Adolphus
Stamey, Lovina - Reade, Pinckney
Stamper, Martha J. - Harwell, Avery H.
Stamy, Eve - Raby, Lawson
Stansill, Jannia - Craig(e), George W.
Starnes, Anna M. - Lail, George

Starnes, Bettie - Graham, Jacob
Starnes, Lovina - Hefner, Elias
Starnes, Salina - Kaylor, Alfred
Starr, Amelia - Reese, William
Starr, Barbra S. - Rader, William P.
Starr, Caroline - Poovey, William P.
Starr, Cary M. - Conrad, John F.
Starr, Cate E. - Rader, Jonas M.
Starr, Ellen - Hudson, Lawrence A.
Starr, Harriet L. - Bowman, G.W.
Starr, Laura - Propst, Avory
Starr, Margaret - Thornburg, A.M.
Starr, Martha - Burris, John
Starr, Mary Ann - Odell, Thomas
Starr, Nancy C. - Bowman, Gilford W.
Starr, Sarah - Cline, Charles A.
Steele, Callie - Penn, Rufus
Stiles, Emeline - McKinzie, William J.
Stiles, Sarah - Kale, Lihue L.
Stine, Elizabeth - Clipard, Marcus
Stine, Harriet B. - Eckard, Guilford R.
Stine, Margaret C. - Isenhour, Philo
Stine, Mary Jane - Little, Lewis
Stine, Matilda C. - Dagenhardt, Wilbern S.
Stine, Nancy - Wingate, Thomas
Stinson, Maggie - Secrest, Hoke C.
Stockton, Emma E. - Caldwell, L.E.F.C.
Stowe, Harriet C. - Clipard, David
Stowe, Kesiah - Bumgarner, John
Stowe, Laura E. - Clark, David H.
Stowe, Mary E. - Keener, Daniel
Stowe, Sarah - Smith, John
Sudderth, Minnie M. - Alexander, F.B.
Sullivan, Bettie - Clinard, Andrew L.
Summerow, Dorah E. - Hinson, Sidney D.
Summerow, Rachel - Campbell, Milton
Summit, A.E. - Callahan, George W.
Summit, Lucinda - Wilson, John Lee
Summit, Margaret Ellen - Drum, Perry Davidson
Summit, Nancy Jane - Rudisill, Thomas
Summit, Sarah J. - Crouse, J.L.
Summitt, B.M.S. - Caldwell, H.H.
Summitt, Catharine - Cline, Pinkney
Summitt, Lena - Yount, Joshua A.

Taylor, Sarah C. - Beal, Marcus
Taylor, Susan - Williams, Thomas
Teague, Mary Ellen - Sherrill, Andrew P.
Teague, Mattie S. - Sherrill, John
Terry, Bettie F. - Moore, Leonidas J.
Thomas, Cenus - Wilson, Robert
Thomason, Emeline - Hawn, Joseph
Thompson, Bettie Ann - Pope, Davant
Throneburg, Margaret-Beard, Jacob Waitsel
Throneburg, Mary - Beard, Blume
Tinck, Susan L. - Arney, Phillip
Tolbert, June - Abernathy, Michael
Tollinger, M. Elizabeth - Beal, Andrew
Townsend, Fridona E. - Cline, Gilbert
Travelstret, Mahala - Yount, David
Travensted, Elizabeth - Travensted, W.M.
Travis, Callie - Beard, J.F.
Travis, Fannie - Hawn, Jacob P.
Travis, Rebecca - Travis, Darius
Troutman, Linea - Sherrill, Thomas
Troutman, Mary E. - Miller, John
Troutman, Rebecca - Caldwell, Lawson
Tucker, Candus - Huffman, William M.
Tucker, Missouri - Johnson, David
Tucker, Nancy - Huffman, Julius
Turbyfild, Carmela - Harwell, Elbert
Turbyfill, Martha M. - Julian, F.P.
Turbyfill, Mary - Drum, Rufus
Turbyfill, Mary - Wilkinson, Thomas F.
Turner, Adaline S. - Cline, Ambrose
Turner, B.C. - Barger, David
Turner, Emeline - Spencer, S.E.
Turner, Harriet - Sigmon, M.A.
Turner, Harriett C. - Sigmon, John L.
Turner, Lidia R. - Sigmon, A.P.
Turner, Mina - Mahue, Stephen
Turner, N.C. - Shuford, P.C.
Turner, S.D. - Lester, Charles H.
Tweksbury, Carrie E. - Howard, John
Vanhorn, Nancy - Drum, Franklin
Wadkins, Mary - Wilson, Jeremiah
Wagner, Catharine L. - Huffman, Daniel
Wagner, J.M. - Bumgarner, A.L.
Wagner, Lovinia - Hallman, William F.

Wagner, Mahala - Ekard, Abel S.
Wake, Elizabeth - Warlick, Lafayet
Wake, Sarah - Starr, Elon M.
Walden, Mary A.S. - Stiles, J.H.
Walden, S. Harriet - Caldwell, Gilbert
Walden, Sepram - Fisher, Carry
Walker, Ada G. - Lyerly, John L.
Walker, Adoline - Raby, William
Wallace, Mary- Williams, Franklin M.
Wallace, Nancy - Gaither, Wiley
Ward, Catharine R. - Berry, Pinckney
Ward, Laura - Golden, Thomas
Ward, Mahala M. - Monday, Fletcher
Ward, Rhoda - Hawn, E.L.
Ward, Sarah E. - Yoder, Moses
Warlick, Eliza - Wade, John C.
Warlick, Francis - Gantt, Joseph N.
Warlick, H.E. - Patten, Robert
Warlick, Matta A. - Roberts, D.w.
Warlick, Minitz M. - Hedrick, Andrew
Warlick, Rachel C. - Seitz, J.C.
Watson, Mary - Martin, Eli J.
Watts, Fanny - Lowrance, Thomas
Watts, Mary - Harrison, Henry
Watts, Malinda - Cansler, Franklin
Watts, Sally - Robinson, Andrew
Weaver, Alice - Killian, Marion M.
Weaver, Anna - Reap, Daniel
Weaver, Anna - Whitener, Levi
Weaver, Eliza - Pope, Lafayett
Weaver, Jane - Ballard, F.A.
Weaver, Levina - Shuford, Israel
Weaver, Linnie A. - Hoyle, John W.A.
Weaver, Malinda - Killian, Luther
Weaver, Martha - Nance, Wiley
Weaver, Mary - Bandy, J.W.
Weaver, Rebecca C.S. - Lafon, Daniel W.
Weaver, Sarah - Hudson, W.H.
Weaver, Sarah E. - Dagenhardt, Robert L.
Weaver, Sarah S. - Michael, J.L.
Weaver, Susan - Leatherman, Stewart
Whisenant, Amanda L. - Seitz, Jones P.
Whisenant, Dovie - Whitener, Absolom
Whisenant, Hulda - Burns, William

Whisenant, Mary - Johnson, Hosea R.
Whisenant, Susan - Propst, Adolphus M.
Whisenant, Susan - Smith, M.A.
Whisenhunt, Catharine - Huffman, Gaither
Whisnant, Jane - Lutz, William
Whisnant, Margarett - Huffman, Hosea F.
Whisnant, S.E. - Deitz, J.L.
White, Candace L. - Winebarger, William J.
White, Emaline - Little, Hinchal
White, Fannie E. - Ekard, John G.
White, Frances C. - Miller, William L.
White, Malinda - Hefner, Sylvana
White, Mattie - Brown, Alfred
White, Rosea M. - White, George L.
Whitenburg, Candace - Huitt, Eleanah
Whitenburg, Elvina - Wilson, David
Whitener, Adaline - Gamble, Henry
Whitener, Alace E. - Rowe, Junius Q.
Whitener, Anna - Sherrill, Ceburn
Whitener, Anna P. - Hawn, Henry
Whitener, Bertha - Mosteller, Levi
Whitener, Bettie - Whitener, Joseph
Whitener, Catharine - Rocket, R.P.
Whitener, Catharine - Wise, David
Whitener, Dora - Miller, William E.
Whitener, Eliza - Davis, John C.
Whitener, Eliza Jane - Baker, David J.
Whitener, Elizabeth - Bolch, John S.
Whitener, Emaline - Seagle, Adam
Whitener, Emma - Whitener, Marcus A.
Whitener, Harriet - Gabriel, Edmond
Whitener, Jane - Abernathy, Samuel
Whitener, Laura - Fry, Buck
Whitener, Maggie E.-Abernathy, David A.
Whitener, Margaret R. - Yount, L.H.
Whitener, Martha E. - Harbinson, Jonas A.
Whitener, Mary - McCaslin, Charlie
Whitener, Mary - Hill, L.H.
Whitener, Mary Ann C. - Smith, Marcus
Whitener, Mary J. - Allen, J.A.
Whitener, Mattie - Rowe, Peter J.
Whitener, Rettie - Morrison, Andrew
Whitener, S.C.E. - Rhine, Eli S.
Whitener, S. Jane - Fry, James C.
Whitener, Sacy E. - Yoder, Daniel
Whitener, Sallie - Winters, Marion
Whitener, Sarah - Crawford, Felix Q.
Whitener, Sarah Ann - Reinhardt, Andrew
Whitener, Susan A. - Ward, John S.
Whitener, Susan J. - Yount, Moses
Wike, Catherine A. - Fincannon, J.W.
Wike, Ellen, McRee, James P.
Wike, Jemima - Moose, G.R.
Wike, Linna R. - Gibson, J.W.
Wike, Margaret - Wike, John L.
Wike, Martha A. - Setzer, Daniel
Wike, Michael (female) - Gibbs, Jonas
Wike, Polly - Gantt, J.J.
Wike, Rhoda - Ingram, Fields
Wike, Sarah - Moose, V.A.
Wike, Scady - Hartzoe, Jacob
Wike, Tolly - Gantt, I.I.
Wilfong, Adoline C. - Miller, Nelson A.
Wilfong, Alice - Ramsour, Rufus
Wilfong, Bettie - Robinson, Miles
Wilfong, Chana - Ramsour, Sidney
Wilfong, Emma - Winkley, Jerry
Wilfong, Harriet - Robinson, Caleb
Wilfong, Julia Ann - Robinson, Sidney
Wilfong, Lettie - Wilfong, Ned
Wilfong, Lucinda - James, George M.
Wilfong, M.E. - Burns, J.H.
Wilfong, Mildred C. - Marshall, Andrew W.
Wilfong, Sarah Ann - Clark, Jeptha
Wilkerson, Sarah E. - Link, Caleb
Wilkie, Caroline - Seitz, Marcus
Wilkie, Ellen - Danner, Hosea A.
Wilkie, L.V. - Miller, John
Wilkie, Mattie - Abernathy, John Eli
Wilkie, Sarah - Bridges, Hosea W.
Wilkinson, Ada Senora - Grice, Francis M.
Wilkinson, Dancey - Armstrong, W.B.
Wilkinson, M.J. - Caldwell, W.J.
Wilkinson, Martha A. - McCombs, James
Wilkinson, Nancy C. - Drum, William A.
Wilkinson, Nancy E. - Martin, John
Wilkinson, Susan Rebecca-Goodson, Martin L.
Wilkinson, Jane - Henson, John

Williams, Mahala - Howard, Nelson
Williams, Margaret - Carrell, G.W.
Williams, Mary - Childers, Henry
Williams, Mary J. - Brown, James M.
Williams, Sarah - Starnes, Columbus C.
Williams, Susan - Caldwell, James R.
Williamson, Hatty - Sherrill, James M.
Wills, Margaret - Angel, Henry M.
Wills, Matty - Dourity, Marcus A.
Wilson, Alace V. - Pence, Hugh A.
Wilson, Allie A. - Shuford, John M.
Wilson, Cairan - Norwood, G.W.
Wilson, Catharine - Miller, Jones
Wilson, Cora - Killian, W.L.C.
Wilson, Delph - Gibbs, Samuel
Wilson, Fannie A. - Reinhardt, J. Edd
Wilson, Jemima - Sherrill, Richard
Wilson, Jinny C. - Deal, Sylvanus M.
Wilson, Julia Ann - Bostain, Norman
Wilson, Laura - Wilfong, Philip
Wilson, Lena A. - Paine, A.B.
Wilson, Lillie - Fields, Thomas E.
Wilson, M.L. - Hill, J.E.
Wilson, Margaret - Angel, George
Wilson, Mary - Robinson, Gabriel
Wilson, Mary A. - Hall, Hugh M.
Wilson, Sarah - Powell, Julius
Wilson, Selia - Hunsucker, Calvin
Wilson, Synthia - Schenk, Monroe
Winebarger, Candace-Deal, Wilbern P.
Winebarger, Catharine - Bowman, Lawson
Winebarger, Delia - Christopher, Jacob
Winebarger, Lorina - Lail, Calvin
Winebarger, Louisa - Davis, H.A.
Winebarger, Mary - Rector, William
Winebarger, Mary C. - Bolch, James H.
Winebarger, Rachel - Dellinger, Sherman
Winebarger, Susan - Duncan, Thomas
Wingate, Phebe - Boyd, R.W.
Winkler, Agnes - Sigmon, Aaron Y.
Winkler, Andy - Cloninger, S.C.
Winnburgh, Elizabeth - Huit, Lewis
Wise, Elizabeth - Hoyle, Eli
Withers, Adoline - Snider, L.F.
Witherspoon, Catherine - Sigmon, David S.
Witherspoon, Eliza - Parker, Samuel
Witherspoon, Elizabeth - Gant, Theophilus
Witherspoon, Emoline S. - Martin, George H.
Witherspoon, Harriet - Hunsucker, Jacob P.
Witherspoon, Harriet - Hunsucker, Jacob P.
Witherspoon, Margaret - Setzer, Patrick
Witherspoon, Margaret - Wilson, Jerry
Witherspoon, Mary J. - Abernathy, James
Witherspoon, Ruannah O. - Freeze, William, Jr.
Witherspoon, Sarah - Propst, D. Franklin
Witherspoon, Susanah - Hunsucker, Marcus
Woodford, Jane - Smyre, Milton
Woodson, Mary F. - Pace, John F.
Workman, Dicy - Rudisill, Philip
Workman, Martha J. - Smith, William
Workman, Mary Jane - Whisenant, John M.
Workman, Sarah Ann - Leatherman, Solomon
Workman, Sarah Ann - Newton, William M.
Workman, Susan - Sigmon, John H.
Wyant, M.J. - Leonard, J.Y.
Wyant, Sarah - Richey, Joseph W.
Wycoff, Mary F.E. - Lowrance, John W.
Yoder, Anna C. - Houser, Elam
Yoder, Eliza - Jarrett, John J.
Yoder, Eliza E. - Yoder, George M.
Yoder, Florence I. - Ramsour, David Henry
Yoder, Frances - Whitener, Philip b.
Yoder, Jane C. - Yoder, Jason E.
Yoder, Julia A. - Propst, Reuben
Yoder, Martha A. - Moore, H.L.
Yoder, Mary Caroline - Jarrett, D.P.
Yoder, Mary M. - Hawn, Amyia A.
Yoder, Rhoda E. - Carpenter, John F.
Young, Martha - Propst, Alfred
Yount, Adline - Carpenter, Richmond
Yount, Amanda - Murphey, James
Yount, Anna - Whitener, Levi
Yount, Anna R. - Cline, Jesse
Yount, Azline - Shook, Franklin
Yount, Carmila E. - Carpenter, P.W.
Yount, Catharine - Matthews, John
Yount, Catharine - Hoke, Q.J.
Yount, Clarinda - Whitener, L.G.

Yount, Clemma O. - Rudisill, Henry P.
Yount, Eliza - Weaver, O.H.
Yount, Elizabeth - Little, George S.
Yount, Elizabeth - Morrow, William
Yount, Ellen E. - Clifton, Thomas C.
Yount, Filecta - Yount, Walton C.
Yount, Florance - Holler, William L.
Yount, Harriet - Yount, James N.
Yount, Jemima A. - Mitchel, James S.
Yount, Laura C. - Long, Johniah
Yount, Leanah - Yount, Jones
Yount, Margaret - Setzer, Marcus
Yount, Mary M. - Hawn, Noah
Yount, Mary S. - Huffman, Joseph
Yount, Rhoda - Bolch, Joseph
Yount, S.A. - Sherrill, John
Yount, Sallie J. - Rockett, Calvin W.
Yount, Sarah Ann J. - Pitts, William P.
Yount, Sarah E. - Coulter D. Monroe
Yount, Sarah J. - Campbell, Robert F.
Yount, Susan C. - Mayberry, Robert

www.ingramcontent.com/pod-product-compliance
Lightning Source LLC
Chambersburg PA
CBHW080404170426
43193CB00016B/2804